Listening to the Customer

Listening to the Customer

Peter Hernon and Joseph R. Matthews

LIBRARIES UNLIMITED

AN IMPRINT OF ABC-CLIO, LLC
Santa Barbara, California • Denver, Colorado • Oxford, England

Library of Congress Cataloging-in-Publication Data

Hernon, Peter.
  Listening to the customer / Peter Hernon and Joseph R. Matthews.
     p. cm.
  Includes bibliographical references and index.
  ISBN 978-1-59884-799-4 (pbk. : acid-free paper) – ISBN
978-1-59884-800-7 (ebook) 1. Libraries—United States—Evaluation. 2.
Public services (Libraries)—United States—Evaluation. 3.
Libraries—Public relations—United States. 4. Libraries—User
satisfaction—United States. 5. Customer services—Evaluation. 6.
Consumer satisfaction—Evaluation. I. Matthews, Joseph R. II. Title.
  Z678.85.H475 2011
  025.10973--dc22   2011002763

ISBN: 978-1-59884-799-4
EISBN: 978-1-59884-800-7

15 14 13 12 11   1 2 3 4 5

This book is also available on the World Wide Web as an eBook.
Visit www.abc-clio.com for details.

Libraries Unlimited
An Imprint of ABC-CLIO, LLC

ABC-CLIO, LLC
130 Cremona Drive, P.O. Box 1911
Santa Barbara, California 93116-1911

This book is printed on acid-free paper ∞
Manufactured in the United States of America

Contents

Illustrations

Figures

Tables

Preface

An organization, such as a library, develops a set of products and services to meet the changing information needs and expectations of its customers in a highly competitive environment of information provision. Many businesses include listening to the voice of the customer as part of their review of existing services and when they plan new ones. The voice of the customer refers to a process of listening to customers, benefiting from what they have seen—including the results in their planning and decision making—and maintaining an ongoing dialogue with them. The literature of library and information science contains numerous articles on libraries as learning and complex organizations, but does not refer to them as "listening organizations."[1] Being an effective listener is not a passive activity. It takes concentration, effort, and active attention, and people appreciate it when others listen to them. When quizzed about acting, many of the world's foremost actors mention listening as a key factor that makes them outstanding at their craft and respected by their peers.

As *Listening to the Customer* discusses, there are a variety of ways to engage in listening and to create a climate of data-driven management based on the results. As Terry G. Vavra points out, the more that survey respondents view an organization as regularly listening to them and valuing what they have to say, even if that organization does not act on everything that customers raise (but explains why not), the more likely they are to share their opinions and perceptions in the future.[2] In other words, those libraries that experience low response rates to surveys probably infrequently listen to their customers and do not engage in a vigorous, ongoing dialogue based on what they are told.

Listening to the Customer discusses a voice-of-the-customer program for libraries and how to collect and use the evidence gathered. A powerful type of data that organizations often collect is the actual comments, both positive and negative, that customers make directly to the library or post on social networks or blogs, most likely ones not sponsored by a library. This book also addresses types of customers and assorted methods for gathering evidence; highlights data reporting to stakeholders and relevant metrics for libraries to report; devotes a chapter to regaining lost customers, known as regain management; and discusses leadership and preparation to meet an uncertain future. Academic and public libraries should not settle on the status quo as good enough. They should try to deliver a customer experience that is more than promised: do not over-promise, but over-deliver! Outstanding customer service is more than what librarians say or do for their customers. It means giving customers a chance to make their opinions known and developing services that meet or exceed their changing expectations.

This book, which is our first collaboration, complements a number of our works highlighted in the bibliography and is a logical outcome of our many years in dealing with customer service and the evaluation and measurement of library services. We do not identify either of us as the author of each chapter; instead, we both contributed content to all chapters, thereby strengthening the book's content. Once we had a draft of the manuscript, we reviewed the content and settled on chapter sidebars, written by practicing librarians, that would reinforce particular messages.

Notes

1. Merryn Rutledge, "The Listening Organization," *Revisions: Ideas for Leaders* 6, no. 1 (winter 2003): 1, accessed August 12, 2010, http://www.revisions.org/newsletters/ReVisionsIdeas_v06n01.pdf.

2. Terry G. Vavra, *Improving Your Measurement of Customer Satisfaction: A Guide to Creating, Conducting, Analyzing, and Reporting Customer Satisfaction Measurement Programs* (Milwaukee, WI: ASQ Quality Press, 1997).

Acknowledgments

We wish to thank the American Library Association and the Association of College and Research Libraries for permission to use the documents quoted in chapter 1, as well as the authors of those quoted documents.

We would also like to thank the authors of the sidebars for their invaluable contributions to this book:

- Shirley Amore, City Librarian, Denver Public Library, Colorado

- Sherry Spitsnaugle, Community Relations, Denver Public Library, Colorado

- Georgia Lomax, Deputy Director, Pierce County Library System, Tacoma, Washington

- Moe Hosseini-Ara, Markham Public Library, Ontario, Canada

- Mary Anne Hodel, Director and CEO, Orange County Library System, Orlando, Florida

- James LaRue, Director, Douglas County Libraries, Castle Rock, Colorado

- Don Mills, Director, Mississauga Library System, Ontario, Canada

- Robert Boyd, Assistant University Librarian for Technology Applications, Santa Clara University, California

- Robert E. Dugan, Dean of Libraries, University of West Florida, Pensacola, Florida

- Melonee Lotterhos Slocum, Manager for Strategic Initiatives, Jacksonville Public Library, Florida

- Carl Thompson, President, Counting Opinions, Toronto, Canada

- Steven J. Bell, Associate University Librarian, Temple University Libraries, Philadelphia, Pennsylvania

1

Listening to and Valuing
Customer Comments

When people feel listened to, valued, and important to a company, it's rare.[1]

Historically, and even today, many academic and public librarians have resisted referring to those using libraries as *customers*; they prefer to call them *patrons*, *users*, *borrowers*, *readers*, *clients*, *visitors,* or some other word acceptable to the organizational culture. As Joe Matthews explains:

> The term *customers* emphasizes the fact that the individuals using the library actually "pay" a real cost (distance to travel to the library, time to visit the library physically or virtually, etc.) and thus must actually make a "purchase" decision. The use of the word customer reminds library staff members that individuals are choosing to visit the library and that they have customer service expectations that must be met or exceeded. In fact, in many cities and counties, it could be argued that library customers are the "ultimate" customers because they have already paid for the service through their taxes.[2]

Peter Hernon and Ellen Altman, who concur, note that "most customers have expectations about service, though sometimes those expectations are unrealistic."[3] Customer expectations are not static and are shaped in a highly competitive environment. As a result, it is important to understand those expectations, determine which ones the organization is willing to meet, and realize that customers are now more demanding than they have been in the past. Further, by implication, customers may use products and

1

services from an organization, but they may not demonstrate loyalty to that organization—
that is, be unwilling to find a replacement for information provision.

KANO MODEL

Named after Noriaki Kano of Tokyo Rika University, the Kano model characterizes
a critical aspect of customer service, namely customer satisfaction. For our purposes,
we might divide organizations and their services into three attribute actually categories:
threshold, performance, and excitement or delight. Any attributes that cannot be classified
into these categories have little or no consequence to the customer.

Threshold attributes are those that do not provide an opportunity for product or service
differentiation. Increasing the performance of these attributes actually lowers customer
satisfaction. The absence or poor performance of one or more attributes, however, results
in extreme customer dissatisfaction. An example of a threshold attribute is the ability to
control the frequency with which a car's windshield wipers are automatically turned on
and off (the intermittent option).

Performance attributes, which are those that customers typically verbalize, improve
customer satisfaction. Conversely, an absent or weak performance attribute reduces
customer satisfaction. *Excitement attributes* are unspoken and unexpected by customers,
but they can result in high levels of customer satisfaction. Their absence, however, does
not lead to dissatisfaction. Excitement attributes satisfy latent needs, the real needs of
which customers are unaware.

Given this characterization, the Kano model (see figure 1.1) addresses the extent of
implementation for three factors:

1. Basic ones: those that are so obvious to customers that they may fail to state
   them overtly.

2. Normal ones: those that customers are cognizant of and can readily articulate.
   Meeting these needs produces satisfied customers, whereas failing to do so
   results in dissatisfied customers.

3. Delighter ones: those that customers may not be aware of, but customer delight
   emerges from meeting them.

The goal of the Kano model is to remind service organizations to go beyond threshold
attributes and embrace the other two types, while recognizing that the elimination of those
attributes might lead to customer dissatisfaction. This may require a trade-off analysis
against cost. Still, cost should not become a rationale for refusing to work on performance
and excitement attributes.

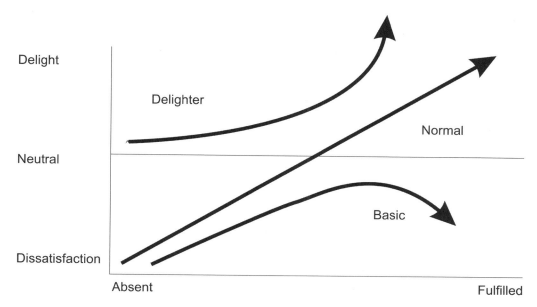

Figure 1.1. The Kano Model

The Kano model is important to remember as libraries try to hold on to the customers they have and to understand how to attract new customers. In essence, the model looks at service organizations as they exist in a competitive environment and instructs them about how to be successful in that environment. (Additional discussion of the Kano model and learning how customers view different service attributes may be found in *The Evaluation and Measurement of Library Services*.[4])

Still, it merits mention that, to evaluate service quality for the digital library at the University of Guadalajara (Mexico), Cecilia Garibay, Humberto Gutiérrez, and Artuor Figueroa combined the Kano model with quality function deployment (QFD), which identifies the information needs (requirements) of customers and is associated with organizational processes (e.g., marketing and product development and design) in order to achieve common goals.[5] (QFD relies on the methods of data collection discussed in chapters 3 through 6.) Although the authors confuse service quality with satisfaction, they note that "the limitation of the Kano model is that it classifies, but does not quantify either numerical or qualitative performance of attributes. Therefore, it is important to use current information of customer requirements that can be obtained by specific surveys and QFD methodology." They add:

> A distinctive feature of QFD is that it establishes customer requirements (*Whats*) and translates them into appropriate technical requirements (*Hows*). Such information is then reprioritized in the Kano model, thus providing a clear understanding of what customer requirements should be improved in order to satisfy the digital library's customers.[6]

CUSTOMER EXCITEMENT WITH THE LIBRARY

Customer excitement results from those factors that surprise and delight customers, without leading to their dissatisfaction. Matthew Dixon, Karen Freeman, and Nicholas Toman, who believe that companies place too much emphasis on delighting customers, would probably characterize excitement in terms of solving problems and avoiding "service failures," which see customers go elsewhere. They note that service failures are four times more likely to result in unsatisfactory and disloyal customers. This means that loyalty is a difficult, if not impossible, concept to create and maintain, and that librarians can never forget the impact of a service experience.[7] Although they limit their observations to organizations specializing in call centers and call-back services, libraries can still benefit from their discussion. Of course, creating customer excitement, delight, and loyalty are all worthwhile goals; the bottom line is the avoidance of service failures. Expressed another way, libraries need to invest in service recovery if they are going to be successful in turning the dissatisfaction deriving from a service failure into the possibility of customer retention. A complication is that such failures may involve customer anger, and managers must be able to handle highly emotional episodes.

Staff members may not realize that a service failure has occurred. As discussed in subsequent chapters, when a customer complains, that person is pointing out an opportunity to fix the problem. When a customer makes comments, those remarks should be reviewed and managers be held accountable for ensuring that the problem does not recur.

WHAT IS A LIBRARY?

Writing in 1933, Pierce Butler answered this question largely by calling the library "a social apparatus for transferring . . . [books—one social mechanism for preserving the racial memory] to the consciousness of living individuals."[8] Numerous other definitions continue to focus on books, but they also note the structure in which those books are housed. There might even be some mention of the organization, the classification of books, and perhaps their preservation. By the late twentieth century, definitions might recognize books as only one type of resource and make some mention of libraries as service organizations. Future definitions are more likely to highlight digital resources while downplaying the physical setting. Still, they might view the library as a place to socialize, read and study, gather and deliberate, and learn—question, challenge, and apply knowledge.

In an environmental scan, the Research Committee of the Association of College and Research Libraries (ACRL) listed the following assumptions for the future of academic libraries:

- "There will be an increased emphasis on digitizing collections, preserving digital archives, and improving methods of data storage, retrieval, curation, and service."

- "The skill set for librarians will continue to evolve in response to the changing needs and expectations of the populations they serve, and the professional background of library staff will become increasingly diverse in support of expanded service programs and administrative needs."

- "Students and faculty will continue to demand increasing access to library resources and services, and to expect to find a rich digital library presence both in enterprise academic systems and as a feature of social computing."

- "Debates about intellectual property will become increasingly common in higher education, and resources and educational programming related to intellectual property management will become an important part of library service to the academic community."

- "The evolution of information technology will shape both the practice of scholarly inquiry and the daily routine of students and faculty, and demands for technology-related services and technology-rich user environments will continue to grow and will require additional funding."

- "Higher education will be increasingly viewed as a business, and calls for accountability and for quantitative measures of library contributions to the research, teaching, and service missions of the institution will shape library assessment programs and approaches to the allocation of institutional resources."

- "As part of the 'business of higher education,' students will increasingly view themselves as 'customers' of the academic library and will demand high-quality facilities, resources, and services attuned to their needs and concerns."

- "Online learning will continue to expand as an option for students and faculty—both on campus and off—and libraries will gear resources and services for delivery to a distributed academic community."

- "Demands for free, public access to data collected, and research completed, as part of publicly funded research programs will continue to grow."

- "The protection of privacy and support for intellectual freedom will continue to be defining issues for academic libraries and librarians."[9]

Not all of these assumptions are limited to academic libraries. The last one, for instance, applies across libraries.

As the library profession reviews these assumptions and contemplates what libraries will become, it is useful to review various future scenarios. *Futures Thinking for Academic Librarians: Higher Education in 2025*, another ACRL publication, presents twenty-six scenarios "organized in a 'scenario space' visualization tool, reflecting the expert judgment of ACRL members as to their expectations and perceptions about the probability, impact, speed of change, and threat/opportunity potential of each scenario."[10]

The authors of *Futures Thinking for Academic Librarians* ask readers interested in a particular scenario to consider the following questions:

- "If this scenario were to exist today, would we be able to leverage it to our advantage? Do we have the resources, staffing, organizational processes, and strategy right now to take advantage of this scenario?"

- "If this scenario were to exist today, in what ways are we currently vulnerable to the change it represents? In what ways are we unprepared, lacking in resources and staffing, or to what degree are our strategies and underlying values unable to respond effectively to the conditions this scenario represents?"

- "Assuming we had all the staffing and resources we need (a very big assumption, we concede), what could we be doing to leverage this trend to our advantage?"

- "What would need to happen—internally and in the external environment—for this vision to become a reality?"[11]

We created the following scenarios, one for an academic library and the other for a public library, for illustrative purposes and to show that other scenarios might be developed. Readers should consider the questions listed above, but they should also discuss the staffing needed to carry out a favored scenario over the next fifteen years. These scenarios comprise *stories* that contain elements or threads that libraries can use as they modify a story and adapt it to local circumstances and link their discussions to their strategic planning and change management. Both of the following scenarios reflect a change in the types of services provided to the library's community, namely the realization that libraries exist in a competitive environment, their public's expectations are changing, and the staff must assume new roles and acquire new skill sets and abilities.

Academic Library Scenario

This scenario, applicable to research university libraries, is one of the five reported in a new book, *Engaging in Evaluation and Assessment Research*, and it reflects a trend among some of the member libraries in the Association of Research Libraries:

Embracing an institutional service role, the library is totally restructured. It has greatly downsized its physical collections and traditional services. The physical space emphasizes group study space and sharing space with selected campus support units (e.g., the writing center). Moving beyond the physical setting of the library, four types of service roles for librarians emerge:

1. Embedded specialists support faculty research teams and projects, and develop the collection and/or provide access to the collection. These specialists might preserve and make accessible online datasets that faculty members produce for their research. Or, they might convert faculty field notes and photographic collections for online access as well as assist faculty in a Web-based sharing of resources with their colleagues at other institutions.

2. Embedded instructional design librarians work closely with academic programs to support mutually agreed-on student learning outcomes that contribute to student learning and faculty teaching, especially in the online delivery of courses and programs. These librarians include visual literacy in their program-level instruction and contribute to the institution's successful methodology for addressing general education learning outcomes.

3. Librarians engage in special projects such as working with the specialists and instructional design librarians to develop digital guides as finding aids and help guides. These librarians do not have a content role.

4. Librarians work in the center for digital initiatives, which produces digital content for use in campus scholarship and teaching, digitizes signature collections from the library's special collections, and offers consultative services to academic units undertaking digital projects.

The same librarians might perform all of these roles or a subset of them as the libraries lack unlimited resources. With this scenario the library assumes an active, nurturing role of information discovery, supporting and advancing teaching and learning pedagogy, and knowledge production for the institution.

To accommodate the service roles, the library further outsources technical services and no longer offers assistance at a traditionally regularly staffed reference desk. Students and others needing assistance in doing research either make appointments with knowledgeable staff members or convey their questions via the library's homepage or text messaging. The library might also manage the institutional repository.

The primary motivations for pursuing this scenario are the:

- changing information needs and information-seeking behaviors of faculty and students, and

- critical role that the library actively plays in student learning.

The library has not gained a larger percentage of the institutional budget and is engaged in re-engineering operations and staff positions. Given the expectation of program and regional accreditation organizations, the library has dramatically shifted its attention to program-level assessment for all students. The library advances the institutional mission and how it demonstrates campus-wide support, while still coping with the shift in student use of databases over the library's OPAC. Depending on the extent to which a library assumes the four service roles without having staff engaged in more than one service role, there is likely a need to expand the number of professional staff members, not necessarily librarians who hold the master's degree from a program accredited by the American Library Association.[12]

Public Library Scenario

We developed this scenario for a Delphi study of public library futures. Entitled "the happening place," it portrays a flexible, dynamic physical space that encourages social interaction among strangers and collaboration using media and information technologies, and provides good quality food/drinks in its café. The book collection not only contains best sellers in print form, but it also provides access to an ever-growing number of e-books. Regarding the media collection, customers can hear music and/or watch videos, and they can download music and videos for limited periods of time.

There is limited reference desk service (the desk is staffed only by paraprofessionals); professional staff rove and receive referrals from the paraprofessionals. Reference service is also provided via e-mail, chat, text, and instant messaging, and through the use of social networks. Programming for children takes place several times a day, and customers are encouraged to present their own programs.

Techno-savvy staff, many of whom probably do not have the traditional master's degree from a program accredited by the American Library Association, provide direct hands-on assistance. Some of them, especially those in nonprofessional positions, might join the reference librarians in roaming the library and interacting directly with customers.

There are numerous meeting rooms of various sizes, which contain a wide variety of technologies, and there are numerous public access computers and self-checkout machines. The library has lots of broadband bandwidth for Internet access, and there is Wifi access throughout the building. Furthermore, there is a dedicated area for creating/editing music and videos, and the library provides assorted computer software programs for public use. Another feature of the library is comfortable seating and a pleasant ambiance. The café provides good drinks and food and perhaps contains a wine bar.[13]

LIBRARIES ARE STILL SERVICE ORGANIZATIONS

Taking a holistic view, being a *service organization* means that all activities, those related to both technical and public services, are directed at the library's customers and meeting their information needs and expectations. *Service*, which extends to the concept of the library as a place of virtual and physical spaces, indicates that a library is more than the sum of its individual services, those operational and those planned. As Matthews notes, "over the course of time, librarians have developed a set of services and created collections based on a set of assumptions about whom they serve and the needs of the community."[14] Yet as information needs, information-seeking behavior, and customer expectations change in an increasingly competitive environment, those services evolve as the library tries to weave itself into the fabric of the lives of its customers.[15]

A number of managerial leaders recognize the shifting role of the library and define their leadership vision in terms of service. They seek staff buy-in to that vision and realize that the workforce of a library will change and require new skill sets. Furthermore, that vision is not the same as the type normally reported on library Web sites. The university librarian at Boston College University Libraries, for example, uses some powerful language linked to the goals articulated in the university strategic plan in pledging a responsive and learning organization that is service focused. Herein is a service-focused vision—one associated with leadership.[16]

In its mission statement, the University Library System at the University of Pittsburgh makes a link to the university's leadership role and stakes out a "collaborative" service role:

> [The mission] . . . is to provide and promote access to information resources necessary for the achievement of the University's leadership objectives in teaching, learning, research, creativity, and community service, and to collaborate in the development of effective information, teaching, and learning systems.[17]

The Seattle Public Library offers a clear indication of a service-oriented mission, with language such as "inform, enrich and empower," "an informed citizenry," "lifelong learning," "nation and around the world," and "reach out to all members." Reinforcing the power of the message expressed in the mission statement is a set of "aims" and "organizational values" (see figure 1.2, p. 10).

In 2007, Penn State University sponsored a conference on becoming the best student-oriented university in the world. The topics covered include, for example, the vision; maximizing student engagement; defining and measuring student-centeredness; the undergraduate and graduate student perspective; changing student demographics; and opportunities, challenges, and best practices.[18] It seems a logical leap for organizations to embrace customer service in their vision statements—to become the best customer-oriented library in the world.

TYPES OF CUSTOMERS

For public libraries, customers comprise registered individuals who have a library card, whereas for academic libraries, such individuals have an institutional identification card or number, but they probably do not have an actual library card. The institutional identification may be honored by consortial partners. Customers might be subdivided into frequent, moderate, and infrequent categories. Another subdivision is that of lost customer, someone who visited the library in person or remotely and has a library card or other form of institutional identification, but for whatever reason, has not used part of the library's collection or service for a long time (perhaps one year or longer). Such a customer might have had a bad experience or readily finds needed materials from another resource (e.g., the Internet). Another classification is the noncustomer or nonuser, perhaps someone whom the library has not yet gained or who has no interest in library collections. Some noncustomers might be enticed to use the library, whereas others will never, under any circumstances, use the library, either in person or virtually.

Our mission is to become the best public library in the world by being so tuned in to the people we serve and so supportive of each other's efforts that we are able to provide highly responsive service. We strive to inform, enrich, and empower every person in our community by creating and promoting easy access to a vast array of ideas and information, and by supporting an informed citizenry, lifelong learning, and love of reading. We acquire, organize, and provide books and other relevant materials; ensure access to information sources throughout the nation and around the world; serve our public with expert and caring assistance; and reach out to all members of our community.

Aims

We intend to provide:

- Services that are understood and valued by the community and result in library use and involvement from the broadest possible spectrum of residents.
- A caring, welcoming, and lively cultural and lifelong learning center for the community.
- Outstanding reference, readers' advisory, and borrower services that are barrier free for users of all ages, regardless of ethnic background, educational level, economic status, or physical condition.
- Collections of enduring value and contemporary interest that are relevant to user needs and readily accessible from every service point.
- A highly trained and competent staff that reflects the rich diversity of our community and that works together to provide responsive service to all users.
- Appropriate technology to extend, expand, and enhance services in every neighborhood and ensure that all users have equitable access to information.
- Facilities that are inviting, safe, and maintained well and that are available during hours of greatest convenience to users and equitably distributed throughout the city.
- Careful stewardship of the public trust, which ensures accountability and makes the most efficient and effective use of funds, both public and private; fosters collaboration, cooperation, and co-location where possible with other agencies; and builds public/private partnerships to enhance services to our users.

Organizational Values

Service to our users is our reason for being. Those who need us most should be our highest priority.

- All employees, volunteers, and Friends of the Library are valued as human beings and for their important contributions to our service.
- We are a learning organization that is open, collegial, and risk-taking; we nurture our talents and each other and constantly reassess our services and methods to adapt to the changing needs of our community.
- We support and defend intellectual freedom and the confidentiality of borrowers' and inquirers' use of the library.
- All library services are provided in a nonpartisan and nonjudgmental manner that is sensitive to and supportive of human differences.
- Both staff and patrons are encouraged to laugh often and out loud.

Figure 1.2. Service-Oriented Mission Statement: Seattle Public Library. From The Seattle Public Library, *About the Library: Mission Statement* (Seattle, WA: Seattle Public Library, 2010), accessed May 22, 2010, http://www.spl.org/default.asp?pageID=about_mission.

Another characterization of customers is internal and external. The former comprise library staff, and the latter represent members of the broader community. Although much of the literature focuses on external customers, it is important to know who the internal customers—anyone who relies on others in the organization for the performance of a function, delivery of information, or completion of a task that is necessary for the delivery of services to others—are and to encourage fellow staff members, up and down the organization, to think that their opinions matter. Further, managers and nonmanagers need to maintain a dialogue, share ideas, obtain buy-in to the service vision, and develop positive working relationships.

MORE ON LOST CUSTOMERS

Most companies lose between 10 and 40 percent of their customers each year, and Internet turnover—those who do not become repeat users of a Web site—is much higher. Regarding libraries, system-wide managers may report hypothetically to the management and staff of individual libraries that

> [w]e just ran the annual purge of patrons whose records have been inactive for over four years (and had neither fines nor overdue notices). A total of 48,000 records were deleted. Since patrons who only use their cards for database/Internet usage do not have the "circactive" date updated, there may be some deleted library cards for patrons who regularly use our library.

A key set of questions is: What does the library do with this information? Do the staff merely note the results, or do they investigate whether the customers are still members of the community and, if they are, do the staff adopt a strategy to win them back? In other words, can libraries determine their defection rate? What is the trend? Is that percentage increasing, decreasing, or constant?

Once regained, how likely is a customer to again become one of those 48,000? Matthews estimates it takes twenty visits for people to become regular customers; those visits might be virtual ones. Clearly, until achievement of the number twenty, they may be unwilling to try the library; they have not yet become regular users. Complicating matters, regular customers can become lost customers, and not all lost customers are good win-back prospects. An important question becomes, "Is there some way to prioritize lost customers and identify those for whom there is highest probable return on the time and resources invested in regaining them?" Without effective segmentation, time, effort, and money will be wasted on locating and contacting lost customers who are poor prospects for win-back.

LIBRARY BRAND

As previously discussed, the public associates libraries with books. Elizabeth J. Wood, Rush Miller, and Amy Knapp point to the OCLC report *Perceptions of Libraries and Information Resources*, which shows that customers place an equal trust in libraries and search engines and the quality of information both provide. However, if they had to choose, they would give the "nod" to search engines. As stated in the report, "it would be delightful to assume that when respondents say 'books' what they really mean to say that books, in essence, stand for those intangible qualities of information familiarity, information trust, and information quality. The data did not reveal it." The report then adds, "the library has not been successful in leveraging its brand to incorporate growing investments in electronic resources and library web-based services."[19] The challenge for libraries, as the authors and the report indicate, is to define and differentiate their place in the competitive information environment.

As both scenarios previously highlighted indicate, the role of libraries is changing. Some libraries now focus more on managing digital datasets that faculty generate under grants or on becoming more involved in digital publishing. The traditional brand is outdated, but the problem of updating the public's perceptions remains. For any library, certain questions arise:

- Is the brand image correct?

- Does that image reflect what the library means to its customers?

- What do customers expect from the library?

Once these questions have been answered, what has the library set as its brand aspiration, and how will the staff try to attain that ideal? Clearly, customer expectations shift and are shaped through a competitive environment of information and knowledge provision. In essence, with the changing information provision landscape, a library wants to create a brand expectation beyond merely being a conveyor of books and to be a critical partner in meeting the mission of the larger organization or institution.

CUSTOMER EXPECTATIONS

Service and quality are interconnected. *Quality* is the manner in which the service is delivered, or in some cases, not delivered. Furthermore, customers form their own opinions about quality and how the organization provides it. Those opinions fall into two categories: (1) service quality and (2) satisfaction. *Service quality* relates to content and context. It refers to obtaining what prompted the visit, and both service quality and satisfaction cover the experience itself: interactions with staff, ease or difficulty in navigating the organization, and the comfort of the physical environment. Service quality, which is an antecedent to customer satisfaction, might also relate to the performance/performance-expectations gap.

Most important, customer satisfaction, like service quality, deals with the interaction between actual customers and the library (or any service provider). *Satisfaction* is a sense of contentment or a state of mind that customers have about a particular library and the extent to which their expectations have been met or exceeded over a lifetime of use (overall service satisfaction) or during a particular visit (service encounter satisfaction). In either instance customer satisfaction measurement requires a comparison of the actual experience to the expected experience.[20]

ARE LIBRARIANS REALLY AWARE OF CUSTOMER EXPECTATIONS?

Those academic libraries that periodically survey their faculty and students using LibQUAL+® (http://www.libqual.org/home) have some awareness of expectations, mostly those related to service quality; it is important to remember that the survey process does not produce high response rates or generalizable data, and that the survey process is not continuous. Those academic and public libraries using Counting Opinion's LibSAT (http://www.countingopinions.com/) rely on online surveys that capture customer satisfaction information on a continuous basis. Some of this information includes the comments that those completing the survey make. In other instances, libraries might develop their own service quality and/or satisfaction surveys or engage their communities through a community survey or forum or a series of focus group interviews.

On the other hand, a number of libraries may have no method of soliciting information about customer expectations. They may assume they already know what those expectations are and regard any formal means of data collection as a waste of time. Furthermore, the libraries' stakeholders may not demand accountability and proof of service improvement. In essence, the library appears aloof, without realizing the likelihood that staff perceptions are outdated. Due to the economic recession of 2008–2011 and its aftermath, unemployment remains high, and a number of members of the community have used the public library to file for social security and other benefits and seek employment. Libraries benefit from documenting these numbers and uses and from demonstrating their relevance to the community. Still, are the services effective? Might there be ways to improve them? Further, how can the answers to such questions be determined without listening to customers?

Listening to customers might have a side benefit, namely that these individuals might react positively to the opportunity and become advocates for the library. As libraries compete in an ever-changing information environment, they need to be attuned to the information needs and customer expectations of their actual and potential customers. They then need to act on what they learn.

CUSTOMER FEEDBACK

Hernon and Altman note that customer feedback can take three forms: comments, complaints, and compliments. *Comments* are value neutral; they point something out or raise an issue, but, if the comment "is critical, it is still expressed with a mild or nonhostile tone."[21] A *complaint*, which can range from a minor annoyance to a major problem, indicates that the service does not meet a customer's expectations, and a *compliment* indicates praise for a service or staff member. A complaint represents an opportunity to create a dialogue with a customer and to make visible improvement in a service.

Each visit to a library represents a moment of truth for that organization. An exceptional experience leads to strong word-of-mouth recommendations, an average experience goes unmentioned, and a negative experience generates strongly unfavorable word-of-mouth comments. People may respond to what others say. Paul Quinn encourages organizations to view customer complaints as similar to an iceberg. The part above the water represents actual complaints to management. The much bigger part below the surface should represent the major concern. Unhappy customers may not share their discontent or the episode with management. Instead, they may tell others who, in turn, notify others. Quinn advises organizations "to develop a multi-channel feedback system," one perhaps associated with the Kano model.[22] The model encourages consideration of data collection methods such as focus group interviews, customer forums, usability testing, examination of search logs, and surveys and interviews. Once the data are collected, it is important to use them to improve the customer's experience. As Jon Anton and Debra Perkins explain, consistent customer feedback to the service organization produces voice-of-the-customer data that "can then be used to initiate strategies that will retain customers, and thus protect the most valuable corporate assets—loyal customers."[23] We take a broader view, namely that libraries, like other service organizations, should not be content to serve present (internal and external) customers. They need to reach out to lost and never-gained customers. The goal should not be merely to meet current customer expectations.

LINKAGE TO STRATEGIC PLANNING

A strategic plan enables a library to show how it serves the mission and vision of the institution or broader organization by setting goals and strategic directions and working to achieve objectives and activities; all of these actions should lead to improved services and better organizational effectiveness and efficiency. In doing so the library, its stakeholders, and its customers gain "a common understanding of where the library is going, how everyone can work to achieve a common purpose, and how the library will measure and report its progress and levels of success."[24]

The library's mission and vision statements, together with the strategic plan, enable managerial leaders to create a culture, one that is variously described as a culture of assessment, learning, or evidence-based decision making. Whatever the name, the purpose is to achieve service priorities that, for instance, the Seattle Public Library, highlighted in figure 1.2 (p. 10), wants to achieve. Such an achievement may require a new workforce, one not limited to entry with a master's degree in library and information science from a program accredited by the American Library Association. James Neal refers to the workforce of a university, research library as consisting of "feral" and presumably "nonferal" librarians. As he explains, a number of university libraries are hiring staff with "advanced degrees in subject disciplines, with specialized foreign language skills, with teaching experience, or with technology expertise, for example, into librarian positions." These libraries are also developing "new professional assignments in such areas as systems, human resources, fundraising, publishing, instructional technology, and facilities management . . . that demand diverse educational backgrounds." The responsibilities that professional staff members, feral and non-feral, have traditionally performed might be transferred to "support staff and student employees."[25]

Such a workforce should consist of individuals who want to provide exceptional customer service, know themselves, embrace the organization's service mission and vision, are flexible, are able to engage in multitasking, see where the organization and their unit is going and how they fit into a changing organization, are comfortable working outside the physical library, collaborate with others in and outside the library, passionately advocate for the library, and engage in leadership in teams and groups.

CONCLUDING THOUGHTS

Data collection that involves direct customer feedback comprises one way of listening to customers. Libraries might place comment cards strategically throughout the library or have a digital or physical suggestion box for anyone to make comments whenever they want. If libraries engage in formal data collection, they might do so sporadically or at regular intervals. As discussed in subsequent chapters, they might also collect some data on a continual basis. The point is that the more frequently they collect data and involve their customers and show those customers that they value or appreciate their input, the more likely customers are to participate in future data collection and to share their thoughts. Once libraries collect data, they owe customers speedy feedback, showing how they acted on the data. The goal is to improve response rates, actively engage customers in an ongoing dialogue about the library and its services (that relates to planning), and become more service oriented, as specified in figure 1.2.

[T]he research we did showed that overall customer satisfaction is declining.[26]

Denver Public Library*

The aroma of fresh-baked cookies wafts through the Denver Public Library's B2 Conference Center on a chilly December Saturday morning. Customers perch on the edge of their seats in the capacity-filled room as they watch Chef Shellie Kark prepare chocolate peppermint pinwheels and Mexican wedding cookies.

The class, part of the library's popular adult cultural programming Fresh City Life, is about baking for the holidays and is the last in a four-part series titled the ABCs of Great Cooking. After the presentation, nearly 100 attendees line up to chat with the chef, sample the sweets, and share their own cooking successes and challenges with each other. Sounds of laughter and chatter fill the room.

At the Denver Public Library, we listen to our customers in many different ways. Not only do we have focus groups, community meetings, surveys, and comment letters, but we also listen to our customers by their actions. When customers show up in droves, they do not have to speak or write a word. We know we are doing something right.

When Fresh City Life was conceived in 2004, few customers thought they would find a cooking demonstration or a knitting class at a library. But today, people flock to the programs, which include everything from Knit-Flix, where knitters gather to create fabulous scarves and watch a movie, to a Nuts and Bolts Basic Bike Maintenance class.

"People are looking for ways to connect," says Chris Loffelmacher, the brains behind Fresh City Life. "There's a real sense of community and fellowship at our programs." Loffelmacher says that he and his colleague, Simone Groene-Sackett, also listen to what customers prefer by their absence. "When customers *don't* show up in droves," he adds, "that also tells us a lot."

Circulation

Another way in which we listen to our customers—when they do not actually speak or write a word—is by observing and monitoring what they check out. These days, that includes thousands upon thousands of CDs, DVDs, e-books, and audio e-books. Manager of Collection Services Mike Eitner says, "We are seeing explosive growth with eBook checkouts." In fact, from January to August 2010, e-book circulation numbers tripled.

Michelle Jeske, Director of Collections and Technology, says we have responded to that increase by shifting resources from more traditional formats to downloadable formats. "To stay relevant," she adds, "we *must* respond to our customers' wants and needs."

Staff also keep close watch on the dusty book report, a report that shows if an item has not circulated for a certain amount of time. Items not checked out for several years are removed. "Removing items that no longer hold interest for our users provides space for our collection to grow and change," says Jennifer Hoffman, Manager of Books and Borrowing. "Maintaining a collection that is fresh and current is one of the most important ways we listen to our customers," adds Eitner. "No one wants to read a computer book from 1985."

Online Survey

Counting Opinions LibSAT, our online customer survey, is one of the most recent methods we have established as a way of listening to our public. The Customer Satisfaction Survey has been on the public Web site since May 2009 and allows us to collect valuable data, both quantitative and qualitative. Customers go online and tell us what they think about their experience at the library. We hear about their thoughts on everything from programming to hours, parking, and a host of other issues.

The Library's Executive Team reviews comments on a quarterly basis. If we hear from one person or a handful of customers about something they want to see changed, we take that into consideration and determine what action we should take. But we are looking for trends rather than anomalies. It is important to review the information over a period of time so we can see a trend as it develops.

We also believe that to keep in touch with our customers, we must communicate the way they do. Librarian Tara Bannon blogs daily about best sellers, movies, yoga classes, scrapbooking, or music. One recent exchange, which shows that we are not just talking *to* our customers but are having conversations *with* them, went like this:

Anonymous:	I'm not usually a fan of blogs, but I think the DPL blogs have potential. I'd recommend doing more of what you did with the Greek Festival promoting something of local interest, such as the Cherry Blossom Festival downtown.
Tara Librarian:	Thank you for the compliment about the blogs! I agree that posts about local events are wonderful. I will be sure to do a post on the Cherry Blossom Festival. Do you have books or movies that you recommend as tie-ins? Thanks for the suggestions and the feedback!

Anonymous: Sticking just to books that focus on traditional Japanese culture, I'd recommend almost anything by Yasunari Kawabata. For movies, recent hit *Departures*, the original Japanese version of *Shall We Dance?* For music, the best place to start is probably the group Kodo. I hope that helps!

Tara Librarian: Thanks again for the great idea! I've got that post up as suggested. Let me know what you think!

Community Meetings

We have also had some serious conversations with the community. In the summer of 2009, we held a public meeting to ask customers their opinions on how to cope with the dwindling budget. What worked well for us was to list three options: reducing hours system-wide, closing branches, or a combination of the two.

We heard the community's preference to reduce hours system-wide. Customers were hopeful that hours could be restored when the economy improved, but believed that once a branch closes, it is closed for good. In addition to the public meeting, we offered an online survey. The results of the survey mirrored the results from the community meeting.

What also worked well was explaining to the public how the decision-making process would work. It is important for customers to know that the final decision rests with the Library Commission, the eight-person governing board of the library appointed by the mayor, and with city council.

Comments Not Always Positive

Asking our customers their opinions means we take the good with the bad. When we recently revamped our Web site, customers wasted no time telling us they had issues. The main source of irritation was the "My Account" option. On the redesigned site, they could no longer check to see where they stood on the holds list, among a few other issues, and they were not happy.

Some of the comments we received were constructive, and others were not as helpful. We responded. Within a week, our Web Information Services team changed the site. "We basically restored the old version of 'my account,' and kept the new version since it has additional features, so customers have their choice," says Jeske. Since then, we have had few complaints. And it is icing on the cake when we receive messages like the following: "I am very impressed with the usefulness of the Denver Public Library's Web site. Nicely done. Will be there to get my library card this weekend!"

Professional Research Firm

From 2005 to 2008, we worked with OMNI Institute, a professional research firm, to gather feedback about our Summer of Reading program and evaluate the effect of the program on children and teens. We learned a great deal, including the fact that 87 percent of parents who responded to the survey believed the program had increased their child's interest in reading "a little" or "a lot."

In 2008 we conducted focus groups with kids, teens, and parents to learn why kids were signing up but not finishing the program. Research showed that kids often lost their booklets and also that there was a better way in which we could distribute prizes. We made some adjustments, which we believe improved the program. Still, the ratio of kids finishing the program remains about the same. We will keep looking for ways to improve the completion rate.

OMNI also conducted customer surveys about our *Tu Biblioteca Hoy* (Your Library Today) program, which addresses the needs of Denver's growing Hispanic population. The surveys told us one thing in particular: customers want flexibility.

Today, families and individuals come and go at our Community Learning Plazas at their convenience, rather than sitting in a classroom setting.

Thank You, Staff

We would like to thank the real experts who pay attention to our customers' needs, and that is staff. They are the heart and soul of the Denver Public Library, and they know our customers better than anyone. Staff across the board listen and respond every single day so that we can provide better library service.

Nearly four million people walk through our doors each year to check out books, movies, or music; research their dream jobs; or attend a cooking demonstration. It is a privilege to be part of our customers' lives. And it is our responsibility to listen and react to what they have to say.

*Shirley Amore, City Librarian, and Sherry Spitsnaugle, Community Relations, the Denver Public Library.

Hearing Voices*

Established in 1946, seven small libraries became the foundation of today's Pierce County Library. As the year 2011 unfolds, eighteen community libraries serve 554,000 people across the 1,800-square-mile service area, which includes unincorporated Pierce County and fifteen cities and towns that have been annexed into the library district. Given the growth and changes in Pierce County communities, the library repeatedly has asked, "What does the community expect from the library today and tomorrow?" The only way to answer is to listen closely to customers.

Executive Director Neel Parikh set the Pierce County Library on the listening path fifteen years ago, when she brought her strong belief in "engaging the customer" to the system. She expects the staff to listen to the public, not to themselves, and to understand the community and its needs and expectations. With the insights gained, the staff determine the best role for the library to play in meeting its mission. Further, she believes it is critical to have in-depth, thoughtful participation from citizens, especially community leaders and those knowledgeable about the communities served and aware of the broad picture. She reframed "getting out into the community" into "engaging the communities," which changed participation from attending meetings and telling people what the library does to becoming embedded in community groups and efforts, listening to the conversation, and connecting the library to that conversation.

In 2004 the library began to develop its next strategic plan. Because the previous planning process was outdated and insufficiently robust, the executive team chose the balanced scorecard, a strategic planning and performance measurement tool, for its structure and result orientation. In creating the scorecard, the team reviewed the library's mission, vision, and values; examined organizational strengths, weaknesses, opportunities, and threats; and identified initiatives and targets that would move the library toward its goals.

As part of that scorecard, primarily the customer portion, the team decided that the only way that the library could "be the community's choice for the discovery and exchange of information and ideas" was to listen and learn from the people and communities. The team decided the library needed to listen to both customers and nonusers and hear and learn from the entire community, not just loyal customers. The library staff needed to interpret honestly and accept what they heard, then apply professional knowledge and judgment to what was learned.

Becoming a customer-focused organization was critical to achieving the vision and serving the entire community. Customer focus can be defined in many ways, but at its core is simply a commitment to actively listen to taxpayers and others, to make decisions in their best interests, and to reach decisions that address the customer's point of view. Following are examples of how the Pierce County Library approached services and decisions by listening to the customer's point of view, as well as the results of those efforts.

Levy Lid Lift: Going to the Voters

Pierce County Library, an independent junior taxing district, is funded by a dedicated property tax levy; this levy provides 97 percent of its revenue. The maximum assessment is 50 cents per $1,000 of assessed property value. As a result of taxing caps set by legislative action and voter initiatives, there is a steady erosion of the mill rate over time. In order to collect money that exceeds the cap (but is still within the maximum allowed), taxing districts in the state (e.g., fire districts, schools, and libraries) must ask voters to approve reauthorizing the millage to a higher rate.

In 2006 the library's levy was 40 cents. It was time to consider the system's response to community growth and changing needs, which were pushing the limits of the current service. The library had not gone to the voters since 1992, when a request to exceed the 50 cent levy maximum failed, and it had been years since the library had asked the voters to lift the levy limit. The library needed to determine if it should ask voters to restore its tax levy, and if so, what it would accomplish with the additional money. As a customer-focused organization, the decision to go to a vote and the service changes that would be funded by the increased revenue would have to be determined by the communities served.

The library engaged the public in setting priorities for the levy through town hall and public meetings, talking with community organizations, market research, and a Citizens' Advisory Committee. The library gathered input on priority services from surveys in all branch libraries and online, public and town hall meetings, library staff, and the Pierce County Library Foundation. A researcher and planner helped the library prepare two direct telephone call surveys to randomly selected adults in the service area to gain further information about library use and the value and importance of various services. The surveys narrowed the list of possibilities that were generated by the earlier public input and provided accurate information and direction about services taxpayers were willing to fund. A second goal of the survey was to determine if the public was willing to pay more to receive services, and if so, how much more. This information helped determine the budget and what the library could deliver.

While surveying was underway, the Citizens Advisory Committee was tasked with reviewing the library's budget and funding options, evaluating public input, assessing staff interpretation of what was heard from the public, and making a recommendation to the library's governing board of trustees about if and when to go to the voters and how much to ask for.

The committee helped craft a proposal that reflected what the community valued most and met the price point that the members believed was acceptable to the public for adding, increasing, or enhancing those services. Throughout the process its members pointedly questioned library assumptions, asked questions, and refused to allow us to slide by on "people love us." They wanted numbers, facts, and specifics.

When the committee was satisfied, the chair recommended to the board of trustees that the library ask voters to fund a levy lid lift. The committee recommended a levy rate of 48 cents (not the 50 cent maximum). The board approved taking the proposal to voters on the September 2006 ballot. That proposal promised the public that, by reauthorizing the levy, the library would be open more hours, provide more books and other materials, increase services for youth, and improve customer service and the technology available for public use. (If the committee had not been supportive, the proposal would not have gone to the voters.) The levy passed by 55.8 percent, raising the library's budget 47 percent—from $17.2 million in 2006 to $25.3 million in 2007.

The committee also advised the staff to develop a short, simple way to report progress in fulfilling the promises and to demonstrate specifically what the public was getting for its money. The one-page *Levy Goals and Benchmarks*, reported to the public quarterly, recorded progress and accomplishments. The library also reported four times to the public in 2007, via brochures and posters, listserv messages, Web site information, and media relations, as it implemented the promises contained in the proposal.

On June 19, 2007, an editorial in the local newspaper, *The News Tribune*, acknowledged the library for its listening and responsiveness to the public: "Pierce County Library users agreed last fall to put up the bucks. Now the Library system is delivering the goods." The editorial continued with details of the levy promises and a description of the expansion of services, including a 20 percent increase in open hours, a 30 percent reduction in wait-time for popular books and movies, added materials and computers, and more reading and homework support for children and teens. In its conclusion, the editorial stated: "That focus on delivering what was promised is plain, responsible stewardship of public dollars. It also will keep the Library system in good standing for the next time it needs voters to reaffirm their support for public libraries."

Pierce County Library 2030: Planning for Future Facilities

As the library began implementing the levy promises in 2007, it convened a nineteen-member community planning team to prepare the next strategic plan. Three two-hour meetings were held during a two-month period, at which the team reviewed the library's strategies and objectives and considered initiatives that would help the library achieve its vision. One outcome was the decision to focus on facilities: "What do our communities need and want in the next 20+ years, and how can the library align its services and buildings to meet those needs?"

A collaborative community process was designed to listen to customers. Group 4 Architecture, Research + Planning, Inc., from San Francisco, was hired to help, because the library needed architect/planning expertise to support this major effort. Building on the levy process, surveys and community discussions were incorporated into the listening phase of Pierce County Library 2030. A staff advisory team gathered internal ideas and issues, and local community meetings attracted 1,200 community members. In addition, five regional community leader advisory groups, composed of leaders invited from cities, communities, organizations, schools, colleges, and other groups, were created. More than 100 leaders attended two interactive workshops, where they identified the needs of their regions and evaluated the library's preliminary recommendations and potential improvement strategies. A key piece of the groups' work was to identify opportunities for development and partnerships between the library and community partners.

Finally, fifty-seven community decision makers were invited to an all-day strategic visioning workshop to identify future challenges for the county and envision how the library could help meet future community needs. Especially valuable were five visions the group created of how the library could contribute to the future of Pierce County communities. Following the workshop, all of the words captured during the day were fed into the word cloud generator (http://www.wordle.net) to create a word picture of the library. It became the cover for the *Strategic Vision Workshop Summary Report* and is regularly used to remind ourselves of how the public views us. The two largest words are *library* and *community*.

While the recession ended any immediate thoughts of a bond for a major facilities project, what the public told the library through the process has been invaluable as we adjust to the new norm of decreased or flat revenue and increased use. The vision that the public painted, and the value expected from the library, inform decisions as we reexamine what we do and how and why we do it. New or expanded buildings are not feasible at this time, but we believe that despite that, "2030 starts now." The work with community leaders also has strengthened the library's connections with cities, agencies, and community groups that are engaged in Pierce County's future and are now alert to opportunities to partner with the library.

Assessing the Collection

The board of trustees has long been committed to maintaining a healthy materials budget. Since 2002, that budget has been set at 16 percent of the overall budget. When the overall budget increased as a result of the successful levy, the materials budget increased proportionately. The library had more books, movies, and music than it had space for these collections. In 2008, eight staff members investigated what people wanted and expected in the collection and how they used the existing materials. Key listening tactics focused on statistics available through the library's integrated library system, Polaris, and conducting surveys.

For the surveys, the library purchased an unlimited-use subscription to Survey Monkey for $200 a year. This tool provided the functionality needed, vendor support, and an ability to process unlimited responses. The surveys targeted on-site users at all locations and service stops, online customers, children, teens, nonusers, staff, and Spanish-speaking customers. In those surveys the public described its use and opinion of the collection. The staff were surveyed about the collection and their experiences in helping customers find (or not find) what they wanted. The study team also reviewed past surveys that asked collection-related questions and conducted informal interviews with users, and the communications department director conducted two focus group interviews with nonusers.

Not all voices are audible: customers send many messages without saying a word, behaving differently from how they say they behave. The team therefore balanced survey responses and anecdotal reports with the statements that customers made through their actions, as demonstrated in circulation and use statistics.

An immediate result of the project was to realign materials' budget allocations by increasing the DVD, audio book, downloadable e-book and audio book, and large print budgets. In 2010 circulation increased 37 percent since 2008, and the overall collection turnover rate increased 15 percent from 2008 to 2009. Information from the collection assessment is critical to making choices with a bigger view and was invaluable during one branch's floor plan redesign, which required a large weeding project when space was reallocated and some shelves were lowered or eliminated.

Listening Is Challenging

Although it is hard to remove the library filter when we listen to customers, responding to our questions may be challenging for the public as well. Carefully crafted questions must help people respond from their point of view as users who are unfamiliar with the possibilities. The public can be conflict averse and not willing to speak up and disagree with us. Customers need a neutral forum that allows them to be comfortable telling their truth. The value of listening becomes clear as we make decisions on how to spend tax dollars and how to best serve communities, then observe the impact of those choices.

*Georgia Lomax, Deputy Director, Pierce County Library System, 3005 112 St. E, Tacoma, WA 98446.

NOTES

1. Karen E. Klein, "Building Customer Relations by Listening," *Bloomberg Businessweek* (June 1, 2007): 1, accessed May 17, 2010, http://www.businessweek.com/smallbiz/content/jun2007/sb20070601_858776.htm.

2. Joseph R. Matthews, *The Customer-Focused Library: Re-inventing the Public Library from the Outside-In* (Santa Barbara, CA: Libraries Unlimited, 2009), 12.

3. Peter Hernon and Ellen Altman, *Assessing Service Quality: Satisfying the Expectations of Library Customers*, 2nd ed. (Chicago: American Library Association, 2010), 4.

4. Joseph R. Matthews, *The Evaluation and Measurement of Library Services* (Westport, CT: Libraries Unlimited, 2007), 267–68.

5. For additional coverage of quality function deployment, see "Quality Function Deployment: Overview," accessed July 31, 2010, http://thequalityportal.com/q_know01.htm.

6. Cecilia Garibay, Humberto Gutiérrez, and Artuor Figueroa, "Evaluation of a Digital Library by Means of Quality Function Deployment (QFD) and the Kano Model," *The Journal of Academic Librarianship* 36, no. 2 (March 2010): 131.

7. Matthew Dixon, Karen Freeman, and Nicholas Toman, "Stop Trying to Delight Your Customers," *Harvard Business Review* 78, nos. 7/8 (July–August 2010): 118.

8. Pierce Butler, *An Introduction to Library Science* (Chicago: University of Chicago Press, 1933), xi.

9. Association of College and Research Libraries, *Environmental Scan 2007* (Chicago: Association of College and Research Libraries, 2008), accessed July 1, 2010, http://www.ala.org/ala/mgrps/divs/acrl/publications/whitepapers/Environmental_Scan_2007%20FINAL.pdf.

10. David J. Staley and Karen J. Malenfant, *Futures Thinking for Academic Librarians: Higher Education in 2025* (Chicago: Association of College and Research Libraries, 2010), 4, accessed July 1, 2010, http://www.ala.org/ala/mgrps/divs/acrl/issues/value/futures2025.pdf.

11. Ibid., 22–23.

12. Peter Hernon, Robert E. Dugan, and Danuta A. Nitecki, *Engaging in Evaluation and Assessment Research* (Santa Barbara, CA: Libraries Unlimited, 2011).

13. Peter Hernon and Joseph R. Matthews, "Public Libraries in the Year 2025" (unpublished manuscript, 2011).

14. Matthews, *Customer-Focused Library*, 5.

15. Ibid., 4.

16. See Boston College University Libraries, "Message from the University Librarian: Welcome to the Boston College Libraries" (2009), accessed September 22, 2010, http://www.bc.edu/libraries/about/universitylibrarian.html.

17. University of Pittsburgh, University Library System, "About Us: The University Library System (ULS) Mission" (2007), accessed May 22, 2010, http://www.library.pitt.edu/uls/mission.html.

18. Penn State University, "Conference to Focus on Becoming a More Student-Centered University" (2008), accessed September 20, 2010, http://live.psu.edu/story/26927.

19. Elizabeth J. Wood, Rush Miller, and Amy Knapp, *Beyond Survival: Managing Academic Libraries in Transition* (Westport, CT: Libraries Unlimited, 2007), 22; Cathy De Rosa, Joanne Cantrell, Diane Cellentani, Janet Hawk, Lillie Jenkins, and Alane Wilson, *Perceptions of Libraries and Information Resources* (Dublin, OH: OCLC, 2005), sections 6, 7, accessed July 26, 2010, http://www.oclc.org/reports/pdfs/Percept_all.pdf.

20. See Hernon and Altman, *Assessing Service Quality.*

21. Ibid., 65.

22. Quintessential Marketing Consulting Pty Ltd ®, "Customer Feedback: The Customer Complaint Iceberg" (2006), accessed May 17, 2010, http://www.quinntessential.com.au/customer-feedback.htm.

23. Jon Anton and Debra Perkins, *Listening to the Voice of the Customer* (New York: Alexander Communications Group, 1997), 5–6.

24. Joseph R. Matthews, *Strategic Planning and Management for Library Managers* (Westport, CT: Libraries Unlimited, 2005), 58.

25. James G. Neal, "Raised by Wolves: The New Generation of Feral Professionals in the Academic Library," *Library Journal* 131, no. 2 (February 15, 2006): 42.

26. Klein, "Building Customer Relations by Listening," 1.

2

Obtaining Staff Buy-In

Training is everything. The peach was once a bitter almond;
cauliflower is nothing but cabbage with a college education.
—Mark Twain, *Pudd'nhead Wilson* (1894)[1]

Developing and sustaining a program of listening to the customer has enormous implications for any library. In short, such a program means a different way of operating—placing the information needs and expectations of customers as the highest priority. Perhaps a better way of stating it is to decide on those information needs and expectations that the library will meet and those that it will regard as highest priority. Data about different groups of customers will have to be gathered, analyzed, synthesized, and discussed to produce an action plan. Implicit within any such plan is the need for staff to operate in new ways and learn new abilities, skills, and knowledge. This means that the library will have to develop and fully support a staff training and development plan.

One's perspective will shape one's perceptions of library customers. A staff member's perceptions are strongly influenced by interactions with a small subset of the customers coming into a library. Staff may claim that they "know their customers and what they want." Based on their interactions with this subset of customers, they might generalize to all of the library's customers. Yet these generalizations, though they may be valid for a specific subset of customers, will most likely be incorrect for all of the library's customers. This is one of the primary reasons why a voice-of-the-customer program can have significant and wide-ranging impact on any library. As discussed in chapters 3 through 6, there are a variety of ways in which librarians can learn more about the different market segments of the library's customers.

Implicit in any staff training and development plan is the explicit approval of the library's top management team. This group of managers must provide continuing and constant encouragement for library staff members to embrace wholeheartedly the training plan. The leadership exercised by this group of managers is key to the success of a library being willing to listen to customers and act on what they say.

LEADERSHIP THROUGHOUT THE ORGANIZATION

Leadership is similar to the words *peace* or *love* in that there are many definitions. In fact, there are more than 100 definitions for *leadership*. It seems that many people refer to library directors as leaders; as Peter Northouse comments, the person in charge of the organization is an *assigned leader*, but that person may, in fact, be more of an administrator or manager than a true leader.[2] Any perusal of blogs maintained by librarians, especially Gen-Xers, indicates that they do not always see their directors as leaders. No study of library directors has discovered a common definition of leadership, nor should we expect to see a single definition. However, common to a number of the definitions are mention of leadership vision, change management, and getting followers to buy into that vision. *Buy-in* refers to implementation of that vision through an action plan.[3] The vision, which must inspire others to want to accomplish it and be included as part of strategic planning, goes beyond the written institutional and organizational mission and vision statements readily displayed on most library homepages. A vision presents a possible and desirable future state of the organization, one that differs from the present state. The vision of leadership permeates the workplace and is manifested in the actions, beliefs, values, and goals of the director and the senior management team. When shared with staff, the vision explains why they should work together to achieve the desired future. Shared with customers, the vision shapes customers' understanding of why they should work with the library to accomplish a better future.

Leadership is not confined to a position but should exist throughout organizations. Naturally, the director should be a true leader, as should the members of the senior management team. Managers at other levels should exhibit some characteristics of leadership, as should everyone in the organization. Those not assigned to formal leadership positions, known as followers, should be willing to serve as leaders when they have the needed expertise. Such a fluid view of leadership should exist in those organizations that rely on teams to accomplish tasks.

J. Richard Hackman believes that effective teams spend a substantial amount of time on team socialization and professional growth. The belief is that socialization and professional development lead to effectiveness and better results. He identifies five conditions that increase the likelihood of team success or effectiveness. The first three conditions refer to the actual design of the team, and the final two reinforce the team's work once in place. It is common for most organizations to stop after meeting the first three conditions. However, effective teams need all five conditions to be present:

1. *A real team*: Necessary for establishing the foundation for the team's future work, this condition involves making sure that the tasks assigned to the team are clear, members work together, the team's authority has been delineated, and membership is stable over time.

2. *A compelling direction*: Someone in authority sets the direction for the team. Although the direction guides the team about what is expected at the end of its work, it does not specify the means by which the team gets there.

3. *An enabling team structure*: The structure is the *shell* of the team; structural features include designing team tasks that motivate members, putting the right people on the team, ensuring an appropriate size to the team, and balancing the mix of members to meet the assigned tasks.

4. *A supportive organizational context*: The goal is to align the rewards, information, education, and technological systems so that they reinforce the team's efforts.

5. *Team coaching*: Such coaching refers to facilitating group process and development. The coach motivates the team, serves as a consultant when team members have questions, and educates members.

Hackman poses a set of questions that characterize each condition (e.g., for the first condition, "How clear are the team's boundaries?"). The answers to these questions determine the extent to which each condition is present in an organization that uses teams.[4] Effective leaders, he maintains, ensure that "the team is set up right in the first place, that it is well supported organizationally and that members have ready access to the kind of coaching that can help them exploit the team's potential to the fullest extent possible."[5] Applying Hackman's framework to libraries, Elaine Martin notes that "effective leaders ensure conditions are in place for teams to be successful"; however, she adds, "leadership behavior or personality is nonetheless an insufficient determinant of effective teams."[6]

Various researchers have explored qualities that leaders should have. Warren Bennis argues that "adaptive capacity is the most important" of these.[7] His choice makes sense, because librarians are engaged in change management and the transition to an unknown future. They must be able to adapt to unanticipated situations. As complementary qualities, we would add those associated with emotional intelligence, which "involves the ability to perceive accurately, appraise, and express emotion; the ability to access and/or generate feelings when they facilitate thought; the ability to understand emotion and emotional knowledge; and the ability to regulate emotions to provide emotional and intellectual growth."[8] In essence, the qualities center on self-awareness and one's relationships with others. Such qualities should exist throughout the organization, with a complete set possessed by the director and the senior management team.

Other than possessing emotional intelligence, directors and the senior management team should be aware of and practice a variety of leadership theories, including, for instance, resonant leadership, which relates to coping with the challenges faced by stress, pressure, sacrifice, and dissonance.[9] A little known, but secondary, leadership theory is applicable to ascertaining and acting on the voice of the customer. This theory, known as *service leadership*, can be used in conjunction with other theories, including, for instance, transformational leadership, situational leadership, authentic leadership, and adaptive leadership.

Service Leadership

Svafa Grönfeldt and Judith Strother present one of the best introductions to service leadership, which they define as "the culture that empowers the organization to strategize its promises, design its processes [service processes regulate the interactions with customers], and engage its people in a proactive quest for competitive advantage." The critical elements of this definition are "culture," empowerment, and "strategize," and this definition relies on a "service-leadership mind-set" that permeates the entire organization; "every employee-customer encounter is considered to be an invaluable opportunity to improve customer service and engender customer loyalty."[10] The organizational culture encourages collaboration "dedicated to the customer" (e.g., team building and staff coaching) and cultivation, thereby helping customers to "reach their full potential."[11] Service leadership envisions customers and employees working together to design service processes that are both effective and efficient in meeting customer needs and expectations.

The literature on customer service discusses the importance of empowering the staff with the authority to make work-related decisions that resolve the information needs of their customer. One example follows:

> Some years ago, as I was checking out of a . . . [h]otel, the couple in front of me complained to the desk clerk of cobwebs in their room. Without any hesitation, the clerk immediately gave them the room at no charge. He didn't have to check with a supervisor or dither about whether to do it or not. He just did it. That is employee empowerment.[12]

Grönfeldt and Strother envision an "empowerment continuum," which ranges from "limited empowerment" to "full license to act." According to them, that continuum (see figure 2.1) asks library leaders to envision the future of their organization and to determine whether or not they favor, for instance, "full license to act." If they do, how will they go about achieving full trust in the staff? This may not be as hard as it seems at first glance. After all, trust is an important quality associated with leadership. No leader wants to lose staff trust; it is difficult to regain.

RESISTANCE TO CHANGE

One of the realities facing any leader is that an organization that embarks on any new project will inevitably encounter some resistance from individuals as well as groups within the organization. Resistance to change is a normal, not an abnormal, reaction of human beings. Yet library mangers are often surprised when there is pushback to a new program, service, or change in the way a process is handled.

Staff members pick up on any lack of enthusiasm by the director and the senior management team to proposed changes. Ensuring that the director and the team are "on board" with any proposed change is fundamental for any planned change. Not only must they "talk the talk," they must also demonstrate through their actions that they are "walking the walk." The literature on change management is clear that many change programs fail due to the lack of clearly defined or achievable objectives and the lack of commitment by senior management. Library directors and the senior management team must lead first by engagement and example.

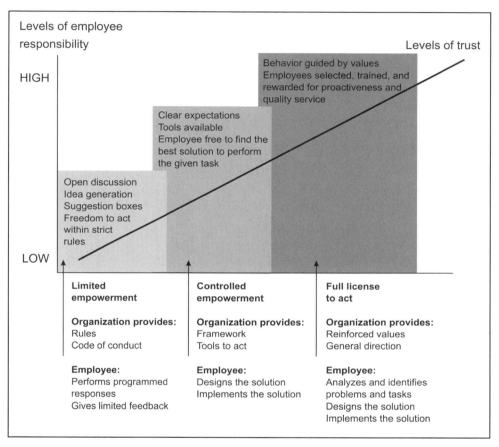

Figure 2.1. The Empowerment Continuum. Reprinted with permission from Svafa Grönfeldt and Judith Strother, *Service Leadership: The Quest for Competitive Advantage* (Thousand Oaks, CA: Sage, 2006), 55.

Winning the hearts and minds of library staff members is the key to any change management program. One important part of winning over staff members is to put together a communication plan that accomplishes five things:

1. Presents the right message

2. Presents it to the right people

3. Presents it at the right time

4. Presents it using the right media or method of delivery

5. Presents it with the right person (who delivers the message)

The messages that will be delivered as a result of developing a communication plan must be conveyed carefully and constantly. Staff members must accept the service vision and the value of the library listening to (and valuing) the voice of the customer. At the same time, it is important to listen to any staff concerns that they raise. After all, frontline staff members deal most frequently with the library's customers, and their involvement and belief in the value of the program are vital to the success of the voice-of-the-customer program.

Pushback from any staff member (or manager) comes in a variety of forms. Consider the following reasons (excuses) to ignore (resist) a proposed voice-of-the-customer program:

- We are overloaded now—simply too busy.

- This is going to cost money—and the library's budget is being seriously cut.

- There is no need to listen to customers—we are too busy as it is.

- This project is doomed to fail—so why put forth any energy?

- Nobody will listen to my concerns.

- We do not have time for anything new.

- There is too much on our plate as it is.

- What a great idea—but no one besides me will be interested.

- There is too much bureaucracy here.

- What do customers know?

- We have a risk-averse culture here.

- We cannot shift resources now.

- We do not really care what customers think or expect.

- This sounds way too complicated.

- You mean I will have to learn about this social media stuff?

- It will die in committee.

- Let us wait for the economy (and our budget) to improve.

- If it is not broken, do not fix it.

- What do you mean? We know what our customers need!

- I have already got enough headaches.

- We have too much change going on now with budget cutbacks.

- Nothing ever changes around here.

- Not another management fad.

- This will mean even more meaningless meetings.

- It will be hard to encourage and sustain the motivation to do this.

- We need to hire an expert to do this or show us how to do this.

- It is not my job.

- They expect me to learn about social media on my own time?

The list could go on and on, but you get the idea.

Implicit in any communications plan is the need to develop a staff-training plan. Some staff members may have to assume new responsibilities and learn about new tools that will be used to gather, analyze, and utilize the information they receive from customers. Two of the areas that will most likely have a big impact in developing a training plan are developing leadership capacity throughout the organization and addressing the topic of social media or social networking.

STAFF DEVELOPMENT PLAN

The hundreds of thousands of new users flocking each day to a wide variety of social media platforms are not exhibiting a new trend in behavior; they are simply illuminating human behavior in an environment where it is possible to measure networking activity. The ease with which individuals can network online has made this human activity faster, more convenient, and more likely to mutate quickly.

Any staff development plan focuses on the skills or competencies that library staff members need now or will need in the short-term future. Aside from traditional customer interaction and customer service skills, increasingly staff members are expected to learn continually about online resources available on the Internet. The concept of applying new online technology tools within any organizational settings has been referred to as Web 2.0[13] and by extension, Library 2.0 within library and information science. As many people adopted and embraced these tools, a shift occurred in how people discover, read, and share news, information, and content. This fusion of sociology and technology has transformed the monologue (one to many) into dialogue (many to many) and has allowed people to move from simply being consumers of information to becoming publishers of information at the same time. This social networking and social media have also been called user-generated content and consumer-generated media. The Web sites included within this broad domain include, for instance, blogs, video- and picture-sharing sites, wikis, and text sharing.

The importance of any library understanding and embracing social networking cannot be overstated. The reason is quite simple: millions of people use these tools daily, and more join daily. Failure to provide a range of online services that will appeal to these millions of users means that the library will become more irrelevant to them.

The importance of social media is illustrated by the following statistical profile of the social networking arena:

- If Facebook were a country, it would be the third most populated in the world (trailing only China and India).

- The number of minutes spent on Facebook per month in 2010 was 500 billion; in 2009, the number was only 150 billion.

- Some 25 billion items (Web links, news stories, photos, video links, blog posts, and so forth) are shared each month on Facebook.

- The amount of video uploaded to YouTube every minute of the day more than doubled from 2009 to 2010.

- Four billion images are hosted on Flickr; this number is thirteen times more than image collections of the Library of Congress.

- The average number of tweets per day on Twitter in 2010 was 27 million; this number is eight times higher than the average for 2009.[14]

Drawing on a convenience sample of U.S. librarians, Curtis Rogers found most use focused on blogs, Facebook, and instant messaging (for reference requests).[15] Webjunction (http://www.webjunction.org/), a Web site for librarians that is designed to explain and encourage the use of technology for libraries, recently conducted an online survey. Because the sample consisted of Webjunction members, most of the respondents were library staff members. The survey asked respondents to indicate the amount of use of ten online tools, including such things as professional or social networking sites, blogs, and wikis. Slightly more than 60 percent of the respondents used one or more of the tools more frequently than quarterly. Most discouraging is the fact that, for many of these tools, the amount of use was "never" (see figure 2.2).[16]

The implications are clear. As Roy Tennant observed on his blog *Digital Libraries*, figure 2.2 is a "graphical representation of an industry that was intentionally marginalizing itself."[17] If staff are not engaged in the same arenas as their customers are, they and the library will be left behind.

A great starting point for any staff development plan is the "23 things" program, originally developed by Helene Blowers (formerly with the Charlotte & Mecklenburg Library and now with the Columbus Metropolitan Library), which asked staff to experiment with a variety of Web 2.0 tools over a nine-week period.[18] While many other libraries picked up on the concept and have encouraged their staff to get involved in learning more about these "things," perhaps a majority of public libraries have not done so. Furthermore, not all staff will complete the list of things to do. The intent of the original "23 things" and the many updates of the list is to ensure that staff members share or use such tools as the following:

- Blogging

- Blog search engines

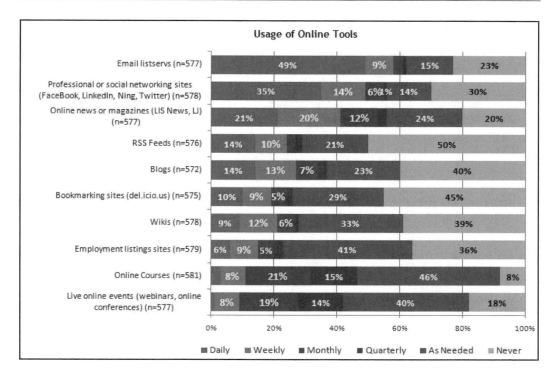

Figure 2.2. Usage of Online Tools. Reprinted with permission, WebJunction, Info@webjunction.org. The figure appears in a Webjunction survey; see http://blog.webjunctionworks.org/index.php/2010/ 07/06/library-staff-report-their-use-of-online-tools/?utm_source=WhatCountsEmail&utm_medium= Crossroads&utm_campaign=2010-07+Crossroads (accessed August 9, 2010).

- Picture, image, and graphic tools (Flickr, http://www.flickr.com/)

- Really Simple Syndication (RSS) feeds and Google Reader for keeping up with blog content and news stories and for sharing items with friends and colleagues

- Library Thing (http://www.librarything.com/) for cataloging books online for free

- Twitter (http://twitter.com/), a social networking and microblogging site

- Facebook (http://www.facebook.com), a social network connecting friends and colleagues

- Tagging

- Wikis

- Cloud apps for sharing images, files, links, music, and videos (Google Apps, http://www.google.com/apps/; Zoho, http://www.zoho.com/).

- Streaming media (YouTube, http://www.youtube.com/)

- Podcast search tools

- Download audio files (e-books, e-audiobooks)

- New learning environments, including Second Life (http://secondlife.com/)

- Group collaboration tools for sharing information and coordinating activities

The key in a "23 things" program is to recognize what activities included in the list will change over time as new technologies and Web sites are introduced and become popular. Staff members need to recognize that next year they might participate in a "five new things" training program. Obviously, there should be recognition and celebration of all staff members who complete all or major parts of any "23 things" program.

A VOICE-OF-THE-CUSTOMER PROGRAM

Figure 2.3 depicts the three broad activities related to implementing a voice-of-the-customer program in either an academic or a public library. The *first activity* is becoming aware of the potential and impact of the program. One of the more important components of this first activity is recognizing that library staff have to listen carefully to a wide segment of customers through data collection methods that libraries have relied on for years. They must also use new tools and learn about the ones they are only beginning to use. Many of the new tools discussed in this chapter are a subset of a broader technology-driven focus that has been called Web 2.0 and/or Library 2.0.

Figure 2.3. A Voice-of-the-Customer Process

The *second activity* is gaining familiarity with Web 2.0 and Library 2.0 technology tools and their possible uses. This is where the staff training and development program should focus. All staff members should be aware of, and familiar with, social network Web sites, blogs, RSS feeds and readers, and mobile devices. Otherwise, they cannot interact with people who daily use these tools and technologies or who want to use them.

In addition to understanding how a specific tool works through the staff member's hands-on learning, it is important for staff to interact with one another to draw out the implications and "so what's?" as they use such tools. The use of Web 2.0/Library 2.0 requires a shift in services, processes, skills, and roles, and that starts with a shift in the mindset for all who work in a library. A new mindset requires viewing the world from several different perspectives and having new and different conversations with library customers.

The *third activity* involves using new knowledge about tools and customers to design, develop, and deliver new services that bring real value to the lives of the library's customers. It is essential for a library to listen carefully to customers and then react in a positive manner to what customers are saying about new services.

Let there be no mistake! Adopting and implementing a "listening to the voice-of-the-customer program" is not for the fainthearted. Embedded in any such program are the elements for a substantial amount of change in any library. For a library that embraces service leadership and truly listens to (and values) its customers, the messages that customers deliver most likely will indicate that the library must change the way it provides some services, possibly eliminating some of them, and introduce some new ones in an attempt to be more responsive to customer information needs and expectations.

CONCLUDING THOUGHTS

Ensuring an ongoing commitment to change management and keeping up with changing customer information needs and expectations will put pressure on libraries, especially those that faced substantial budget cuts resulting from the economic recession of 2008–2010 and its aftermath. The recession and the declining resources that ensued should not lessen the commitment to a service vision and how best to meet customer needs and expectations. At the same time, it is important to empower the staff to better serve customers, develop effective teams, and develop effective organizational leadership. Staff development programs might examine the culture of service that companies such as L.L. Bean, the Ritz-Carleton Hotel, and Nordstrom provide. There is ample literature on the philosophy of customer service each provides, and from the assorted writings, libraries could identify similarities and dissimilarities and what might work the best for them. The senior management team should also engage in succession planning as the group looks to the future and plans position reengineering and staff qualities that will best serve the library of the future.

> *A company is people.... [E]mployees want to know ... am I being listened to or am I a cog in the wheel? People really need to feel wanted.*
> —Richard Branson[19]

NOTES

1. The Quotations Page. "Mark Twain," accessed August 10, 2010, http://www.quotationspage.com/quote/30207.html.

2. Peter G. Northouse, *Leadership: Theory and Practice*, 5th ed. (Thousand Oaks, CA: Sage, 2009), 5.

3. See Peter Hernon, ed., *Shaping the Future: Advancing the Understanding of Leadership* (Santa Barbara, CA: Libraries Unlimited, 2010).

4. J. Richard Hackman, *Leading Teams: Setting the Stage for Great Performances* (Boston: Harvard Business School Press, 2002).

5. Ibid., 258.

6. Elaine Martin, "Team Effectiveness and Members as Leaders," in *Making a Difference: Leadership and Academic Libraries*, ed. Peter Hernon and Nancy Rossiter (Westport, CT: Libraries Unlimited, 2007), 128.

7. Warren Bennis and Patricia W. Biederman, *Still Surprised: A Memoir of a Life in Leadership* (San Francisco: Jossey-Bass, 2010), 160.

8. John D. Mayer and Peter Salovey, "What Is Emotional Intelligence," in *Emotional Development and Emotional Intelligence: Educational Implications*, ed. Peter Salovey and David J. Sluyter (New York: Basic Books, 1997), 10.

9. See Peter Hernon, Joan Giesecke, and Camila A. Alire, *Academic Librarians as Emotionally Intelligent Leaders* (Westport, CT: Libraries Unlimited, 2007).

10. Svafa Grönfeldt and Judith Strother, *Service Leadership: The Quest for Competitive Advantage* (Thousand Oaks, CA: Sage, 2006), 5.

11. Ibid., 269.

12. AllBusiness.com, "Customer Service Experience: Employee Empowerment Contributes to the Customer Service Experience," accessed August 12, 2010, http://www.allbusiness.com/sales/customer-service/3876268-1.html.

13. Darcy DiNucci first used the term Web 2.0. See Darcy DiNucci, "Fragmented Future," *Print* 53, no. 4 (1999): 32. See also Eric Knorr, "Fast Forward 2010—The Fate of It," *CIO* (May 15 2004): 14–19.

14. Data provided courtesy of Marta Kagan, as covered in "What Is Social Media Now?," accessed August 9, 2010, http://www.slideshare.net/mzkagan/what-is-social-media-now-4747765.

15. Curtis R. Rogers, "Social Media, Libraries, and Web 2.0: How American Libraries Are Using New Tools for Public Relations and to Attract New Users," in *German Library Association Annual Conference in Frankfurt, June 2nd to 5th, 2009,* accessed August 9, 2010, http://www.slideshare.net/crr29061/social-media-libraries-and-web-20-how-american-libraries-are-using-new-tools-for-public-relations-and-to-attract-new-users-second-survey-november-2009.

16. For Webjunction survey results, see http://blog.webjunctionworks.org/index.php/2010/07/06/library-staff-report-their-use-of-online-tools/?utm_source=WhatCountsEmail&utm_medium=Crossroads&utm_campaign=2010-07+Crossroads, accessed August 9, 2010.

17. Roy Tennant, "An Industry in Search of Failure," *Digital Libraries* (blog), July 3, 2010, accessed September 19, 2010, http://blog.libraryjournal.com/tennantdigitallibraries/2010/07/13/an-industry-in-search-of-failure/.

18. Helene Blowers, "Public Library of Charlotte & Mecklenburg County," *LibraryJournal.com* (March 15, 2007), accessed August 13, 2010, http://www.libraryjournal.com/article/CA6423431.html.

19. "Lesson #1: Be a Good Leader," accessed August 10, 2010, http://www.evancarmichael.com/Famous-Entrepreneurs/592/Lesson-1-Be-A-Good-Leader.html.

3

Methodologies (Structured and Solicited Approaches) for Gathering Voice-of-the-Customer Data

Research is formalized curiosity. It is poking and prying with a purpose.[1]

This is the first of four methodological chapters, each of which has a different focus (see figure 3.1, p. 42). *Structured* and *solicited* approaches refer to formal methodologies in which librarians directly seek customer input about the services they provide, the extent of customer satisfaction, relevant information needs, and areas requiring service improvement. These methodologies can be either quantitative (generating numbers for which measurement is possible) or qualitative (any information that can be captured but is not numerical in nature). Data collected using either or both quantitative and qualitative methodologies are appropriate for the evaluation and assessment of library services.

The more an organization listens to customers and customers think an organization acts on what they say, the more likely customers will readily share their expectations. Terry Vavra notes that there are different customer groups, namely current customers (e.g., high-value, special-interest, and vocal/conspicuous ones), past and potential customers, and competitors' customers.[2] The same methodologies would not be relevant among all of the groups (or those discussed in chapter 1), and the methodologies tend to emphasize self-reporting—what people want to reveal about themselves. One problem is that their impressions are not always accurate. Further, any method of data collection has both strengths and weaknesses; the investigators need to identify the weaknesses and take corrective action as needed. The result might be the use of more than one method of data collection so that the library gains deeper insights into its actual and potential customers as well as those it is trying to regain.

	Structured	Unstructured
Solicited	**Chapter 3** Surveys: Customer satisfaction and service quality Focus group interviews, exit interviews, and community forums Mystery shopping	**Chapter 4** Comment cards and comments posted on Web site Comments made in customer satisfaction surveys Suggestion boxes
Unsolicited	**Chapter 5** Sweeping observation Customer ratings on third-party Internet sites Analysis of telephone calls, letters, or e-mails: complaints, compliments, suggestions for improvement	**Chapter 6** Blog posts Comments on social networking sites Comments made to staff Text messaging for a quick response

Figure 3.1. Methodologies Discussed

This chapter covers survey research in the form of survey or questionnaire distribution and interviews. Relevant surveys focus on customer expectations in the form of service quality and satisfaction, while interviews might be one-on-one, focus group, or exit interviews. A type of interview might be the exchange between library directors and the community in community forums. Going beyond self-reporting, the library might engage in mystery shopping, namely the employment of customers who visit libraries anonymously and describe their experiences.

This chapter provides an overview of survey research but does not duplicate the coverage provided in *Assessing Service Quality, The Evaluation and Measurement of Library Services*, and *Engaging in Evaluation and Assessment Research*.[3] The sources listed in figure 3.2 also complement the coverage, and we recommend that readers review such works prior to carrying out data collection.

Cox, James, and Keni Brayton Cox. *Your Opinion, Please! How to Build the Best Questionnaires in the Field of Education*. Thousand Oaks, CA: Sage Publications, 2008.

Creative Research Systems. "Survey Design" (2010). Accessed July 2, 2010. http://www.surveysystem.com/sdesign.htm.

Creswell, John W., and Vicki L. Plano-Clark. *Designing and Conducting Mixed Methods Research*. 2nd ed. Thousand Oaks, CA: Sage Publications, 2010.

Grigoroudis, Evangelos, and Yannis Siskos. *Customer Satisfaction Evaluation: Methods for Measuring and Implementing Service Quality*. New York: Springer, 2010.

Holstein, James, and Jaber F. Gubrium. *Inside Interviewing: New Lenses, New Concerns*. Thousand Oaks, CA: Sage Publications, 2003.

James, Nalita, and High Busher. *Online Interviewing*. Thousand Oaks, CA: Sage Publications, 2010.

Klave, Steinar, and Svend Brinkmann. *InterViews: Learning the Craft of Qualitative Research Interviewing*. 2nd ed. Thousand Oaks, CA: Sage Publications, 2010.

Krueger, Richard A., and Mary Anne Casey. *Focus Groups: A Practical Guide for Applied Research*. Thousand Oaks, CA: Sage Publications, 2009.

Marshall, Catherine, and Gretchen B. Rossman. *Designing Qualitative Research*. Thousand Oaks, CA: Sage Publications, 2010.

Oliver, Paul. *Understanding the Research Process*. Thousand Oaks, CA: Sage Publications, 2010.

Quirk's Marketing Research Review. "Mystery Shopping Resources" (Eagan, MN: Quirk Enterprises, Inc., 2010). Accessed July 2, 2010. http://www.quirks.com/market_research_topics/mystery_shopping.aspx.

U.S. Government Accountability Office (previously General Accounting Office, Program Evaluation and Methodology Division). Special Publications: Evaluation Research and Methodology.
- *Case Study Evaluations*. Transfer Paper 10.1.9 (1991). Accessed July 2, 2010. http://archive.gao.gov/f0202/143145.pdf.
- *Designing Evaluations*. PEMD 10.1.4 (1991). Accessed July 2, 2010. http://archive.gao.gov/t2pbat7/144040.pdf
- *The Evaluation Synthesis*. PEMD 10.1.2 (1992). Accessed July 2, 2010. http://archive.gao.gov/t2pbat6/146601.pdf
- *Using Structured Interviewing Techniques*. PEMD 10.1.5 (1991). Accessed July 2, 2010. http://archive.gao.gov/t2pbat7/144388.pdf

Williams, Kawana, Jasmine Plummer, and Myrna Hoover. "Preparing for a Telephone Interview" (Tallahassee: Florida State University, Career Center). Accessed July 2, 2010. http://www.career.fsu.edu/img/pdf/guides/Telephone%20Interview%20Preparation%20Guide.pdf.

Willis, Gordon B. *Cognitive Interviewing: A Tool for Improving Questionnaire Design*. Thousand Oaks, CA: Sage Publications, 2005.

Yin, Robert K. *Case Study Research: Design and Methods*. 4th ed. Thousand Oaks, CA: Sage Publications, 2009.

Figure 3.2. Relevant Research Literature

SURVEYS

With any survey, those conducting the study make an imposition on participants; they are requesting a favor—thoughtful completion of the instrument. For this reason, it is important to explain the value of the survey, why the library wants their input, and how the results will lead to improved service delivery or the creation of a new service that responds to an actual or potential demand. Further, the library will also have to consider whether or not to provide an incentive for participation. The goal is not to accept whatever response rate emerges or to be surprised that there may have been few respondents (commonly less than 40 percent); a response rate is defined as the percentage of survey invitations that results in completion of the instrument. Finally, whatever the results, the library should thank the participants and in a prompt manner show them how the results inform planning, decision making, and improved service. Once a library listens to its customers on a regular basis, it is more likely that response rates will increase over time, that is, if listening results in better service and customers perceive the library as engaged in an ongoing dialogue. Through regular listening and creating a dialogue with customers, librarians should expect a response of no less than 65 percent!

Following are some principles to follow in constructing a cover letter and a data collection instrument:

- Explain the value of the study and acknowledge the imposition placed on respondents (the accompanying cover letter; using a search engine, check terms such as "cover letter research study" and incorporate the results into the cover letter actually used).

- Avoid respondent fatigue. Keep to a limited set of questions; do not make the instrument too long.

- Pay careful attention to the wording of the questions and their sequence. Word the questions clearly, avoid the use of jargon, and allow one question to lead to the next. Respondents should be instructed where to go if they skip a question. A common fault is insufficient attention given to the measurement scale when the investigators want respondents to provide a checkmark for the appropriate response. For instance, if choices include *never*, *sometimes*, and *rarely*, what is the difference between *sometimes* and *rarely*?[4]

- Conduct a pretest. Gather a group of librarians and nonlibrarians (no more than eight to ten) and ask them to comment on each question. Do they find the questions clear and not open to interpretation? They might also comment on the clarity of the response options.

Types of Error

Because social science research and measurement are susceptible to error, those engaged in evaluation research should be aware of, and address, sampling error, which refers to statistical errors that appear as a result of determining the sample of customers to study. *Sampling* is a process by which evaluators select part of the population, and probability sampling enables them to estimate values of the population from the sample. Different types of sampling error (the difference between a sample estimate and the result that would have been obtained had the entire population been studied with the same methodological procedures) can be classified into coverage, measurement, and sampling errors:

- *Coverage errors* occur because the population was incorrectly defined. Such errors also result from inadequate sampling frames and low response rates.

- *Measurement errors* are due to poor-quality interviewing; poor respondent recall; and mistakes in transcription and data coding, entry, and analysis. Measurement errors are sometimes referred to as administrative errors, and they encompass questionnaire errors, which are errors in the content and the structure of the data collection instrument (e.g., wording, scales, and the order of questions).

- *Sampling errors* are a function of sample size and, in the case of small populations, the relationship of the sample size to the population.

Other errors include the following:

- *Nonresponse errors*, which refers to the bias caused by members of the sample who are not included in the actual survey. Such errors depend mainly on how the survey was implemented.

- *Respondent errors*, which occur when customers do not give accurate information due to misunderstandings, lack of knowledge, guessing, loss of interest (particularly in cases of lengthy surveys), or faulty memory (trying to reconstruct something from the past).

- *Interviewer errors*, which result from interviewers who affect the reliability of customer answers (e.g., by not following instructions, by commenting on questions, or by reinforcing particular response patterns).

- *Misrepresentation errors*, which encompass exaggeration and lying.

Customer Expectations

The Gaps Model of Service Quality (see figure 3.3, p. 46) offers service organizations a framework to identify services in the form of the gaps that exceed (or fail to meet) customers' expectations. The model posits five gaps that reflect a discrepancy between customers' expectations and management's perceptions of these expectations (Gap 1); management's perceptions of customers' expectations and service quality specifications (Gap 2); service quality specifications and actual service delivery (Gap 3); actual service delivery and what is communicated to customers about it (Gap 4); and customers' expected service delivery and the perceived service delivered (Gap 5).

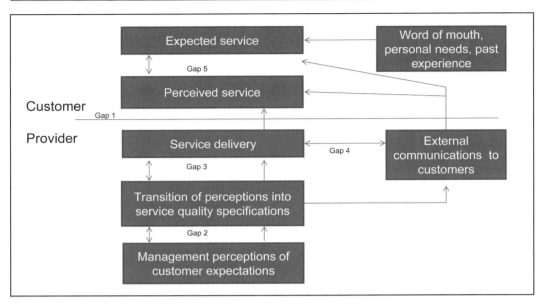

Figure 3.3. The Gaps Model of Service Quality. Adapted with permission from A. Parasuraman, Valarie A. Zeithmal, and Leonard L. Berry, "A Conceptual Model of Service Quality and Its Implications for Future Research," *Journal of Marketing* 49, no. 4 (Fall 1985): 44.

Although all of the gaps may hinder an organization from providing high-quality services, the fifth gap is the basis most frequently used for a study of either satisfaction or service quality. Studies of both examine the discrepancy between customers' expectations of excellence and their perceptions of the actual service delivered. Expectations are defined as *desired* wants, the extent to which customers associate a particular attribute with an excellent service provider. They also comprise subjective judgments of service performance.

Both satisfaction and service quality apply to internal as well as external customers. Library staff, as are employees of any organization, are often referred to as the lifeblood of the organization, and as such no *business* wants them to be dissatisfied.

Satisfaction

Satisfaction focuses on a specific transaction (becomes a sense of contentment with an actual experience) or, in the case of overall satisfaction, is a judgment collected over time from encounters with a service provider. Satisfaction judgments are emotional reactions to any experience or a collection of experiences. Further, satisfaction is a measure of how customers perceive service delivery and its possible shortcomings. In essence, satisfaction is a *diagnostic tool* for reviewing different customer experiences and for locating and resolving problems.

Service Quality

Service quality is an evaluation of specific attributes, and librarians often associate this cognitive judgment with LibQUAL+®, which the Association of Research Libraries introduced and a number of libraries worldwide have used (see http://www.libqual.org/home; for sample screens of the instrument, see http://www.libqual.org/about/about_survey/sample).[5] For a specified period of data collection, the survey examines three aspects of library service:

1. Affect of service: Assessing the attitudes and abilities of employees.

2. Library as place: Evaluating the library environment and its facilities.

3. Information control: Having customers navigate the library and its resources on their own terms.[6]

Contrary to popular opinion among academic librarians, LibQUAL+® is neither a survey of customer satisfaction nor a measure of an information literacy outcome. The survey might include three questions that the designers equate with satisfaction:

1. In general, are you satisfied with the way in which I was treated at the library?

2. In general, are you satisfied with library support for my learning, research, and/ or teaching needs?

3. How would you rate the overall quality of the service provided by the library?[7]

"Treated" in the first question assumes the customer interacted with staff, while the second question tries to cover both faculty and students and three separate activities. Missing are questions such as, "Would you recommend the services of this library to others?"; "Have you recommended the services of this library to others?"; and "How likely are you to reuse the services of this library?" To set up a comparison necessary to gauge satisfaction, there should be questions such as, "Overall, how important is this library to you?" and "Overall, how satisfied are you with the services of this library?"[8]

Five questions, labeled as "information literacy outcomes questions," are not linked to any learning goals formulated at the course, program, or institutional level on which faculty and librarians mutually agree. These questions/statements comprise a form of indirect assessment, meaning that students merely report their perceptions. The intent of student learning outcomes is to measure changes in student knowledge, abilities, and skills over time—at the course level or throughout a program of study. The specific statements covered in the LibQUAL+® survey follow:

1. "The library helps me stay abreast of developments in my field(s) of interest."

2. "The library aids my advancement in my academic discipline or work."

3. "The library enables me to be more efficient in my academic pursuits or work."

4. "The library helps me distinguish between trustworthy and untrustworthy information."

5. "The library provides me with the information skills I need in my work or study."[9]

Community Surveys

Public libraries use community surveys to determine the information needs of the community and patterns of library use. Such surveys might involve probability sampling of library card holders; such sampling requires that every element in the population has a known probability of being included in the sample. Library staff might draw a simple random sample of cardholders. Or they might use a systematic sample, taking every nth element from a list until the total list has been sampled, or a cluster sample, dividing a population into clusters or groups and then drawing a sample of those clusters. Cluster sampling might involve the use of a geographic information system (GIS) and detailed data on the city or a portion of it. The sample selected might be of households, perhaps those with or without members who hold library cards, for a precinct, school, or other geographical characterization. The sample might focus on educational level attained, number and age of children in the household, or numerous other possibilities. As an alternative, the survey might be posted on the library homepage and broadly promoted in the community or conducted as community intercepts at local shopping malls or other high traffic locations. Such surveys, however, might be associated with nonprobability sampling: samples that cannot be generalized to any population.

A survey of Seattle Public Library users, "anyone who used the Library in the past six months," and nonusers, conducted by Berk & Associates, is an example of a community survey. Approximately 33,000 people—roughly 5 percent of the population over the age of five—were surveyed. They learned about the survey through e-mail messages sent to cardholders who had e-mail accounts, finding the survey on the library's Web site, and other methods of promotion. The results were reported in an article in *The Seattle Times* titled "Survey Shows: At 7.3 Million Visits a Year, Seattle Loves Its Public Libraries." The article reflects positively on the library and its value to the community. One change relates to materials use: "A/V material (DVDs, music CDs and audiobooks) grew from 19% of total circulation in 2000 to 49% in 2009. And that figure does not include digtal and downloadable media."[10] When asked how they would spend a hypothetical $10 on library resources, respondents "directed $5.40 to books and print resources, $3.14 to A/V, and $2.49 on online resources."[11]

As part of its strategic planning, the library complemented this survey with community open houses ("to gather input on priorities and new directions the Library should consider") ; public forums ("Technology and Its Impact on the Future of Libraries" and "The User Experience in the 21st Century Library," which were used to explore topical issues); "discussion groups with teens and service providers who work with youth, teens, older adults, immigrants and refugees, and the homeless"; and a library staff survey designed to solicit ideas about how best to shape future services.[12]

Markham Public Library*

Gone are the days of making assumptions on a gut feeling or using anecdotal evidence to make decisions. Also gone are the days when libraries could assume that since they are the only game in town, customers will continue to use them regardless of the services they provide. With shrinking budgets and the scrutiny placed on spending those budgets, it is more important than ever to ensure that the funds are being spent on what customers want, and to get it right the first time. Decisions need to be based on data, both quantitative and qualitative. Both can be used to tell a story, but it is easier to tell the story when it does not require interpretation and is actually in the customers' words. Numbers are good, but when you need to convince your funders that you need the funds, the voice of the customer (or in a municipal environment, the voice of the constituent) can be even more powerful.

Here is the scenario: The library board and municipal council question the budget submission to increase the operating hours for the library system. The key question is, "How do you show or prove the need?" Usage may be good during the regular hours the library is open, but is the library popular at other times? (The question might refer to use of the library's homepage.) The library is considering adding hours on Friday evenings, or extending Sunday open hours to year-round service. The branches have never been open on Fridays beyond 5 p.m., but they have been open evenings from Monday through Thursday. On the other hand, the library system is open seasonally on Sundays, and the managers believe that year-round Sunday hours provide a better return-on-investment (ROI) than extending Friday hours into the evening. There is much that needs to go into the decision-making process, including operational and staffing costs, the impact on overall service, use and circulation statistics, and wouldn't it be nice to add actual customer comments to build the case? Now imagine if the library has access to more than 8,000 customer comments about the services that the library offers. The voice of the customer adds credence to the request to extend hours of operation.

Markham Public Library (MPL) uses Counting Opinions, producer of an online customer satisfaction survey, to gather both qualitative and quantitative data. The survey runs on the library Web site on an ongoing basis (http://www.markham.ca/mpl/onlineserv/cowelcome.asp). On a quarterly basis, a concerted effort is made to gather additional feedback. This is done in the form of a splash page, which appears each time a customer accesses the library's Web site.

MPL has been running the survey since 2005. Over this period we have gathered an enormous amount of feedback in the form of quantitative data and customer comments. As of September 2010, there were almost 8,000 survey responses—importance and satisfaction ratings with respect to programs, services, staff, facilities, policies, and so on. In addition to the ratings, customers provide comments. This powerful voice of the customer is used for everything from supporting budget requests to making decisions on services, programs, and policies.

The survey is set up so that the results can be broken down by branch and by context (e.g., staff, facilities, collections, programs, and services). Customers can provide feedback and request follow-up as necessary. Managers in charge of each branch receive alerts, conduct the follow-up, and engage the customer in a conversation. They are also responsible for tracking both the data and comments for their individual branches, while a senior administrator does the same on a system-wide level. Because the comments can be categorized and searched, the whole process is efficient and accessible. The comments serve as an ongoing "Tell Us What You Think" survey and not only provide a quick snapshot of the mood of the customer but also cumulatively provide trends and feedback that can be used for decision making, planning, and budget requests.

The budget request scenario outlined above is not fictional. In 2007, MPL made a pitch to extend Sunday service hours to year-round operations. At the time, we had been running the customer satisfaction survey for two years. A quick search of the customer feedback portion of the data gathered over that time period resulted in fifty different customer comments requesting to have Sunday hours extended. An entire business case was created, and the additional service was costed out. Still, the most powerful piece was the five pages of comments appended to the submission. What better way to tell your story than to have customers tell it for you? Here is a sample of the actual comments that were a part of the submission:

- "May we know the rationale for libraries to close on Sundays for FOUR months during summer? It is such a huge loss to so many people, like myself, who use the library on Sundays after Church."

- "The libraries, as everybody know, are not solely there for children in school, if the closure relates to summer holidays. Even some schools open during the summer holidays so that children have a proper place to congregate, not to mention the meaningful and educational libraries on a Sunday."

- "The libraries are a refuge when the weather is biting cold in winter and people have nowhere else to go."

- "The libraries play so crucial a role in a community that no funding should be spared for the Sunday opening."

- "The libraries may have this Summer Sunday closure practiced for a long time. But that does not have to be continual in view of the huge social changes since then."

- "[W]e now live in a different time and it is so frustrating that the library is closed on the very days designed for leisure."

- "The hours of operation need to be revamped. . . . [S]ome people enjoy a quiet Sunday in the summer reading a book."

- "Please continue the Sunday service from October to May; and don't let anyone ever convince you that the Internet will replace the library or the librarian."

- "I would like to see the hours of operation extended during the weekends and have Sundays open for use year-round."

- "The hours need to be extended on weekends. The grocery stores are open longer than the libraries and that's when there are so many stores."

Imagine how powerful five pages of similar comments would be. It makes it very difficult to ignore the need when the need has a voice. So how does this story end? At a time when funding for other municipal services was being cut and reduced, the library was successful in getting approval for the additional annual operating funds to provide year-round Sunday service.

Since then, MPL has used the voice of the customer to set service levels, improve services, and determine our success. However, it is not just enough to ask, you need to listen and act to make a difference. Give customers a voice and do not underestimate the power of their words.

*Moe Hosseini-Ara, Markham Public Library, Ontario, Canada.

INTERVIEWS

One-on-One Interviews

One-on-one interviews might be conducted face-to face, over the telephone, or using the Internet, such as with Skype. However the survey is conducted, it is important to minimize the amount of imposition time and to explore ways to get people to accept that imposition. The goal is a high response rate and extensive coverage of the topic addressed. Most often, the interviewer asks open-ended questions and probes the responses. However, if interviewers use closed-ended questions, they ought to avoid reading a long list of options and asking the respondent to rank them most to least important. Furthermore, there may be a desire to force respondents to select from among certain choices; however, when doing so, it is important to know that the choices are meaningful. Jolene Smyth, Don Dillman, Leah Melani Christian, and Michael Stern found that respondents favor more options "and take longer to answer in the forced-choice format than in the check-all format." Still, they discovered that "the forced-choice question format encourages deeper processing of response options and, as such, is preferable to the check-all format."[13]

Focus Group Interviews

The literature on focus group interviews is extensive, and libraries often use this methodology. Some of the critical issues discussed in the literature are the number of questions to ask, the selection and number of participants, the role and value of an objective moderator, recording responses, and any follow-up with the respondents in which they validate the transcribed record or reflect on the findings since the interview was conducted.

Focus group interviewing is often associated with exploratory research and affords an opportunity for people to play off what others say. The result is a deeper understanding of some issue or problem. These interviews involve the use of open-ended questions. In some instances, the investigators preselect the five to seven questions they will ask, and in other instances, they ask the initial question and raise subsequent questions based on what the participants say.

Most often the investigators want a transcript of the entire conversation and will not rely on brief notes taken during the session. To produce that transcript, the session might be audio-recorded, and the investigator might have someone else prepare that transcript. When this occurs, the investigator should validate the accuracy of the transcription and be actively involved in its preparation. Investigators want to remain close to the dataset and not have too many layers between them and the voices of the participants.

Telephone Interviews

Telephone interviewing, which was in vogue from the 1970s through the mid-1990s, is hard to conduct on a large scale. The pitfalls are that interviewers may not be well trained and have pleasant voices, they frequently engage in multiple call-backs, phone numbers for a sample are harder to obtain as people switch from landlines to cell phones, people rely more on caller ID to screen calls, and busy people are seldom home. Most important, the interview should be short; however, some respondents may want to chat and not care about the length of time. For businesses, the response rate is less important than actually selling merchandise; in such situations a response rate of 1 percent may be acceptable—generating a respectable number of sales.

Exit Interviews

Typically such interviews are associated with departing employees, who voluntarily resigned, were laid off, or were fired, and the meeting they have with someone from the human resource department. The purpose of these interviews is to gather frank feedback about working conditions and employee retention.[14] In some instances, the purpose is to give disgruntled employees an opportunity to vent in an effort to avoid litigation. Such interviews complement employee satisfaction surveys.

Exit interviews might also apply to customers who are leaving the library and are asked to express their satisfaction with the experience. Such interviews might also be known as exit surveys or customer intercepts. Those libraries engaged in such intercepts should address the following questions:

- About what do we want feedback?

- How many customers do we want to interview?

- How do we go about selecting the customers to participate?

- What do we want to know?

- How do we approach those customers?

- How long should the interview last?

- Where will the interview be held?

Instead of just focusing on the experience, staff might test customer awareness of services the library offers or see if customers have unfulfilled information needs; are leaving the location having used a service or borrowed material; have examined any of the promotional materials and self-help guides; or have visited other libraries recently, and for what purpose(s).

Community Forums

Libraries, especially public libraries, host community forums, for example on economic or disaster recovery. Some libraries have used such forums to engage the community in discussions about library services and facilities. The keys to a successful community forum are

- marketing and promoting the event,

- having an experienced and knowledgeable meeting facilitator to keep the discussion flowing and on-topic, and

- keeping the discussions to a few specified topics.

Libraries might announce forums and engage participants in matters of concern to them. Managerial leaders cannot control the questions asked, but they should anticipate that certain individuals may attend and have their own agenda.

MYSTERY SHOPPING

The business community (e.g., hotels, banks, restaurants, grocery and retail stores, job announcement Web sites, and the travel industry) and some academic and public libraries have used mystery shopping, also known as secret shopping, silent shopping, and test shopping. Recently, the U.S. Government Accountability Office conducted an undercover investigation of for-profit colleges and their recruiting tactics. "Admissions and financial aid officers," it was found, "engaged in unethical and sometimes illegal practices, all in the interest of persuading students to enroll and obtain financial aid." These results, and the accompanying video, were turned over to the inspectors-general for the U.S. Department of Education for possible legal action.[15]

Mystery shopping, a useful tool to counteract professional blinders that library staff place on the services they provide and on the library environment, provides a fresh customer-centric perspective on a wide range of aspects about the library and its services. Mystery shoppers, who are anonymous customers hired to report on their expectations of the facilities and the service provided, might be asked to rate and comment on library parking, landscaping, the condition of the facility, cleanliness of the facility and bathrooms, staff characteristics (e.g., helpfulness, friendliness, approachability, knowledge, and appearance), layout of and wayfinding in the library, the process to register for a library card, computer use, and so forth. Mystery shoppers might also evaluate call centers or telephone services that library staff provide (e.g., referrals to other departments without being cut off).

The library can develop a checklist of specific things that mystery shoppers must observe and of how to rate the library. Mystery shopping in such a situation involves an impartial method of data collection that describes the actual experiences of customers, some of which might be unsatisfactory, and identifies areas for service improvement. When the shoppers relate their expectations, however, a subjective component of the study emerges.

Vanessa Czopek appears to be the first to introduce the application of mystery shopping to U.S. libraries. The Stanislaus County Free Library system, with a main library located in Modesto, California, was shopped in 1996 by a representative of the Modesto Chamber of Commerce, who found the service provided "less than stellar." The results of the mystery shopping experience were shared with all staff. Once the set of questions was refined, a mystery shopper visited all twelve branch libraries. One conclusion is that mystery shopping became a catalyst for developing customer service standards; figure 2 of Czopek's article reproduces those standards.[16] Based on her article and subsequent writings, as well as the experiences of one of the authors, figure 3.4 (pp. 56–57), provides a checklist of questions and issues that libraries typically ask a mystery shopper to include in the rating of a facility.

Some Libraries Using Mystery Shopping

An examination of the literature reveals that mostly public libraries have engaged in mystery shopping. Examples of these libraries are the Arapahoe Library District (Englewood, CO), Madison County Public Library (Berea, KY), Orange County Library System (Orlando, FL), the Monroe County Public Library (IN), the Stanislaus County Free Library (CA), and nine public libraries in Michigan.

Mystery Shopping Practicalities

Though mystery shopping might be combined with an unobtrusive evaluation of a specific library service, such as reference, in most cases this is not done. Mystery shopping is typically used to gain an independent perspective on how the library is perceived rather than to focus on how well the library performs a specific service. In short, mystery shopping is typically about the library and its services and not about how well specific staff members are doing.

The library should carefully design the agenda or checklist of questions and the rating scale for the shoppers to use after considering how the staff will use the data gathered. The library should also determine if it has budget to upgrade or improve its facilities, signage, provide staff training, and so forth, if the mystery shoppers offer negative comments in these areas. It seems foolish to identify areas mystery shoppers will review and rate when there is no budget to implement change. Clearly, the results and the process itself should be linked to staff development, the service culture of the organization, and the service vision of the library's managerial leadership.

MYSTERY SHOPPER CHECKLIST

The shopper may use a scale of 1 (*very poor*) to 10 (*outstanding*) for each item on the checklist. Another scale might be 1 (*very hard*) to 10 (*very easy*). Alternatively, the library could develop a rubric (perhaps with five categories) that describes possible outcomes.

Finding the Library

• Were signs indicating the location of the library clearly visible?
• Was there a sign indicating whether the library is open or closed?

Parking

• Were empty parking spaces available in the parking lot?
• Did you park on the street?
• Did you have to pay for parking?

Entrance

• Was the entrance to the library attractive?
• Did a staff member welcome you as you entered?
• Was the entrance cluttered with flyers and handouts?

Wayfinding

• Were the signs clear and understandable?
• Could you easily determine the location of the:
    Restrooms?
    Drinking fountain?
    Book return area?
    Children's area?
    DVD collection?
    Fiction collection?
    Magazines?
    Audio books?
    New books?
• Did you find any handwritten or computer-printed signs?

Attractiveness/Cleanliness

• Was the inside of the facility attractive?
• Did you feel comfortable in the library?
• Was the library cluttered?
• Was the air temperature in the library too hot or too cold?
• Were the restrooms clean and free of clutter?
• Were the restrooms odor free?

Figure 3.4. Mystery Shopper Checklist

Library Card

- Was it clear from signage how and where to sign up for a library card?
- Did you need to ask a staff member how to get a library card?
- Was the form clear and straightforward?
- Were you welcomed as a new library cardholder?

Find a Book

- Could you easily find a book about travel to a foreign country?

Use a Computer

- Was the process to sign up to use the computer simple?
- What was the wait period to use a computer?
- Was a staff member nearby to provide assistance if needed?

Seek Assistance

- Could you easily identify a staff member?
- When you approached a staff member, did he or she
    Make eye contact?
    Smile?
    Ask how he or she could be of assistance?
    Ask if you needed further help?
    Dress in a professional manner?

- When you asked for assistance in finding a book about cooking (for example):
    Did the staff member walk with you to find the area where the books are shelved?
    Did the staff member point or provide directions to where to find cookbooks?
    How would you rate the total interaction with the staff member?

Web Site

- Log on to the library Web site. Do you find the overall appearance attractive?
- Can you find information about upcoming events at the library?
- Can you easily find what electronic resources (electronic journals and databases) are available?

Overall Impressions

- Rate your overall impression of the
    Staff members
    Physical facility
    Books and other materials in the library
    Use of a computer in the library
    Library Web site

Figure 3.4. Mystery Shopper Checklist (*Cont.*)

The library should consider a number of issues as it prepares for the use of mystery shoppers, such as the following:

- Should the library use a commercial mystery shopping firm, students from a nearby university, or staff from another library? Staff from another library will be knowledgeable about library services, but they may consider some things "normal" about which a first-time visitor would be puzzled. In our opinion, a library will most likely get the best "first-time impressions" if it uses a commercial service firm. Using a commercial mystery shopping firm is fairly inexpensive ($25 to $50 per shopping visit). The costs vary depending on the number of "shops" (visits by a mystery shopper) the library would like to receive over a stated period of time.

- Should the shoppers be trained, or visit the library "cold?" Mystery shoppers who visit restaurants for the prestigious Michelin Guide (http://www.michelinguide. com/us/index.html) must receive extensive training, so the intershopper ratings are quite high (that is, several shoppers will rate the restaurant with the same score or number of stars). Most library shoppers will most likely not receive any training and thus reflect a true first impression reaction.

- Should the shoppers be *library literate*, or should they be infrequent users or have never used the library? A library literate shopper may not *see* things that the infrequent library customer may find confusing or annoying.

- How many shops should a facility receive within what time period? A facility should receive more than a single shop, but the optimum number is partially dictated by the budget. Several libraries have decided to use three shops, believing that this number gives them a fairly accurate representation of the facility and services being delivered.

- How closely should the demographic characteristics of the shoppers be matched to the overall demographics of the community? The age and gender of the shoppers influence their view of the shopping experience.

- Will the shopping be repeated over time? How often? These questions recognize that improved customer service is an ongoing activity and that any data collected may lose value over time.

CHARACTERIZING THE RESULTS

As discussed in *Viewing Library Metrics from Different Perspectives* and *Engaging in Evaluation and Assessment Research*,[17] stakeholders often prefer to see data displayed in a visual form so that they can quickly see trends. One concept relevant to this chapter and the book that these works do not cover is the concept of a Net Promoter Score (NPS).

This concept, which Fred Reichheld of Bain & Company developed, measures overall customer loyalty. It focuses on a single question: "How likely would you be to recommend Library X to a friend or colleague?" The word *promoter* in the concept's name refers to heavy or very frequent library users who take delight in encouraging their friends and colleagues to visit or use the library and its resources and services.

The NPS is the percentage of promoters minus the detractors, those customers who feel so badly treated that they cut back on the frequency of their library use, switch their use to other libraries or competitors, or become lost customers. On a ten-point satisfaction scale (e.g., with end points of *extremely unlikely* and *extremely likely*), detractors answer with a number no higher than "6." Customers who mark a "7" or "8" are considered neutral and do not factor into the score. Promoters are those who provide a "9" or "10."

People cannot always provide a meaningful number. If that is the case, it is important to collect qualitative data in which they explain their answers. In some instances, library staff might ask supplementary questions to determine if the score was due to staff friendliness, approachability, and so on.

Using customer satisfaction data from fifty-three public libraries in the United States and Canada, Matthews found that the average NPS score was a quite high 70.9 percent. The NPS ratings ranged from a high of 73.2 percent to a low of 21.3 percent. The data at the branch level were even more variable. Across all of the libraries, promoters are typically adults who are very frequent library users, whereas detractors are typically students who are first-time library users.[18]

The NPS is often associated with telephone surveying, and it is a means to narrow the range of questions asked in order to minimize the imposition on those surveyed. Still, the application of the score has its detractors, who believe it is not always the best predictor of service results and who question the value of one simple output metric. On the other hand, the statistic could easily be displayed as a dashboard showing a perception over time.

CONCLUDING THOUGHTS

In conducting the type of data collection covered in this chapter, librarians must decide on the frequency of data collection. Counting Opinions, a commercial producer of a satisfaction survey, has created a product in which libraries can engage in continuous data collection, analysis, and use. Except for such a survey, libraries typically engage in data collection on an irregular basis.

One important methodological option in conducting management research is the use of qualitative methods for data collection and analysis. Qualitative research emphasizes understanding complex, interrelated, and/or changing phenomena. Combined with quantitative methods, libraries receive a rich dataset relevant to understanding the voice of their customers. Clearly it is important to put all of the voice-of-the-customer data in a single place to facilitate analysis and gain a deeper understanding of the library's customers and their true expectations.

Inquiry is fatal to certainty.[19]

Orange County Library System*

The Orange County Library System (OCLS) values the voice of the customer and elicits our customers' comments at every opportunity (e.g., through customer surveys).

Customer Surveys

Customer surveys help us formulate an accurate picture of how our customers see us. "The surveys provide a reality check between how we think we are doing and how the customers think we are doing."[1] A humorous look at customer surveys was created by staff and can be found at http://www.youtube.com/watch?v=XTwvrAtHsZA.

OCLS uses ad hoc customer surveys from time to time for specific inquiries. The most recent ad hoc Zoomerang survey we conducted was "The Library Misses You," to reach out to those customers who had not used us for a while. In April 2010 we sent an e-mail survey to those customers who had not used their cards between January 1, 2009, and December 31, 2009. Though a number of the respondents indicated they had moved out of our service district (thus explaining some of our door count drop), 82 percent responded that they would be back in six months. One even said, "I miss you too!"

In dealing with our shrinking revenues, we asked our customers to complete an online survey on our Web site to give us feedback in deciding the cuts to make to manage the revenue reductions we faced in the 2009 fiscal year. They let us know what they could do without and what they could not. We received over 200 responses. We considered this feedback as we determined where we would position our cuts by evaluating the public's tolerance for service impacts.

As a regular surveying tool, OCLS has been using Counting Opinions' LibSAT to elicit, tally, compile, and analyze customer feedback since the fall of 2005. The Web-based survey is available internally from a number of personal computers in each location. Generally, each location has one dedicated station from which patrons can participate in the survey. The survey asks customers if they want a follow-up contact. This is an important feature of the software. If customers would like to receive a response, we need to respond and close the dialogue loop. Our response is timely and personal, with forty-eight-hour response time as the rule.

LibSAT has a powerful reporting side for analyzing responses in a number of ways. OCLS has been using LibSAT's Net Promoter Score (NPS) to report to the library board of trustees monthly. One reason we like the Net Promoter

Score is that it allows us to compare ourselves not just to other libraries but also to other industries. An NPS of 9–10 means the respondent is a loyal customer. A score of 7–8 denotes a passive user, and 0–6 indicates a detractor. To arrive at a score, take the percentage of customers who are promoters and subtract the percentage of those who are detractors. A score of 75 percent is considered very high. "The Net Promoter Score is our lead indicator, the customer canary in the mine of customer relationship management."[2] The scores are gathered and displayed in some of our locations. The customer service ranking of each branch can be posted and demonstrated in an easily understood manner. Managers find the net promoter scores are a good way to track customer service performance of their facility. The scores have become rather competitive, with each branch manager claiming bragging rights for the top NPS of the month. The number of surveys gathered initially was quite small, so small incentives were introduced to encourage customers to take the time to take the survey. A larger number of surveys has helped to give a more realistic and balanced voice to complainers. The number of surveys taken has grown steadily since then and is meaningful enough to give validation to the numbers.

Statistical Analysis

We also listen to the customers through analysis of our statistics. We look at how the collection is used, which programs are popular, and which classes fill up fastest. We use our monthly statistics to look at usage trends.

Community Beta Testers

OCLS has been soliciting customer input during the development and testing of major new digital products, starting with the development of OCLS Mobile, our iPhone enhanced mobile Web site. As customers increasingly interact with us through electronic means, we have begun soliciting customer input for a Web site usability test. The beta testers are asked to perform a series of tasks. Staff observers monitor and measure their progress in order to streamline and improve the usability of the library's Web site. We have a whole page devoted to soliciting beta testers (http://www.ocls.info/beta/default.asp?from=pb):

Beta Testing FAQ

What is a Beta Test?
Beta testing usually starts when the basic features and tools are essentially complete, but there's still work to do on fine-tuning the software, design, navigation, etc.

What do Beta Testers do?
First they use the product or service that is currently being tested just like anyone else would use it. Often times Beta Testers get to use or see a product or service before anyone else.

Second, they give us valuable feedback about how they used it, their likes and dislikes and any comments or concerns. All this feedback is used to create the best product or serivce we can.

How do I become a beta tester?
If you would like to participate in one of the beta tests simply click the "I want to participate" link or send an e-mail to betatester@ocls.info. Please include your name and library card number. You'll be notified by e-mail if you've been selected. Remember, you will need to be a library card holder. Not a card holder? Sign up now.

Do I need any special equipment?
Each test will be different, and may

Usability Testers Needed
We are looking for usability testers to help us make our website even better! Participants will be asked to perform a series of tasks on the library's website under the observation of a library staff member. But don't worry! There's no grade and there are no right or wrong answers. Participants will be given a small gift for their efforts! All usability tests will take place at the Orlando Public Library in downtown Orlando and are estimated to take one hour. Participants must be 18 or older and have a library card in good standing. Ready to sign up? Just answer a few questions and we'll contact you if you are selected to participate.

OCLS Alerts
We've developed powerful new mobile software to allow reminder and courtesy notices about classes and materials to be sent to your mobile devices.
Sign up period has expired

iPhone/iPod Touch Enhanced Catalog
Help us test this exciting new way of searching the catalog using the iPhone/iPod Touch enhanced interface. Be one of the first to help test this newly developed mobile application for the OCLS community.
Sign up period has expired

Mystery Shopper

OCLS has been using mystery shoppers since 2003 to evaluate and analyze our service, as well as to call attention to and reward those individuals who have given excellent service, as determined by the mystery shopper. While initially there was trepidation on the part of staff about being shopped, that hesitation quickly evaporated when it was made clear that this was a reward program designed to improve customer service. All locations are shopped once a month. The reports are compiled and shared with the manager and staff.

The shopping company uses a standard questionnaire to evaluate each location. The shoppers assess the facility in terms of attractive displays, neat stacks, and overall cleanliness. They measure and record how staff do on standard customer service behaviors (e.g., friendly greetings, offers to assist, and personal service). They also evaluate more library-specific customer service transactions, such as the checkout and check in experience, informational help provided, and staff recommendations for other library services or programs.

An overall score is assigned to each shop as well as different subcomponents. The shops are an effective way to get an objective view of a library experience. The shopper reports are a record of users interacting with staff, complete with specific time and place of the shop and details of the interactions. Managers use the reports as a tool to coach and train employees. The shops can help identify the strengths and weaknesses of staff as well as the general impressions users might have based on their experience.

Our original shopping program used an involved rewards program that offered staff choices including cash, gift cards, and paid time off. More recently, we streamlined the program to make it less cumbersome to administer by providing time off as the only reward. The rewards are awarded using a 90 percent benchmark. If a department's shop exceeds the 90 percent benchmark, the employee earns two hours' paid leave. If the shop does not reach the 90 percent threshold, it is considered a coaching moment and does not involve a reward.

A video created by staff explains the mystery shopper program. It was part of a presentation made by Edgewater Branch Manager Kelly Pepo at the ALA annual 2008 program in Anaheim, California. It can be found at http://www.youtube.com/watch?v=a963XqXN8V0 and http://www.youtube.com/ocls, on the sidebar as Mission Possible: Secret Shopping at OCLS.

Overall scores are tracked for each location. This benchmarking allows each branch or department to see how it is doing in comparison to others.

OCLS presents an annual award for the best customer service by a department or branch, based on the mystery shopper points earned. This positive reinforcement acts as an incentive and encourages team motivation toward improving and maintaining top customer service.

Staff Day Training

Our organizational values speak to customers and customer service: respect, excellence, and integrity. These are all part of how we lay the groundwork for staff to listen to library customers. Training opportunities have been regularly presented to staff regarding customers and customer feedback. OCLS focuses on having a single consistent message in terms of policies and procedures. OCLS also focuses quite heavily on the positive, on what we can do. Past speakers have included the following:

- Joan Frye Williams, who talked about trends and customer service. She has been a successful librarian, consultant, vendor, planner, trainer, evaluator, and user of library services. Since 1996 she has been an independent consultant specializing in innovation, technology, and the service needs and preferences of nonlibrary "civilians."

- Simon Bailey, whose book, *Release Your Brilliance* (HarperCollins, 2008), gave sound advice and focused on tips, tools, and techniques staff need to bring about organizational brilliance and produce brilliant results.

- Janelle Barlow, coauthor of *A Complaint Is a Gift* (Berrett-Koehler, 1996), explained how to use customer complaints as a valuable feedback resource to overcome customer dissatisfaction, increase communication, expand customer loyalty, and find solutions to problems.

Comment Cards

Comment cards are perhaps the oldest way we have heard from our customers. They have been used at OCLS for over two decades. Every location and every service desk has them. When customers want to share their opinions, they are given a form to share their comments. Each customer is given a timely response, provided there is a card number, return address, or e-mail address. We also use a virtual customer comment card on our Web site. It works in the same fashion and is available for customers to comment on any aspects of our service.

Our Questline Call Center takes comments from customers any time the library is open. The Questline Service helps customers with account questions, as well as answering reference questions, walking customers through some of our virtual services if they need help, and providing staff-placed holds and guidance on material selection. About 5 percent of their calls relate to customer feedback, although customer feedback is built into every single interaction with Questline staff. About 85 percent are account questions. Our commitment to the patron is to respond to all comments, whether in print or delivered virtually. Generally most contact is made within twenty-four hours. Many people are accustomed to complaints dropping into a black hole. We find that even with a very unhappy patron, we make great strides by contacting them quickly regarding their concerns.

We also categorize these concerns so that we can track the areas to which we need to pay particular attention and compare them over time. Fortunately these "comments" avenues also bring us good news. We frequently receive compliments for individual staff or locations. To get the good news out, we have set up a "Kudos" network in house. When compliments and kudos are received, they are sent via e-mail to all staff. When staff open their inboxes, there is some encouragement there in the form of appreciation from our users.

Our Web site (http://www.ocls.info) provides our customers with several opportunities to share their feedback. The "Contact Us" link, highly visible on the upper navigation bar, gives our customers a variety of methods to get in touch (see the table on page 65).

Comments	Have a comment or suggestion? Send your e-mail to comments@ocls.info.
Comentarios/Sugerencias	¿Tiene usted un comentario o sugerencia? Envíe su correo electrónico a Comentarios@ocls.info.
Circulation	If you have a question about your library card account, PIN, fines, information change, lost card, etc., send an e-mail to circulation@ocls.info.
Help Desk	Having trouble using the catalog? Send us an e-mail at helpdesk@ocls.info.
Suggest-A-Title	Want to request that we add a certain title to our collection? Titles not found in the catalog can be suggested with the Suggest-A-Title form.
Web Site	Have a question, suggestion, or comment about the Web site? Send an e-mail to webmaster@ocls.info and let us know. Any issues related to your online library card account should be directed to circulation@ocls.info.
Administrative Team	If you have comments, questions or suggestions to share with the members of our Administrative Team please feel free to contact them at comments@ocls.info: Mary Anne Hodel, *Library Director and CEO* Debbie Moss, *Assistant Director and Division Head for Technical Support* Bob Tessier, *Comptroller* Craig Wilkins, *Public Service Administrator* Renae Bennett, *Public Service Administrator* Wendi Bost, *Public Service Administrator* Carla Fountain, *Human Resources Manager* Eric Atkinson, *Information Systems Department Head* Tracy Zampaglione, *Public Relations Administrator*

Over the years, using a number of trainers and training techniques and through a variety of methods, OCLS has taken customers seriously and consistently tried to listen to them. This has made a difference in connecting with customers and cemented the relationship between our users, taxpayers, and the library.

Notes

1. Debbie Moss, "And the Survey Says . . . Strengthening Services through Surveying (presentation made at the American Library Association Annual Meeting, Washington, D.C., June 28, 2010).

2. Ibid.

*Mary Anne Hodel, director and CEO of the Orange County Library System, Orlando, Florida.

NOTES

1. ThinkExist.com, Quotations, "Zora Neale Hurston, American Folklorist and Author," accessed July 2, 2010, http://thinkexist.com/quotes/zora_neale_hurston/.

2. Terry G. Vavra, *Improving Your Measurement of Customer Satisfaction: A Guide to Creating, Conducting, Analyzing, and Reporting Customer Satisfaction Measurement Programs* (Milwaukee, WI: ASQ Quality Press, 1997), 63.

3. Peter Hernon and Ellen Altman, *Assessing Service Quality: Satisfying the Expectations of Library Customers*, 2nd ed. (Chicago: American Library Association, 2010); Joseph R. Matthews, *The Evaluation and Measurement of Library Services* (Westport, CT: Libraries Unlimited, 2007); Peter Hernon, Robert E. Dugan, and Danuta A. Nitecki, *Engaging in Evaluation and Assessment Research* (Santa Barbara, CA: Libraries Unlimited, 2011).

4. See Delbert C. Miller, *Handbook of Research Design and Social Measurement* (Newbury Park, CA: Sage, 1991); Vavra, *Improving Your Measurement of Customer Satisfaction*.

5. LibQUAL+® is under the umbrella of StatsQUAL®, which offers a series of evaluation tools (see http://www.statsqual.org/home). DigiQUAL, another of these tools, modifies and repurposes LibQUAL+® to evaluate digital services.

6. For background information, see C. Colleen Cook, "A Mixed Methods Approach to the Identification and Measurement of Academic Library Service Quality Constructs: LibQUAL+™" (PhD diss., Texas A&M University, 2001); Martha Kyrillidou, "Item Sampling in Service Quality Assessment Surveys to Improve Response Rates and Reduce Respondent Burden: The LibQUAL+® Lite Randomized Control Trial" (PhD diss., University of Illinois at Urbana-Champaign, 2009), accessed September 2, 2010, http://libqual.org/documents/LibQual/publications/lq_gr_2.pdf; Association of Research Libraries, "LibQUAL+®: Publications" (Washington, DC: Association of Research Libraries, 2010), accessed September 2, 2010, http://www.libqual.org/publications.aspx.

7. University of Texas at Austin, Library, *LibQUAL+® 2008 Survey* (Washington, DC: Association of Research Libraries, 2008), 35, accessed July 3, 2010, http://www.lib.utexas.edu/sites/default/files/vprovost/2008_LibQUAL_Institution-Results.pdf.

8. Hernon and Altman, *Assessing Service Quality*, 145.

9. University of Texas at Austin, Library, *LibQUAL+® 2008 Survey*, 35.

10. Susan Gilmore, "Survey Shows: At 7.3 Million Visits a Year, Seattle Loves Its Public Libraries," *The Seattle Times*, July 30, 2010, accessed August 8, 2010, http://www.resourceshelf.com/2010/07/31/public-libraries-community-survey-results-released-seattle-wants-more-from-its-libraries/. See also Norman Oder, "Survey in Seattle Shows Satisfaction, Generational Change, Huge A/V Circ," *LibraryJournal.com* (August 3, 2010), accessed August 8, 2010, http://www.libraryjournal.com/lj/home/886208-264/survey_in_seattle_shows_satisfaction.html.csp.

11. Oder, "Survey in Seattle."

12. The Seattle Public Library, *Community Survey Summary* (July 28, 2010), accessed August 8, 2010, http://www.spl.org/pdfs/about/community_survey_summary.pdf. The appendix of this publication reprints the survey instrument.

13. Jolene D. Smyth, Don A. Dillman, Leah Melani Christian, and Michael J. Stern, "Comparing Check-All and Forced-Choice Question Formats in Web Surveys," *Public Opinion Quarterly* 70, no. 1 (2006): 66.

14. See Susan M. Heathfield, "Perform Exit Interviews: Exit Interview Questions," *About. com: Human Resources* (2010), accessed June 9, 2010, http://humanresources.about.com/od/ whenemploymentends/a/exit_interview_2.htm.

15. Jennifer Epstein, "Congress's 'Secret Shopper'," *Inside Higher Ed* (August 3, 2010), accessed August 8, 2010, http://www.insidehighered.com/news/2010/08/03/gao. See also Gregory D. Kutz, *For-Profit Colleges: Underscore Testing Finds Colleges Encouraged Fraud and Engaged in Deceptive and Questionable Marketing Practices*, GAO-10-948T (Washington, DC: Government Accountability Office, 2010), accessed August 8, 2010, http://www.gao.gov/products/ GAO-10-948T.

16. Vanessa Czopek, "Using Mystery Shoppers to Evaluate Customer Service in the Public Library," *Public Libraries* 37, no. 6 (November/December 1998): 370–71.

17. Robert E. Dugan, Peter Hernon, and Danuta A. Nitecki, *Viewing Library Metrics from Different Perspectives* (Santa Barbara, CA: Libraries Unlimited, 2009); Hernon, Dugan, and Nitecki, *Engaging in Evaluation and Assessment Research*.

18. Joseph R. Matthews, "Customer Satisfaction: A New Perspective," *Public Libraries* 47, no. 6 (November/December 2006): 52–55.

19. ThinkExist.com, Quotations, "Will Durant, American Writer and Historian," accessed July 2, 2010, http://thinkexist.com/quotation/inquiry_is_fatal_to/157487.html.

4

Methodologies (Unstructured and Solicited Approaches) and the Presentation of Data Collected

It is easy enough to drive customers away.[1]

This chapter focuses on data collection that can be characterized as unstructured and solicited (see figure 4.1). The library solicits customer feedback by providing customers with opportunities to share their comments (criticism, praise, comments, and suggestions for improvement). Almost every library has had the occasion to receive unstructured and unsolicited, as well as solicited and unstructured, comments and feedback about the library. These comments might be conveyed through comment cards left throughout the library for customers to complete, if they so desire. Comments might also be posted in a suggestion box available on the library's homepage or made through an open-ended question on a survey directed at library customers. The most common method is the library's request for an individual to complete a customer satisfaction survey (and the customer can respond to an open-ended question). It merits mention that this chapter complements but does not duplicate "Managing the Three Cs (Comments, Complaints, and Compliments)" in *Assessing Service Quality.*[2]

Despite the best of intentions and lots of training, no academic and public library delivers stellar service to every customer every time. Jan Carlzon, the chairman of Scandinavian Airlines System (SAS), called each interaction between the airline (airplane, facilities, and staff) and the customer a "moment of truth." This phrase was a rallying call for the SAS staff to start delivering high-quality service as the airline transitioned from a lackadaisical government-run organization to a for-profit company.[3] It is encouraging to note that, after eighteen months of training and making some significant investments in equipment, the airline was voted the best airline in the world.

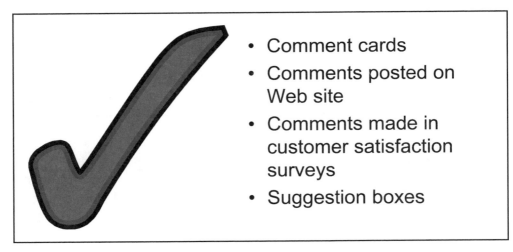

- Comment cards
- Comments posted on Web site
- Comments made in customer satisfaction surveys
- Suggestion boxes

Figure 4.1. Topics Discussed in the Chapter

Organizations that deliver world-class service examine each moment of truth in an attempt to determine what problems might occur. Once identified, they seek to modify that moment before the customer experiences a service failure and goes to another service (information) provider or tells others about the failure.

Surprisingly, the vast majority of customers does not expect library staff members to be perfect. The customers do, however, expect them to fix things when they go wrong (as things inevitably do). Customer complaints are simply a fact of life for any organization. One consulting firm found that 96 percent of unhappy customers say nothing to the company; however, they share their dissatisfaction with family, friends, and coworkers (twenty or more people will hear a customer's story).[4] This negative word-of-mouth advertising causes some people to stay away from a business or a library.

In addition to the usual set of questions that frequently appear on a library survey (asking respondents to rate facilities, services, staff, and so forth), there typically is one or more open-ended questions that ask respondents to provide additional textual information if they are so inclined. Interestingly, many surveys find that 38 percent or more of the respondents do answer the open-ended questions.[5]

COMPLAINTS

Because customers will have complaints, the important question is, what is the library going to do about them? Two approaches seem prevalent:

1. View complaints as a *failure* and as something to be resolved quickly and then forgotten. Often the same problems and complaints recur because the library does nothing to correct the underlying cause. This approach reflects an inward-looking, library-centric view of the world.

2. *Welcome* complaints and regard them as opportunities to learn something from the customer's perspective and, assuming customers identify themselves, to begin a dialogue with those who took the time to comment. The library might review the policies and training that led to the complaint and determine if there are ways to improve the service experience. This approach reflects an outward-looking, customer-centric view of the world.

Rather than becoming defensive, library staff members and library management should embrace complaints as gifts. A complaint provides feedback about how the library is doing (in reality, the library is not doing too well, since someone is complaining). As Pete Blackshaw observes, when an organization does really well, customers share that positive experience with perhaps three people. When that organization does poorly, however, they likely tell hundreds or thousands of people about their experience and might do so through social networks.[6]

COMPLIMENTS

Customers should be encouraged to offer compliments as well as complaints. Compliments provide a positive, emotional reward for service well performed and for efforts to improve the library's ambiance.

One customer at McDonald's wrote a lengthy letter of praise in which she revealed useful information, namely that she is a repeat customer and does not want to see a price increase. She also specifies her service expectations. She writes,

> [I] don't ask that much from a fast-food restaurant: just fresh food, a quick turnaround, and competent, friendly service. Sometimes, to my delight, the experience exceeds my expectations. I'm writing about such an experience with the counter staff at one of your restaurants.
>
> When I visited the . . . store . . . , the people there were so nice and helpful. I am a mother of three small children, who are very active, and they talked to them and adored them. Everyone there was wonderful. The playroom was also very clean and well kept up with. Thank you.
>
> Let me tell you a little bit about myself and my dining habits. I eat at your restaurant fairly often, and I usually spend about $20.00 on a meal there. The main reason I eat there is because I've eaten there in the past and enjoyed it. While I'm pleased with McDonald's Corporation, I don't know whether I'd pay more to eat there.
>
> This experience reminded me why I think so highly of your restaurant. Because of this, I will certainly return there to eat, and I'll definitely urge others to go there.
>
> Please pass along this compliment to everyone who should see it.
> And keep up the good work![7]

In preparing this chapter we studied numerous testimonials that customers wrote to various businesses and posted on the Internet. We also reviewed numerous comments made to public libraries and discovered that the testimonials tend to be far shorter than the McDonald's example. Perhaps because library staff frequently do not wear name tags, it appears to be uncommon for customers to point out specific individuals.

WAYS TO COMMENT

Customers might make their comments orally to staff, and in such cases, they merit capturing. Such recording becomes difficult if staff view the comment as critical of themselves and suspect that management will penalize or criticize them. A more common means of recording comments is in written form (paper and pencil or inserted into a digital format); see figure 4.2 (pp. 74–75) for a set of comments based on the library's branding. However, increasingly customers might make their comments through a social network and pressure the organization to change policies and procedures.

The problem with any of these methods is that the number of respondents is small. Libraries need to encourage comments, perhaps by placing widgets throughout their homepage that invite a dialogue with customers and encourage them to share their comments. Still, it is important to remember that, although the number of comments posted on social networks may be small, they are likely to reach many more people, as Blackshaw points out (see note 6).

SUGGESTIONS

Suggestions might include complaints or compliments, but they might also suggest areas for service improvement. Asking library customers to make suggestions about how to make the library more responsive to the needs of customers is an obvious but seldom used approach for libraries truly interested in listening to the voice of the customer. Some libraries may ask staff to make suggestions for improvement, but most staff suggestions focus on making process improvements rather than suggesting new services.

Though the number of suggestions that a library is likely to receive is small, this approach should not be discouraged, and staff should think *outside the box*. Off-the-wall suggestions might provoke the staff to consider something that will really generate much interest among library customers.

With widespread use of the Internet, many organizations employ blogs and their Web sites to encourage active participation with customers in the development of products and services. For example, Lego embraced a group that is knowledgeable and passionate about Lego bricks, and the Seattle-based Starbucks created a digital suggestion box, called MyStarbucksIdea.Com, where individuals may submit their ideas for products or services, discuss the ideas of others, and vote on their favorites. More than 180,000 people have registered, and more than 80,000 suggestions have been submitted.[8]

A number of companies have developed software that allows a community of customers to become actively involved in making suggestions, commenting and ranking suggestions, and generally becoming a real partner with the organization. In addition to writing about ideas, some companies encourage their active customers to take pictures and videos of things that are memorable as well as problematic. Other companies that actively engage their customers and solicit their suggestions include Intuit (QuickBooks community, Quicken community; http://community.intuit.com/quickbooks) and the online company Threadless (http://www.threadless.com/), which makes funny and satirical T-shirts that site members design and approve. Each week, there is a design contest on the Web site to determine what T-shirts will be produced next. The members vote, the winners get printed, and the T-shirts sell out, sometimes in just days.

SUGGESTION BOXES

Suggestion boxes might be displayed in the library in high traffic areas, where the public is most likely to notice them, and be included in a prominent place on the Web site and Web pages. The library might have signage throughout the building calling attention to a phone number and the telephone suggestion box, where customers can post their comments.

The principal challenge facing the suggestion box is that it is a closed and locked system. That is, every suggestion placed in a suggestion box is not made visible for all to see. Even if the library posts most of the suggestions/questions along with the library's response, not every suggestion is posted.

John Lubans Jr. has used an interesting approach, namely a "suggestion answer book," a three-ring binder in which every question and suggestion, along with the library's response, is visible for all to see. This more transparent approach relies on the fact that most library customers are allies and not the enemy.[9]

COMMENT CARDS

The customer comment card is a great way to collect testimonials and receive complaints. Disgruntled customers generally need an outlet to express their dissatisfaction. A conveniently placed customer comment card could prevent the unhappy customer from complaining to a third party, assuming the customer self-identifies and the library makes prompt contact. One public library director tells a story in which she wrote a letter to a complaining customer and that person was surprised to receive such a letter. In fact, the person declared, "I filled out many comment cards, and this is the first time I ever received a response." This person then made a donation to the library.

Comment cards are a passive means of data collection, but one that should not be ignored. In hotels these cards are left in the rooms and dining facilities for customers to complete. In the case of libraries, there is often a pile of them at various service locations. However, the question arises, "What do customers do with the cards when they fill them out?" Do they leave them in the hotel room, at the restaurant table, or on a service desk, or do they return them to a staff member? What happens to the cards once they are returned?

Share a Compliment

Please convey my appreciation to:

NAME:_____

DEPT._____

COMMENTS:

Share a Compliment

Please convey my appreciation to:

NAME:_____

DEPT._____

COMMENTS:

Share a Compliment

Please convey my appreciation to:

NAME:_____

DEPT._____

COMMENTS:

Figure 4.2. Public Library Comment Cards. Reprinted with permission from Catherine McDonald, the Lucius Beebe Memorial Library, Wakefield, MA.

Suggestion/Complaint

Suggestion/Complaint:

Would you like a response?   Yes   No

How can we contact you?

Where Wakefield Connects
LuciuS
BEEBE
Memorial Library

Suggestion/Complaint

Suggestion/Complaint:

Would you like a response?   Yes   No

How can we contact you?

Where Wakefield Connects
LuciuS
BEEBE
Memorial Library

Suggestion/Complaint

Suggestion/Complaint:

Would you like a response?   Yes   No

How can we contact you?

Where Wakefield Connects
LuciuS
BEEBE
Memorial Library

There are many examples of comment cards posted on the Internet, and a number of companies help tailor the content to the specific needs of the organization. The key is to limit the content to a few questions and encourage those completing the form to self-identify. These cards provide general opinions, but they are no substitute for formal surveys that contain a comment question. If these surveys are conducted continuously or at repeated intervals, they provide trend data.

OTHER FORMS OF COMMENTS

Those Posted on Web Sites

A comments and suggestions page on a library Web site typically states: "Use the form below to send comments, concerns, or suggestions." There might be a note stating that other forms are available to send a reference question; to inquire about library services; to ask about renewals, holds, and patron accounts; to recommend the purchase of a specific title; or to provide feedback about the Web site. The page then calls for the comment and perhaps some contact information: e-mail address or phone number and perhaps the name of the individual. It is helpful to indicate how long it will take for customers to receive a response. Whatever time selected should not be too long.[10]

Libraries should make it easy for customers to locate the Web page to make comments, by placing a link to the suggestion or comments box on the opening screen. When they click on the box, they should not encounter a message like this:

Our **Web site** and e-mail use "cookies" and similar means to gather information. . . . We welcome your **comments** but we reserve the right to remove any content **posted** at any time.

The customer is not informed whether these are session cookies (removed after one use) or persistent cookies (permanently attached to one's computer). The notice about removal might suggest that if the staff did not like the response, they will delete it. Perhaps the removal statement needs clarification. The important point is to encourage customers using the library homepage to share their comments, both positive and negative, as well as suggestions for service improvement.

Comments and Suggestions Made in Surveys

Open-ended questions in a customer satisfaction survey are generally quite helpful in that they allow respondents to expand on a particular topic: the staff, the facilities, the programs, the services, and so forth. By adding one more question to the questionnaire, management and staff members see the library better from the perspective of the customer:

- Please describe the most memorable thing that took place when you last visited the library; or

- Please describe the most memorable thing that took place during your visit today.

Responses to either question are gems and should be treated like gold. The answers provide real insight about what is important to customers. Even more revealing is to have all library staff members complete this question and have management compare responses with those from the customers. Most likely there will be major differences, illustrating that staff often do not know the customers as well as they think.

It is also important to provide a clear option (perhaps a check box) that allows respondents to choose "Nothing memorable happened." Clearly, visits may not comprise a remarkable experience—something worthy of special note.

WHAT ARE LIBRARIES DOING?

One of the authors reviewed all of the Web sites of public libraries in California to determine if they offer a form to make a compliment, comment, or complaint. Only 18 percent do so as a means for the customer to communicate with the library. Even fewer libraries have a form that would allow customers to suggest a title for purchase by the library.[11]

CONCLUDING THOUGHTS

Customers assume various roles. These might include the customer as one of the following:

- **A resource.** The customer as a source of ideas has been studied and is discussed in the innovation literature.[12] One of the challenges is that most customers are passive and accept the status quo. However, if encouraged to think outside the box and reflect on their experiences in other settings, they can be a good source of ideas for improving products or services. In some cases, a staff member may have a conversation with a customer, who may make a suggestion that, if captured in some way and forwarded to an appropriate individual, can be a useful source of ideas.

- **A co-creator.** Customers may also be active participants as co-creators of new products and services. They may be involved in designing service activities and testing service development activities and procedures. Southwest Airlines involves customers who fly frequently in the selection process when hiring new flight attendants (and there is a waiting list of customers who want to be involved). Clearly, many people are still involved in creating *Wikipedia*, developing open software, sharing photos on Flickr, and so forth.

- **A user.** Customers may play an important role in product or service testing (e.g., beta testing a new software release), and many companies find customers willing to share their experiences and expertise in the support of a specific product. And of course, customers may provide feedback as respondents in a customer satisfaction survey.[13]

Listening to the Patron:
When We Begin the Beguine*

At the Douglas County Libraries, we listen to patrons in various ways that might be characterized as formal and informal. All service begins with a conversation. That conversation becomes, at some point, the reference interview: the process through which library staff help patrons discern the path of their curiosity. The conversation might begin as soon as patrons step through the doors. It might start as we find them wandering through the stacks. It might take place at a service desk. It might be on the phone or through e-mail. This relationship-building process is what leads to everything else: whether a service transaction or a moment of simple human connection.

There are also many internal conversations. Staff meetings, continuing education sessions, and library conferences allow us to pool frontline insights and hold them up like eggs to the candles of professional research.

Statistics

All we know of the world is the result of observation and extrapolation. We see, then we make meaning. Librarians are ceaseless collectors of data. We can break down our circulation by Dewey number and format. We can track the busiest times of day at checkout stations (self-check or staff-assisted). We can count the number of Web site or database logins and calculate the average length of a session. We know how many people walk through our doors per day. These kinds of numbers enable us to track what people actually use and what they do with what we offer. There is a certain segment of our user base that does not directly speak to us very often. This is how we listen to them.

In addition to our own internal records of use and patron behavior, there is also a wealth of demographic data available from the U.S. Bureau of the Census and geographic information systems (GIS). There is a growing and complex web of psychographic information on consumer and lifestyle behavior that can also reveal trends or emerging needs. In general, libraries have moved from the passive collection of inputs to the calculation of outputs. The latter metrics (e.g., circulation per capita, program attendance per capita, and reference or computer use) begin to get at the issue of library performance. These metrics also highlight those areas where a library might not be *listening* as well as its peers. Statistics keep us honest. The next level of statistics is outcomes, real and measurable changes in the well-being of our communities. That attention to our social environment is another way to listen to our patrons.

Comment Cards

All of our seven locations offer green comment cards at each service station. This half-page form gives patrons a chance to praise, critique, or otherwise pass along some comment or question to us. Patrons can either do so anonymously, or request follow-up.

Surveys

Surveys are our most formal tool for listening. There are many kinds:

- **@ the library**. My favorite survey is to stand just outside the library and ask people as they leave, "May I ask you what you used us for today?" Sometimes the information is surprising; we found one year that the third most important reason people came to the library was to meet someone. That greatly accelerated our understanding of the library as community hub. There is an obvious bias here, of course; we only get to talk to those people who physically appear in our space.

- **Online**. Growing in popularity (mainly because it is so easy to tally the results through the use of various electronic survey tools) is the online survey. Our preference is to keep things brief, just three to five questions. A new statistical discovery is that we now have as many virtual visitors as physical. There is some overlap between them, but it is not total: Some folks who walk in our physical doors never use our online databases or Web site, and vice versa. The bias here, of course, is toward those people who are reasonably savvy about technology. But over time, that starts to look like the general population.

- **Phone polls**. We have, typically around election time, paid people to conduct phone polls. Here, the focus tends to be more on our approval rating ("How well do you think the library handles your tax dollar?"), planning priorities (e.g., "Please rank the importance to you of the following: more children's storytimes . . . "), and willingness to provide additional financial support ("If you were voting today, would you vote for or against a one mil increase in your property tax?"). We have also done follow-up calls for specific projects, such as business reference support. Our recent creation of a contact center has given us another tool for such surveys, although we have not used it that way yet.

- **Mailers**. Another one of my favorite surveys was a "Why Did You Leave Us?" mailing. We noticed an odd trend: A fair number of people applied for library cards but apparently never used us again. We sent a sample of them a letter saying we had noticed that and wondered if they did use us, but not in ways we could track, whether we had disappointed them in some fashion we were keen to discover, or whether they had just moved away. The key findings, by the way, were that these people tended to be students living in other library jurisdictions who just needed us for one assignment, or people who used us to get cards so they could access various databases. Nowadays, we know how to register database access as a use. We also got a wonderfully touching and funny letter back from a woman "seduced by AOL," although she vowed to change, to come back to the real world of people and print, and she did. We have also done twice-a-year mailings of eight-page magazines, which often encourage feedback in a variety of ways.

Focus Group Interviews

A few years back we used GIS data to find people who did not have library cards. We invited them to neutral ground for pizza to find out what was going on with their lives. With one group of teens, we learned that they did not use the library because they preferred the smell of community: coffee. This led, in one case, to a coffee stand in the library foyer.

Video Traffic Analysis

Another kind of survey is the video sampler. Most of our libraries now have security cameras. We find that by watching them at high speed, we can see traffic patterns that otherwise escape us. We can see where some display areas work well and others do not. We can see where patrons get confused about their choices, bunching up in little knots of ambivalence. We can even see that some of our service standards (e.g., make eye contact with and smile at everybody) fall through the cracks sometimes.

Media

I write a weekly newspaper column and appear (along with other staff) on local radio and TV shows. I often solicit (or receive unsolicited) public comment on library directions through letters to the editor or radio show call-ins.

Complaints

A profoundly useful source of patron information comes from complaints. These days, we tend to get them through e-mail, usually addressed to our board of trustees. That link is on our Web site and seems to get more use than those links directly addressed to staff. These complaints are routed to the director as a first responder, but both complaint and response go also to the board president, ensuring that our governing body hears about problems, too. If there is a pattern of complaints, that is likely to generate a conversation at the senior management level. A request for reconsideration (attempt to remove or restrict materials or services) is another form of complaint that can reveal important patron concerns.

Community

We also listen to our patrons through the process of community connection to our governing body, a lay board of trustees. These volunteers are all active in their communities. As director, I ask them regularly about what they hear about their communities, the better to match our services to those patterns. Our board tends to be composed of people who use the library, too, so their own changing patterns of use provide another kind of focus group.

I believe that getting librarians out into the community, acting in a more organized way to *catalog* community issues, is the future of our profession. Our staff have recently developed a community reference project tracking tool: a blog that through multiple entries, tagging, and regular review begins to tease out hidden or early information needs that might never have landed at a reference desk, but are of vital importance to the communities we serve.

Professional Awareness

Another way that we listen to patrons is through reading newspapers; participating on blogs; engaging in RSS feeds and reports; watching TV, film, and videos; listening to music; and attending a host of cultural, political, and other social events. All of these activities are part of an ongoing community scan.

Elections

Another way we listen to the community is at the ballot box. As OCLC's report, *From Awareness to Funding*, has shown,[1] there is a difference between use and support. Although not all public libraries have the opportunity to go direct to the voters, funding decisions by authorizing agencies (the ones who write the checks) provide a powerful form of speech, and it cannot be ignored.

Doing Something

Ultimately, of course, it is not enough to listen. We have to turn what we have heard into something we have learned. Then we have to translate that understanding into action. Listening to the patron is like listening to your dance partner. "Leading" and "following" can pass back and forth between you in remarkably swift and subtle ways. But the goal is the same: the celebration of synchronous movement.

Notes

1. OCLC, *From Awareness to Funding: A Study of Library Support in America* (Dublin, OH: OCLC, 2008), accessed October 3, 2010, http://www.oclc.org/reports/funding/.

*James LaRue, Director, Douglas County Libraries, Castle Rock, CO.

Mississauga Public Library*

Public libraries are always looking at how to evaluate their services and answer the following questions:

- How well are we doing?
- Are the numbers up?
- What do this month's statistics show?

Once the numbers are collected and reported, they are usually forgotten. If they are *good*, we might promote them; if they are *bad*, we tend to ignore them.

Measuring a library's performance has many shades. One area in which data should always be collected is customer feedback. Such data are not as easy to collect and use as circulation or attendance figures, but a good customer satisfaction rating is the ultimate performance measure. Two questions arise: "How do we gather the comments of customers?" and "What if they only complain?"

The Mississauga Library System, a public library in suburban Toronto serving 750,000 residents, recognizes that contact with customers is an important part of every library employee's duties. The library listens to its customers in a number of ways. The library adopted a *one-stop* philosophy years ago. The intent was to enable staff to remove barriers to good service on the spot, without involving other levels of supervision and thereby avoiding a real frustration for the customer. Each public service level identifies common customer problems and the group, everyone from shelver to reference librarian, examines those problems. The suggested changes to policies and practices empower staff to resolve more issues with customers. The result is both happier customers and happier staff.

The library uses traditional ways of hearing from customers, including:

- complaints, and sometimes compliments, by telephone to *the person in charge* as a result of an unsatisfactory experience with the library;
- complaints on comment forms that are always readily available in all eighteen branches and are regularly responded to by the local branch manager before being forwarded to the public service manager for collation; and
- complaints by e-mail regarding library service or policy;

Managers collate the feedback for system-wide attention. If the customer provides contact information, the appropriate manager promptly responds. Frequently the resolution is shared with elected officials or library board members. As well, the issues are discussed at staff meetings and used to develop staff training priorities.

The library's staff training focuses on customer contact at all levels of staff. The reality that the customer is also *their boss* is emphasized at every opportunity. Staff are trained to practice *roving reference service*, which brings them into increased contact with customers and results in amazing feedback. A friendly, "Are you finding what you are looking for?" can lead to an in-depth conversation on how well the library is meeting a user's needs. It can also allow staff to inform the customer of coming plans and new developments in the library. Impromptu discussions can cover everything from the latest electronic services to washroom maintenance. Of course, compliments are equally telling.

Another regular library practice designed to hear from the customer is ad hoc customer surveys. These are conducted over the year to listen to customers in specific locations or on specific topics in order to guide a decision or help in setting objectives. Staff members approach a representative number of customers with a few questions on the issue at hand. A choice of verbal or written response is offered. Issues have included the state of the library generally, quality of staff assistance, use of time spent in the library, availability of needed resources ("Did you find what you were looking for?") and the overall quality of that visit to the library. A simple, "What one thing would have improved your visit today?" always elicits an amazing number of suggested improvements.

Feedback from customers collected through such simple exit surveys has identified lack of awareness of library services and resources as the major need of customers. Despite ongoing promotion through the usual means (flyers, posters, bookmarks, newspaper advertisements, screen savers, and staff buttons), many comments identify unawareness as the main customer issue. This just confirms the need for a strong ongoing publicity effort for any public library.

In Mississauga the residents have ample access to the members of the library board. The library trustees make contact with residents a key part of their duties. Numerous means are used, including

- open monthly board meetings, widely advertized across the community, with a delegation item on every agenda;

- library board *open houses* at various branches during the year to enable board members to visit the branch, see it operating, meet branch staff, and meet local residents over coffee and dessert;

- library board meetings held at branch libraries when there are key local issues or plans for changes at that location;

- regular seminnual reports to city council by the board chair, which are broadcast on the local cable channel;

- an annual community forum each fall to focus on needs and plans for the coming year, to which other local agencies and partners are invited;

- a library board Web page that encourages resident feedback and comment on the library's plans;

- a major review of library services every five years, with extensive citizen input designed to foresee needs ahead and to plan for them; and

- an annual set of objectives for the library's management based on wide stakeholder consultation throughout the year.

The Mississauga Library System considers the library trustees to have two main duties: to learn continually about the library and its achievement of its stated objectives and about the community's needs for and satisfaction with the library. Both roles require the board members to use their limited time in effective communication with the library's customers, both internal and external.

Library staff approach their duty to listen to the customer through a number of means in addition to those already mentioned. Branches hold "customer appreciation days" each year to create even more contact with the customer. These allow the staff to meet customers in a more relaxed, social way over refreshments and to welcome newcomers and share the library's plans.

All branches provide materials-suggestion forms around the library. Users looking for specific items can complete a form and submit it. All requests are followed through with either a hold being placed on the newly acquired item or an interlibrary loan request being offered. Customers can also conveniently suggest purchases through the library's Web site.

A partnership with the local cable channel allows staff to regularly appear on the local current affairs program to promote the library. The program includes a call-in segment to allow residents to voice their kudos or complaints. Experience again has shown that unawareness of library services is the biggest barrier to customer satisfaction.

One voice of the customer that carries great weight is the feedback from the city's elected politicians. They have ongoing contact with a wide variety and number of residents, and as a result their view of the library can be telling. They can also be effective advocates for the library in their community work, so keeping them informed of and involved in their local library is vital to customer satisfaction.

Community contact at the staff level includes the usual speaking engagements and attendance at community events. The library has a variety of tabletop displays and PowerPoint presentations ready to go. Such efforts seem to be the most effective way to attract new library members.

The Mississauga Library System has consciously developed partnerships across the community with like organizations and works to maintain these links through regular contact and involvement in library initiatives. The library board invites a partner organization to make a short presentation at each library board meeting on the group's operations and how well the library is meeting that group's needs. The group in turn gets to hear about the library board's goals, objectives, and current plans.

The system knows that its success depends on how well it is meeting the community's needs. Customer feedback has set the library's current priorities for change: better awareness of the library's services, more inviting and functional space, and the need to keep up with technology. Of course kudos and compliments are always welcome. They tend to mention the helpfulness of staff, the excellence of the collections, and the variety and quality of programs.

Constant acknowledgment of the importance of customers' comments to all library stakeholders validates the importance of listening to the voice of the customer.

*Don Mills, Director, Mississauga Library System, Ontario, Canada.

The notion of listening to the customer's voice involves a wide range of activities, so that the organization can discern and understand the complete breadth of the message. Capturing the comments of customers, from a variety of sources, is only helpful if those comments are then carefully analyzed. As discussed in the previous chapter, the comments provided in customer satisfaction surveys are clearly going to be different from those provided by individuals who are asked to make suggestions about how to make the library more responsive to their assorted information needs.

> *Complaints that customers bring directly to businesses are the most efficient and least costly way of getting information and understanding customer expectations about services and products.*[14]

NOTES

1. Janelle Barlow and Claus Møller, *A Complaint Is a Gift: Recovering Customer Loyalty When Things Go Wrong* (San Francisco: Berett-Koehler Publishers, 2008), 20.

2. Peter Hernon and Ellen Altman, *Assessing Service Quality: Satisfying the Expectations of Library Customers*, 2nd ed. (Chicago: American Library Association, 2010), 65–82.

3. Jan Carlzon, *The Moments of Truth* (New York: Harper, 1989).

4. Robert G. Sines and Eric A. Duckworth, "Customer Service in Higher Education," *Journal of Marketing for Higher Education* 5, no. 2 (1994): 1–16.

5. Frank Biss, Counting Opinions, e-mail message to Joseph R. Matthews, June 9, 2010.

6. Pete Blackshaw, *Satisfied Customers Tell Three Friends, Angry Customers Tell 3,000* (New York: Doubleday, 2008).

7. Planetfeedback, "Complimenting the Staff," 2001, accessed July 2, 2010, http://www.planetfeedback.com/mcdonalds/employees/complimenting+the+staff/20861.

8. Douglas Quenqua, *Starbucks' Own Good Idea* (Chicago: American Marketing Association, 2009), 23–25.

9. John Lubans Jr., "Where Are the Snows of Yesteryear? Reflections on a Suggestion 'Box' That Worked," *Library Administration & Management* 15, no. 4 (Fall 2001): 240–45.

10. For an example of how such a page might look, see Colorado State University Libraries, "Comments and Suggestions," 2009, accessed July 3, 2010, http://lib.colostate.edu/help/comments.html.

11. For an example of a relevant form, see Hernon and Altman, *Assessing Service Quality*, 80.

12. See Clayton M. Christensen, *The Innovator's Dilemma: When New Technologies Cause Great Firms to Fail* (Cambridge: Harvard Business School Press, 1997); Eric Von Hippel, "Lead Users: A Source of Novel Product Concepts," *Management Science* 32, no. 7 (1986): 791–805.

13. Ibid.

14. Barlow and Møller, *A Complaint Is a Gift*, 22.

5

Methodologies (Structured But Not Always Solicited Approaches) and Analyzing Study Findings

The best way to find out whether your customers are satisfied is to ask them.[1]

As shown in figure 5.1 (p. 88), the methodologies discussed in this chapter are designed to capture information that is structured and often solicited. As in the other methodological chapters, the goal is to pursue different ways to gather data useful to better serving library customers. It is important to remember that some methodologies are more appropriate to external customers than they are to internal customers. The latter might focus on surveys and interviews. Those discussed in this chapter apply to external customers.

BUILDING SWEEPS AS AN OBSERVATION TECHNIQUE

Typically, researchers have explored the use of public spaces in shopping malls, restaurants, and other social settings. Libraries, as Lisa Given and Gloria Leckie point out, contain a public space, one in which individuals engage in assorted social, educational, recreational, and informational activities. They recommend data collection that uses spatial data analysis, a "useful method for mapping the physical layout of libraries and information centers to examine . . . how individuals make use of that space." The results of studying *seating sweeps* "may be used for short-and long-term facilities planning, to match information services to users' information behaviors, or to re-design the social activity space of libraries according to the usage patterns of different types of patrons."[2]

- Sweeping observation
- Customer ratings on third-party Internet sites
- Analysis of telephone calls, letters, or e-mails: complaints, compliments, suggestions for improvement

Figure 5.1. Topics Discussed in the Chapter

A study of seating sweeps is a means of data collection that does not involve interaction with library customers. Staff members merely record what people are doing in public spaces, and answer these kinds of questions:

- What spaces are they using?

- Are they alone or interacting with others?

- In what interactions are they engaged?

More specifically, seating sweeps

> capture particular types of data, including the following: who was using the library (i.e., gender and approximate age), the activities in which those individuals were engaged (e.g., reading, writing, talking, eating, sleeping, and using library computers), the library location in which those activities occurred (e.g., book stacks, computer terminal, printer, and public telephones), and the personal belongings that those individuals had with them (e.g., briefcases, cell phones, laptop computers, food and drink, and baby carriages).[3]

To conduct such a study, investigators need to develop a checklist that profiles users, lists the type of possessions they bring into the library and the types of activities in which customers are engaged, and contains a location code (e.g., for the circulation desk).[4] The investigators might also have a copy of the floor plan so that they can mark where people are standing or sitting. For example, are they sitting alone at a table or with a group?

Before engaging in data collection, it is important to determine the time frame for conducting sweeps. In setting the time frame, the investigators must decide if they want to generalize the findings to a certain period of time (e.g., an entire school term or month), and then within that period, if they want to use a random sample—each element in the population has an equal chance of being included in the sample—or a systematic sample—selecting every nth item for a list until the sample has been drawn—to narrow the time frame to certain days and hours), or if they want to arbitrarily select certain times during a day to collect data (nonprobability sample). They also need to decide if the same person or several people will mark the checklist and floor plan. Further, they need to determine if they will sweep the entire library, parts of it, or particular service areas. If different people are involved in data collection, to what extent is there inter-scorer reliability—consistency in marking among them? If they decide to approximate customer age, how will they do so, and how accurate are the estimations?

Given and Leckie point out that:

> Observed behaviors may not match what individuals say that they do on a written or oral survey and therefore may be able to provide concrete evidence to support a particular library design or certain types of policy decisions (e.g., are the computers really "always busy" as some patrons claim, or are they only very busy at certain times of the day). . . . [I]t is vital to be mindful of the fact that, although observation studies can provide an insightful glimpse of "what" is happening in libraries, they do not indicate "why" patrons do what they do; researchers must assess important "why" questions through a triangulation of other methods (e.g., questionnaires or personal interviews) to investigate the full range of patrons' attitudes and motivations.
>
> . . . [T]here are many ways that researchers may extend this approach to obtain a much more dynamic and rich picture of individuals' behaviors. Observational shadowing of particular library patrons, for example, gives a much more detailed view of patrons' library use, but this approach comes with two issues that researchers must resolve. First, the shadowing approach is quite time-consuming (resulting in a much smaller sample of individuals than was reported in this study). Second, this approach is highly intrusive, so the data collection would necessitate a higher level of care toward individuals' privacy within the library space. Another possible extension of the seating sweeps method is that of time-space mapping, or the ability to follow individuals through the library space and map their activities over the course of a day (or a week). This approach would provide libraries with a much better sense of which areas of the library are more heavily used (by whom and when), which pieces of furniture obstruct people's movements throughout the space, where best to place information technologies, why certain areas are favored for study or reading, or which areas of the library to designate as "quiet" zones for private study. Again, although potentially fruitful, the method would be labor intensive and possible only with a small sample.[5]

SOME OTHER METHODOLOGIES

Usability Testing

Under the umbrella of usability testing are *inquiry*, *inspection*, and *formal usability* testing. When libraries inquire about customer preferences, expectations, and experiences, they typically rely on focus group interviews, one-to-one interviews, and surveys administered online or distributed to those visiting the library. When they engage in interviewing, they can ask follow-up questions and, in the case of focus group interviews, participants interact with the comments that others make. The inspection method refers to heuristic evaluation, which involves a systematic inspection of a user interface design for its usability. There might be cognitive walkthroughs, the purpose of which is to check specific characteristics (e.g., conventions for spelling variables versus procedure calls) and ensure that there is no violation of system-wide procedures. The designers of a Web site, database, or information system, and perhaps other specialists, often substitute for customers, and they perform tasks as they navigate the site, database, or system. In formal usability testing, participants are observed as they perform given tasks. The goal is to improve the appearance, layout, and navigation of information contained on that site, database, or system.

From the customer's point of view, libraries might engage in inquiry and formal usability testing. A review of the literature shows that, for the latter, the number of test questions does not exceed twelve. During the actual observation of user navigation of a Web site or Web sites, database, or online public access catalog, the sequence of steps that participants take to answer questions is recorded, synthesized, and used to diagnose problems, not to test subjects' knowledge of libraries and information literacy skills. As well, comments they make during and after the session might be captured, analyzed, and used in the ongoing improvement of the site, database, or system.

It merits mention that the U.S. government views usability testing as an example of best practices that a number of agencies (e.g., the General Services Administration, the Social Security Administration, the Bureau of Labor Statistics, the Census Bureau, the Department of Homeland Security, and the Internal Revenue Service) build into the Web development lifecycle and the ongoing maintenance of Web sites. The agencies might use all three types of usability testing, and a government portal, Usability.gov, notes examples of lessons that agencies have learned (see http://www.usability.gov/government/lssnslearned/index.html). They have also applied usability testing to instant messaging (see http://www.usability.gov/government/lssnslearned/imlearned.html). Finally, a number of excellent articles, books, and Web page discussions explain how to conduct usability testing, mostly formal usability testing, and how to use the results for product improvement.

Anthropological Evidence Gathering

The University of Rochester, under the guidance of Nancy Foster and Susan Gibbons, has engaged in numerous studies using ethnographic methods to study undergraduate student use of the library and how the library fits into student life on campus. The goal was to increase the frequency of library use and to improve both the design and layout of the physical library as well as student experiences using library services. Once flipcharts were placed in public areas to which two questions were appended ("Why do you like to come here?" and "What is missing?") , and students wrote assorted comments. From those comments, the staff learned that they needed to announce the location of electrical outlets on the library's Web site and to create "a new webpage that indicates the location of good study spaces within the main library. The spaces are arranged by the 'zones' . . . 'Quiet', 'Collaborative', and 'Comfy'."[6]

Next, a cultural probe, which studies people in their own environment, provides a way to extend the amount of time needed to observe participants as they gather needed information. For this qualitative methodology, participants use a camera or a notebook to record their information-seeking processes and jog their ability to recall what they did. The evidence gathered provides a richer record showing what they did. As Tracy Gabridge, Millicent Gaskell, and Amy Stout point out,

> Students took pictures, captured screen shots, and recorded notes of what steps they followed every time they looked for information related to their academic life over the course of a specific week. They were then asked to bring the photos, screen shots, and notes to an interview and to use those images and words to jog their memories about the details of what they did.[7]

These researchers found the insights they gained useful in improving online services and aiding students in being more effective and efficient in their information seeking. For instance, students were often "unaware of the vast array of relevant and helpful information and tools available to them from the . . . Libraries," and, as numerous other studies have documented, "students prefer to discover things on their own and not to ask for help, except from trusted peers. It is critical that every interaction with the . . . Libraries be positive in order to overcome this barrier as well as to allow the . . . Libraries to become part of the students' networks of trusted resources."[8]

Additional insights might emerge from asking customers to sketch a map of the library or a portion of the library from memory, to see what they are aware of and can recall. Such insights reveal their familiarity with and knowledge of a library and perhaps a service of particular importance to them.[9] A variation of this is to give a map to customers, undergraduate students in this case, and ask them, for a predetermined time period, "to mark their movements" on campus—to indicate "when they arrived at each place and when they left it."[10] One finding is that the participating students "often eat on the run" and that, because the library allows food and drink in the building, this policy "might be a contributing factor to the heavy use made of the library, especially by undergraduates."[11]

Finally, a library's Web site might also be reviewed through the use of mystery shopping or focus group interviews, or by asking customers to provide a written critique of the library's homepage. For instance, they might be given a photocopy of the opening screen and be asked what they would like to see.[12]

CUSTOMER RATINGS

Web sites devoted to online shopping frequently adopt a method of customer feedback known as *customer ratings*. Once customers make a purchase, they are asked to rate their shopping experience, perhaps on a scale of one to five, with five being the highest. Once the average has been tallied, the business receives an overall rating that it displays on its homepage. Because higher customer ratings presumably encourage future sales and low ratings have a negative effect, staff are often reminded about the importance of the ratings and instructed in ways to improve them. The transactional logs generated from online visits are regularly reviewed, and once problem areas are identified, they are corrected.

Such ratings complement satisfaction surveys and other means of data collection. Most important, they provide a single statistic. If that number fluctuates or never reaches a five, managers become concerned. Most likely, they review the number on a weekly basis and want to ensure the highest number possible.

If libraries engage in a similar rating, they can make direct comparisons to competitors that rely on customer ratings. Any rating should not be regarded as a competitive gimmick but rather as another tool for improving customer service and the *library experience*. As a variation of customer ratings, a library might ask a group of people to rate its Web site using a variety of features (e.g., appearance). Depending on the focus of the ratings, the results might be treated as confidential. A possible problem is that others may discover what is going on and demand access to the findings, especially if one aspect studied relates to filtering.

CREATING A DATABASE

If a library intends to use comment data in a systematic way, it should identify and create a single repository of data so that they can be examined on a regular basis and so that the library can handle ad hoc data analysis requests. The library might store the textual information in a word-processing file or another file specifically designed for storing and analyzing textual information. A cloud-based solution also exists, meaning that a library might ensure the migration of the system from an in-house data center to an Internet-based service that others may adopt, perhaps set up by a professional association, consortium, and so forth.[13]

Counting Opinions (http://www.countingopinions.com) offers LibSAT, which allows a public or academic library to store and review open-ended responses to a customer survey. Authorized library staff members can view each record online, assign responsibility for follow-up, and produce printed reports. There are ample opportunities for libraries subscribing to this service to "drill down" from the data characterized through some descriptive statistics and displayed visually to the actual comments that respondents make.

In addition, a quick search of the Internet reveals a wide variety of social media management software programs that operate on Windows, Macintosh, and Unix systems. Some are free, and others require payment.[14] As libraries invest more in capturing and analyzing customer comments, they will need to assign a staff member to ensure that the data, especially comments written on a paper form, are converted to an electronic format so that they can be included in the library's "compliment, comment, and complaint" database.

Hearing from Our Customers with No Words Spoken*

Santa Clara University's (SCU) $95 million Harrington Learning Commons, Sobrato Technology Center and Orradre Library, first opened its doors in March 2008. It is located in Silicon Valley, where the cost of start-up cash is often shockingly high and the expectations for return on such an investment can be just as lofty. For those of us who work in this state-of-the-art building, our responsibility and obligation is to meet the expectations of our students, administrators, and faculty.

What does *state-of-the-art* mean? At SCU, the investment resulted in nearly 200,000 square feet across four levels with all sorts of the latest green features (e.g., energy-efficient lighting and raised flooring to reduce cooling and heating costs). Our users will find a Learning Commons on two levels that includes 68 high-end computers and 11 media stations, with over 200 total computers in the building; a faculty development lab; a multimedia lab; video editing suites; and videoconferencing abilities. Particularly popular are the twenty-five collaborative workrooms with built-in technology for network and wireless access, projection and video capture capabilities, along with walltalker® whiteboard wallpaper for floor-to-ceiling note-taking.

Like every other library, we monitor log files, gather database statistics, track Google Analytics (and play with the graphs), and report every statistic known to humankind that libraries are called upon to do. We listen to students through formal and informal channels. We are on a three-year cycle with LibQUAL+®. More informally, we receive feedback in person; over the phone; through e-mail, chat, and texting through "Ask a Librarian"; via a comments/feedback online forum; and through a good old-fashioned suggestion box at our Learning Commons help desk. We hear and learn a lot from our customers even when they do not speak to us. All we need do is watch and observe.

There are five easy lessons we have learned from our customers:

1. Do not be so loud at the Learning Commons Desk. The cold stares from nearby students are not accidents. In our effort to provide cradle-to-grave service at our chief service point, we can be loud to the point of distraction.

2. The investment in machines with dual monitors is paying off. Look at the student who no longer has to toggle back and forth between Facebook and his or her Excel spreadsheet for accounting. There is no need to toggle when you have two screens. Social media are not a distraction; they are the fabric of life of the community—both globally and on the campus.

3. There is no such thing as too much collaborative space. SCU invested plenty in the two dozen collaborative workspaces. As each quarter draws to an end, they are all booked all of the time; even during the middle and beginning of the term, they are in demand during prime meeting time. Students work in teams, and teams need space.

4. There is no place like home, or the library, when finals roll around. You need your own space. And you need it for hours on end. SCU's library remains open twenty-four hours/day through the final exam period, and the energy and nerves are palpable. The head count at 3 a.m. is remarkable.

5. The good stuff, such as the furniture, is used and gets worn out. The planning involved in creating this space took untold hours in discussions, in exacting detail, about the type of furnishings to be used. In the end, this became part of the experiment: What furniture would be best suited for this space, and how would it be used? Answer: The worn-out chairs and sofas, after just a couple of years in business, are preferred.

Observation is critical. There are many lessons that the staff working in our new space can learn simply by paying attention to our customers. Fortunately, we do not have to speculate whether or not we are, in fact, picking up on their signals correctly. We take every opportunity to confirm our suspicions, and our patrons have been generous with their time providing regular feedback, formally and informally.

Shortly after opening, a building survey was conducted to get a first read on the services and space now available. The results of the quick poll confirmed our observations:

- 95 percent of respondents thought a time limit was necessary for the twenty-five collaborative workrooms, with a majority suggesting a four-hour limit for groups.

- Respondents also suggested the qualification "for group use only," because many rooms were being occupied by just one user when our building was brand new. Interestingly, it was a nearly split decision when asked, "Would you feel comfortable asking an individual using a group study room to leave so your group could utilize the room?"

- 70 percent preferred PC over Mac.

- Few students were making use of the Macs in the training/instruction and multimedia labs.

- Nearly 70 percent knew that all Macs ran both the OS and Windows operating systems, and half thought that it was easy to use the dual boot Macs.

- Three-quarters of our library customers bring their own laptops into the building to use as their computers.

- Regarding support services, the vast number were "satisfied" or "very satisfied" with network access, power, and printing in the new space.

- 86 percent recommended that we designate some "quiet spaces" in the building. They also had some ideas about what should be banned in the quiet spaces, starting with cell phones but even including "quiet" conversations and typing on keyboards.

This type of feedback is useful. With our suspicions confirmed, we have made adjustments in the room reservation system. The changes ensured that reservations could not be modified or deleted by someone else (sad but necessary, unfortunately). Reservations for collaborative study rooms were limited to a total of four hours per day in any combination of times.

Our regular participation in LibQUAL+® also verified a real problem with noise in the new building. This problem had been anticipated and discussed with architects in the program planning for the new building, and it was recognized that the Learning Commons, by design, was meant to foster collaboration and interaction (read: noise). The upper floors were intended, even in the architectural drawings, to be the quieter space for focused work and reading. With this in mind, the aim was to spread the word through the digital signage and table tents strategically placed on tables and carrels, promoting the upper floors for quiet study space.

Just as the PC replacement program guarantees that the machines in the building (PC and Mac) are no more than four years old, the idea is to repair and replace the furniture on a regular basis, too. Worn-out furniture is not such a bad thing. We strive to create an inviting, welcoming, and comfortable learning and study space and, after two and one-half years in operation, the condition of some furniture clearly indicates that we are on the right path. An interesting side note is that the furniture travels throughout the building, sometimes riding in an elevator and ending up on a new floor! While we had ideas, along with the architects, about where the furniture belonged, we might not be so right. The lesson is clear: watch and learn.

Looking to the future, we know we have much to learn from our library users at Santa Clara University. We will continue our observations, confirm our suspicions, and take the necessary steps to provide better service and improved space in support of the university's chief aim to promote student learning. One challenge is to enhance our communication channels to receive and respond more quickly and efficiently to user needs, so like many others, we have begun to reach out through every possible means: in-person, phone, e-mail, text, chat, social media, and mobiles. Still, we should not underestimate the power of observation.

*Robert Boyd, Assistant University Librarian for Technology Applications at Santa Clara University.

As the database grows in size, the library may wish to obtain and use a text analysis software package. Text analysis software programs identify frequently occurring phrases and concepts and make it possible to sort the results by branch location, date range, and so forth.[15]

If the survey respondents or individuals who complete a paper comment card include a telephone number, address, or e-mail address, the library has an obligation to prepare a response to these individuals. All too often, these queries and the responses are placed in a file (paper or electronic) and promptly forgotten. Wherever these records are typically placed, there is only one type of record, paper or electronic. As a result, each of these repositories becomes a silo of data that are rarely examined on a periodic basis to discover if any new patterns or trends have emerged. One purpose of a comprehensive database is to prevent the continuation of silos.

ANALYSIS OF OPEN-ENDED QUESTIONS

If the number of respondents with comments exceeds 100, then it becomes a time-consuming task to identify any trends or patterns. One solution is to develop categories and then assign each open-ended comment to the appropriate category (e.g., parking, facilities, collections, services, staff, programs, policies, and technology) and subcategory (e.g., facilities: equipment, seating, and so forth; policies: hours of operation, fees and fines). If the library tracks these comments over a period of time, it will discover the areas in which customers have concerns, and the library should take corrective action.

Figure 5.2 (p. 98) displays some of the comments that the customers of one public library, with a main library and a number of branches, made when they completed the LibSAT survey. Counting Opinions dates each comment and codes it to a category and subcategory. The comments reported in this chapter do not deal with staff members. Although some might be negative, many are not; for instance:

- "I come to the library once or twice a week and have been doing so for 15 years. I have mostly high praise for the facility, staff, and equipment."

- "This is a great library! The staff goes out of their way to answer my questions."

- "Wonderful big new building, helpful staff."

Furthermore, from a satisfaction perspective, some customers mention what they "love" about the library. For example:

> Love the self-checkout. Is there a way to rotate the selection of DVDs? Love the "New Fiction" section. Love reserving materials to pick up. My kids can be independent here with these services. Thank you!

The length of the responses in the database ranges from a few words (e.g., "more seats!") to a couple of lines, to one that exceeds 160 lines. The very long comment discusses different services and offers concrete recommendations for improvement, concluding the short essay by saying "Good luck." Some common themes emerge from the comments reported in figure 5.2: The public wants more computers, does not feel entirely safe in the building, has concerns about the presence of the homeless in the building, finds cell phone use a distraction and the Web site hard to use, and thinks parts of the building are unclean.

1. Since more people are using the library these days, there should be a time limit on use of daily newspapers. Also, there should be lighting on long table next to 5th floor paging desk. Self check-in does not give specific information on receipts.

2. Desks are too high for laptop use. Internet too slow (pages fail to load). No soft seating. Books I want never available.

3. I need . . . [this library] as I need to survive in this beautiful city. Thanks.

4. Far too many homeless sleeping and living in the Main Library branch. Far too many.

5. There is much too much noise in the library. Cell phones should be banned (put up signs), and librarians should do a better job of keeping the noise level down. I've been complaining about this for the past couple of years and have seen (and heard!) no real change.

6. Please bring back some padded chairs. Please bring back the original café, or improve the present one.

7. On Fridays please open library earlier. I usually come in the mornings.

8. Allowing cell phone use is always an issue. Why is the staff so soft about that? The problem is especially acute at computer terminals.

9. Don't like new Web interface. Much more confusing. Good selection of books. Would like to get my friend a card so she can access databases, but she is not from California.

10. Extend operating hours (for study space especially). Bathrooms should be on every floor. Too many homeless in the library, feels unsafe sometimes. Higher security or more security personnel [in] every area.

11. Should be more quiet.

12. Clean computers, more computers, clean facility, odors.

13. No suggestion box, ongoing problem with unisex bathroom not improved, dirty and wet floor (flooded almost), no security, crowded seating for computer users.

14. Buy more books for teens, comic books, and computers.

15. I use your Web site on a daily basis. Love your e-mail alerts.

16. It is extraordinarily difficult to find items in the library due to the unusual lack of signs. Last time I looked for a book I had to ask three people, after I had written down the call number. There are not enough catalog terminals in the audiovisual area, and more self-checkout stations would always be appreciated. Bathrooms are disgusting.

Figure 5.2. Survey Comments. Courtesy of Counting Opinions. See also University of New Hampshire Library, "Comments," accessed July 3, 2010, http://www.library.unh.edu/comments/viewcomments.php.

Some of these problems have simple solutions. For instance, for a hard-to-use Web site, the library can engage in usability testing and see how the public navigates the Web site. It may be that the homepage needs reorganizing and changing colors, but which ones?

The same type of analysis might apply to comments received through social networks, e-mail messages, letters, and comment cards. In fact, as already discussed, the library should place all comments in a single database but retain the ability to sort by method via which the comments are received. It could be beneficial to examine comments in their entirety and to share them with stakeholders. Actual comments may create a positive impression as customers show their support for the library and its services. The library might weave comments together into compelling stories.

CONCLUDING THOUGHTS

As libraries encourage customers to complain and to offer compliments and suggestions, they could demonstrate transparency, perhaps by devoting a Web page to what they learned and what corrective action has been taken. They might do the same on social networks. Instead of providing dense tables, they could create stories (what the customer said, how the library responded, and the reaction from the customer) that they can share. Furthermore, they should explore the use of dashboards, which are visual charts (e.g., a bar chart or some type of gauge showing a simple statistic related to recent trends). Such dashboards (see chapter 8) might bring critical information to decision makers as they review the effectiveness of departments and the entire organization.

Your interest in competitors' customers is in how they rate the competitor. These ratings levels provide you with an invaluable benchmark with which to interpret ratings given to your product and services by your customers.[16]

NOTES

1. F. Jon Reh, "Customer Satisfaction Survey" (About.com: Management), accessed July 8, 2010, http://management.about.com/od/competitiveinfo/a/CustomerSatSurv.htm.

2. Lisa M. Given and Gloria J. Leckie, "'Sweeping' the Library: Mapping the Social Activity Space of the Public Library," *Library & Information Science Research* 25, no. 4 (2003): 366. See also Gloria J. Leckie and Jeffrey Hopkins, "The Public Place of Central Libraries: Findings from Toronto and Vancouver," *Library Quarterly* 72, no. 3 (July 2002): 326–72; Gloria J. Leckie, "Three Perspectives on the Library as Public Space," *Feliciter* (In special issue devoted to "Library Space, Planning, and Architecture") 50, no. 6 (2004): 233–36.

3. Given and Leckie, "'Sweeping' the Library," 375.

4. Ibid., 374.

5. Ibid., 383.

6. See Nancy F. Foster and Susan Gibbons, *Studying Students: The Undergraduate Research Project at the University of Rochester* (Chicago: American Library Association, 2007), 21.

7. Tracy Gabridge, Millicent Gaskell, and Amy Stout, "Information Seeking through Students' Eyes: The MIT Photo Diary Study," *College & Research Libraries* 69, no. 5 (November 2008): 512. See also Foster and Gibbons, *Studying Students*, 40–47. Page 41 presents the twenty items that students might photograph. One of these is "a place in the library where you feel lost."

8. See Gabridge, Gaskell, and Stout, "Information Seeking through Students' Eyes," 521–22.

9. Mark Horan, "What Students See: Sketch Maps as Tools for Assessing Knowledge of Libraries," *The Journal of Academic Librarianship* 25, no. 3 (May 1999): 187–201.

10. Foster and Gibbons, *Studying Students*, 36.

11. Ibid., 53.

12. Ibid., 48.

13. For an example, see Jyoti Namjoshi and Archana Gupte, "Service-Oriented Architecture for Cloud-Based Travel Reservation Software as a Service" (paper presented at the 2009 IEEE International Conference on Cloud Computing), accessed June 19, 2010, http://www.patni.com/media/345097/SOA_for_Cloud_based_Travel_Reservation_SaaS.pdf.

14. See, for example, http://www.textanalysis.info/ for more information about available software options.

15. Ibid.

16. Terry G. Vavra, *Improving Your Measurement of Customer Satisfaction: A Guide to Creating, Conducting, Analyzing, and Reporting Customer Satisfaction Measurement Programs* (Milwaukee, WI: ASQ Quality Press, 1997), 65.

6

Methodologies (Unstructured and Unsolicited Approaches)

Want your problem redressed quickly? Gripe about it on Twitter.[1]

This is the last of four methodological chapters, each of which has a different focus (see figures 3.1 and 6.1, p. 102). Unstructured and unsolicited approaches refer to unsolicited comments that library customers make, primarily on Web sites. These comments, which will likely reflect the extent of customer satisfaction, offer specific observations about what customers have seen, the quality of their interactions with staff, and the adequacy of the collections and facilities. Such comments may be seen by few members of the staff; however, in some instances, they might be observed by millions of people. Picture, for example, a disgruntled customer who received poor service from an airline employee and the airline itself and then registered a complaint posting compelling videos of his bad experiences, which million of people have viewed. Given the negative public reaction, the company is forced to admit its error and try to prevent further damage to its image.[2]

Comments might be posted on library and other blogs or social networks; made directly to a library staff member; or sent as a text message to friends, colleagues, and perhaps library staff or management. In most cases, staff are trained to encourage customers to complete comment cards, and some actually follow through on this. Many customers, however, will ignore this suggestion and simply make their comments directly to the staff member. The extent to which all of these comments are captured and recorded in some way determines the extent to which the library is learning about the full spectrum of customer experiences. In fact, most unsolicited and unstructured comments will be made using Web sites. Among the more likely sites where customers post comments are the following:

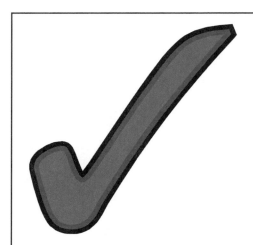

- Blog posts
- Comments on social networking sites
- Comments made to staff
- Text messaging for a quick response

Figure 6.1. Topics Discussed in the Chapter

- Blogs: There were more than 152 million blogs at the end of 2010.[3]
- Video postings on YouTube
- Comments on social networking sites such as Facebook, Twitter, and MySpace
- Wikis
- Community-focused Web sites, including Angies List and so forth
- Chat with friends

In almost all cases, the people making these comments, whether anonymously or by revealing their identity, are frustrated and doing the posting because of the way they were treated.

This chapter covers ways to capture comments made to library staff members as well as the unsolicited comments and observations made on a variety of Web sites. Discovering the existence of comments made about the library is the hardest part of any job for someone tasked with learning the true voice of the customer. Learning what others are saying about the library, both good and bad, however, is essential in terms of listening to the customers.

DISCOVERY TOOLS

To locate and monitor customer comments, library staff should regularly check the following sources:

- Google
- Twitter alerts
- Yelp.com

By searching Google, a staff member could discover what is being said about "Your Town Public Library" or "My University Library." For example, a search for the "San Diego Public Library" returns some 56,700 hits using Google (on July 1, 2010). Trying to discover comments that customers make about their library experiences seems like a daunting task, given the number of blogs, Web sites, and other sources that permit digital postings. Complicating matters, local newspapers and radio and TV stations might report on news stories on the library. Even adding the word "comment" to the Google search request still retrieves some 11,600 hits. And adding the word "awful" will result in shifting through some 2,420 hits. Still, in the first page or two several very useful sites do emerge. The *San Diego Reader*, a local "freebie" newspaper and Web site, had an interesting story about the public library called "No Shushing in This Library."[4] Linked to the story were a plethora of readers' comments, both positive and negative, about specific library branches and their services. All of these comments should become a part of a central database that the library maintains.

A more effective strategy is to use the Google Alert service (http://www.google.com/alerts), which sends the designated person e-mail message alerts any time something matching his or her search profile has been entered. The library may need to revise and refine its search profile until it generates useful results on an ongoing basis.

Similarly, libraries might use Twitter Alerts (http://tweetbeep.com/). These alerts might capture conversation about the community and what people are doing and what they like and do not like. In essence, libraries form impressions about the "general 'feel' of the community."[5]

While library staff monitor these sites, they should not forget sources such as Yelp.com, which provides reviews by categories for major cities. For instance, it is possible to enter "libraries" or a similar term in the general search box. For a particular city and its suburbs, comments are arranged by library. One result produces the following comments, "A bit miffed by the $1 charge for DVD rentals and the charge for inter-library loan—but I guess it goes toward providing the service that I enjoy" and "This library is my home away from home. I love it here. The librarians are friendly and always willing to help you find what you're looking for." Josh Hadro offers some specific suggestions on how a library can open the doors of Yelp more effectively in a recent article. He provides specific directions on how to register your library if it is not already.[6]

OTHER WAYS TO DISCOVER CUSTOMER COMMENTS

Not surprisingly, there is a host of other tools that a library can use, on an ongoing basis, to learn more about the voice of the customer. Among these tools are the following:

- Social search engines

- Finding information on blogs

- Searching on Twitter, microblogs, and lifestreaming services

- Message boards and forum search tools

- Conversations and comments search tools

- Social news and bookmarking search tools

- Brand monitoring tools and techniques

Social Search Engines

A social search engine typically checks multiple social media sites and, in some cases, allows the library to set up an RSS (Really Simple Syndication) feed. In most cases, these sites use multiple simultaneous searches to deliver their results, and in some instances, the library's friends and friend of friends can be alerted to respond to queries. Among these social search engines are the following:

- **Aardvark** (http://vark.com), which is a way to find people, not Web pages, who have specific information to answer a posted question.

- **Addictomatic** (http://addictomatic.com/), which creates a custom page with the latest buzz on any topic.

- **Keotag** (http://www.keotag.com/), which has some great tools for bloggers, is a service that easily allows a person to discover links from several bookmarking sites based on preferred search terms.

- **monitorThis** (http://alp-uckan.net/free/monitorthis/), which allows someone to subscribe to twenty different search engine feeds at the same time.

- **OneRiot** (http://www.oneriot.com/), which is a real-time social buzz search engine. OneRiot search results are influenced by what people share on Twitter, MySpace, Digg, Facebook, and elsewhere.

- **Pipes: Social Media Firehose** (http://pipes.yahoo.com/pipes/), which tracks brand or product mentions on numerous social media sites, including Flickr, Twitter, FriendFeed, and Digg.

- **Samepoint** (http://www.samepoint.com/), which is a conversation search engine that relays what people are discussing.

- **Serph** (http://serph.com), which reflects what people are saying in the blogging world about any key word of interest.

- **Social Mention** (http://www.socialmention.com/), which is a social media search and analysis platform that aggregates user-generated content from across the universe into a single stream of information.

- **Scour** (http://scour.com/), which integrates search results from Google, Yahoo, MSN, and OneRiot on one page. By blending user feedback with proven search algorithms, the Scour community helps shapes the Scour brand of results.

- **Whos Talkin** (http://www.whostalkin.com/), which is a social media search tool that allows users to search for conversations surrounding the topics that they care about most.

Finding Information on Blogs

Other search engines focus solely on searching the more than 144 million blogs. Among these are the following:

- **Ask.com** (http://www.artikiz.com/?o=0&l=dir), which was originally called Ask Jeeves, enables people to get answers to questions.

- **Blogdigger** (http://www.blogdigger.com/index.html), which uses syndication technologies (e.g., RSS and Atom) to index blog content and make it available for search.

- **BlogLines** (http://www.bloglines.com/), which enables others to subscribe, read, and share any updates from their favorite news feed or blog.

- **BlogPulse** (http://www.blogpulse.com/), which is an automated trend discovery system for blogs and analyzes and reports on daily activity in the blogosphere.

- **Google Blog Search** (http://blogsearch.google.com/), which is a favorite site for many people and reports on the activity of various logs.

- **IceRocket** (http://www.icerocket.com/), which searches across blogs, MySpace pages, news sources, and videos.

- **LJSeek** (LiveJournal Seek; http://www.ljseek.com/), which is a blog search service.

- **Technorati** (http://technorati.com/), which indexes millions of blog posts in real time and searches them in seconds. It enables organizations to set up alerts to capture what is written about them.

Searching on Twitter, Microblogs, and Lifestreaming Services

Many organizations use Twitter and Twitter-related tools as a way to provide immediate customer service. For example, recently one of the authors was standing in line at the airport waiting to get on a Southwest Airlines flight. The guy next to him (we were at the end of the A group or first to go onboard) was muttering and texting a message to Twitter. He was agitated because he was not first in line (he had paid for a business class ticket)! Shortly thereafter he received a Tweet asking him to go to the podium, where he was given an apology, placed at the start of the line, and given a free drink ticket. To say he was a delighted customer would be an understatement.

Aside from searching directly using the Twitter search options, especially the advanced search options, several other alternatives are available, including the following:

- **Flaptor – Hounder** (http://hounder.org/), which is a complete open-source search engine. "Hounder crawls the web targeting only those documents of interest, and presents them through a simple search web page."

- **FriendFeed Search** (http://friendfeed.com/search/advanced), which is a "cross-network activity aggregator" and more fun to use than the phrase "cross-network activity aggregator" implies.

- **Twazzup** (http://www.twazzup.com/), which, by operating a leading real-time news platform, makes it possible to filter the news out of live Internet content.

- **Tweefind** (http://www.tweefind.com), which is a Twitter search engine that displays results based on users' ranking. The Tweerank, an "engagement score" that is assigned to any Twitter user, is assigned dynamically and changes daily.

- **Tweetizen** (http://www.tweetizen.com/), which is a simple Web-based tool designed to help filter the daily influx of tweets and to find easily those that are relevant.

- **Tweetscan** (http://tweetscan.com/), which searches Twitter, Identi.ca, and other sites.

- **Tweetzi** (http://tweetzi.com/), which is a simple yet powerful tool for searching Twitter. It has special functions for finding useful information, media, and links.

- **Twigly Channel** (http://www.twingly.com/), which searches Twitter, Jaiku, Identi.ca, and more.

- **Twilert** (http://www.twilert.com/), which is a Twitter application that enables a company to receive regular e-mail alerts of tweets containing its brand, product, and service; it goes well beyond the use of common keywords.

- **Twitalyzer** (http://www.twitalyzer.com/), which is the social media industry's most popular, most widely used analytics application.

Message Boards and Forum Search Tools

In this arena, the following are common tools:

- **BoardTracker** (http://www.boardtracker.com/), which is a forum discussion search engine that enables brand and reputation monitoring, social media analytics, and visualizations, and offers an alerts service.

- **Omgili** (http://omgili.com/), which is a forum search engine for finding communities, message boards, and discussion threads about any topic.

Conversations and Comments Search Tools

There are a number of tools in the conversation and comments area that can retrieve relevant information, including the following:

- **Artiklz** (http://www.crunchbase.com/company/artiklz), which aggregates discussions and comments from a number of services (e.g., Digg, Reddit, FriendFeed, and Delicious).

- **coComment** (http://www.cocomment.com/), which is a service that manages and researches conversations and notifies the individual when there is a response.

- **BackType** (http://www.backtype.com/), which is a tool that charts the number of tweets and other comments related to a company or an organization.

- **ConvoTrack** (http://convotrack.com/), which is a comment aggregation app that tracks comments and conversations surrounding any blog posting. It shows comments from Twitter, FriendFeed, Digg, Reddit, HackerNews, and other blogs.

Social News and Bookmarking Search Tools

Social news and bookmarking sites have search capabilities and other services that let them simultaneously search multiple sites. Among these are the following:

- **Del.icio.us** (http://delicious.com/), which is the largest social bookmarking site

- **Digg** (http://digg.com/), which is a site to discover and share the best content from across the Web. It is a place where people collectively determine the value of content.

- **Diggio** (http://www.diigo.com/), which places a bookmark in other social bookmarking systems and enables someone to find search terms on a page, highlight them in different colors, and search everyone's archives by title, URL, notes, or full text.

- **Delizzy** (http://delizzy.com/), which searches all content, including title, description, and page content for all identified bookmarks.

Brand Monitoring Tools and Techniques

The following are among the tools for monitoring the library's brand:

- **HowSociable** (http://www.howsociable.com/), which tracks the presence of product brands, companies, and organizations on thirty-two social Web sites and calculates their "visibility" score (scores range from 0 to a maximum of 1,000). "We took a set of benchmark results using one globally recognised traditional brand and gave it a score of 1000. To ensure that even small, local brands would register we made it a sliding scale. For example, Coca-Cola has around 8,000 times more photos mentioning them on Flickr compared to our company Inuda, but we still get a score of 10 for having some photos rather than getting 0."[7]

- **Trendpedia** (http://www.trendpedia.com/), which monitors social media, buzz tracking, brand measurement, and blog trends.

Incidentally, the visibility score for the Library of Congress is 858; for the Seattle Public Library it is 325. Wouldn't it be helpful for libraries to determine their scores? Caphyon (http://www.advancedwebranking.com/) provides a detailed overview of the type of visibility report that might be generated.

APPLICATION EXAMPLE

The authors took a couple of actual public libraries and traced them through the various Web pages highlighted in this chapter. A caveat is that the search ability of each page may not be precise and might yield coverage of topics that are tangential. Suppose, for instance, that a library had the name "Newton" or "Franklin" in its title. The search might produce anything related to Sir Isaac Newton or Benjamin Franklin.

Because some of the search engines extract Web pages, the library sees how it is portrayed on each site. What pages have been highlighted? Does the library want to find ways to complement the coverage, or is it satisfied with the image presented? Some of the photostreams available at the libraries that we examined highlight people (staff, customers, auditorium speakers, or musicians), wildlife in the vicinity of the library (e.g., deer, rabbits, or turkeys), and showings in the art gallery.

It is possible for library staff to post questions about the library and try to generate a community discussion. Of greatest concern is the visibility score (see HowSociable, http://howsociable.wordpress.com/). In one state, the score for a public library located in a large town was 38 (on the date we looked); for a public library in a city with a renowned college it was 25; and for a competitive city with a well-known university it was 15. It is unfair to compare these scores to those for the San Francisco Public Library (248), Cleveland Public Library (181), University of California at Los Angeles (72), and Simmons College Library (31). Nonetheless, the score of 15 suggests that the public does not associate that public library with a Web presence and digital access to collections and services. Perhaps repeating the same search today might show an increase. If this were so, what happened in the meantime?

CONCLUDING THOUGHTS

As this chapter indicates, libraries should not ignore the comments that customers post on Web sites. These sites reveal the public's thoughts about the community in which they reside and indicate what they think about various businesses and services. Together with the comments made directly to the library through its homepage or on a satisfaction survey, the staff can gain a better understanding of what customers tell others. The critical issue is one of monitoring and capturing as much information as possible; this is especially true of the actual comments that customers post. The library can use what customers actually say as a persuasive voice to document their expectations and demonstrate the perceived value of the library to the community. Given the digital availability of these comments, it is not that difficult to move them into a general database. At the same time, the library should begin a dialogue with those posting comments. What is the most effective way to reach them and thank them for their comments, both positive and negative? The key is to start an ongoing dialogue. Most likely those posting comments will be surprised that the library is paying attention and contacting them. Here is a way to build customer delight and loyalty.

> *[M]any companies . . . have started devoting resources to social media monitors, who aim to respond to an angry tweet within 60 minutes.*[8]

NOTES

1. Steven J. Snyder, "The Customer-Service Express Lane," *Time* 176, no. 4 (July 26, 2010): 56.

2. For example, James Lawrence participates in triathlons to raise money to build dams in Africa. On a recent trip home, he flew one airline that busted his expensive, competition bicycle and then refused to accept responsibility. More than 25,000 viewers saw his videos on YouTube.com in the first three weeks following the accident (see http://www.youtube.com/watch?v=axDgcfPUnXM, accessed July 1, 2010). Dave Carroll had his checked guitar destroyed by another airlines. More than one million people have viewed his videos on YouTube.com (accessed July 1, 2010).

3. See the *Doug Ross @ Journal* blog, accessed February 9, 2011, http://directorblue.blogspot.com/2011/01/internet-by-numbers.html.

4. See the San Diego Reader Web site, accessed July 1, 2010, http://www.sandiegoreader.com/news/2008/jun/18/cover/.

5. David Lee King, "The Social Web and Libraries: Twitter Alerts," 2008, accessed July 10, 2010, http://www.davidleeking.com/2008/08/09/the-social-web-and-libraries-twitter-alerts/.

6. Josh Hadro, "Is Your Library Up on Yelp?" *Library Journal* 136, no. 2 (February 1, 2011): 28–29.

7. How Sociable? Brand Visibility Metrics (WorldPress.com), "How Visibility Score," 2008, accessed August 20, 2010, http://howsociable.wordpress.com/.

8. Snyder, "Customer-Service Express Lane," 56.

7

I Was Once Lost But Now . . .

Your competitors are making it easier than ever for your customers to leave you.[1]

How library staff members refer to their customers is an important issue that deserves discussion in every library. What word do they use, and why does that word matter? In *The Customer-Focused Library,* Joe Matthews addresses this issue more fully than we do here or in chapter 1.[2] The choice of how to describe and refer to customers (e.g., customers, patrons, guests, clients, visitors, members, or users) has an emotional impact on staff as well as on those using the service organization. The word *customer* highlights the fact that the individuals using the library actually *pay* a real cost (distance to travel to the library, time to visit the library physically or virtually, and so forth) and must actually make a *purchase* decision. Individuals weight their expectations of the benefits they will receive versus the costs that they incur before making a decision to go to the library, either physically or virtually. The word *customer* reminds library staff members that individuals choose to visit the library and have customer service expectations that must be met or exceeded.

WHO ARE YOUR CUSTOMERS?

Understanding and being able to answer this question is the obvious first step. Who uses the library's physical or electronic resources and services? Who among the library nonusers might become a customer? How can nonusers be reached most effectively? Should the library expend marketing resources in an attempt to lure nonusers to the library?

If we were to ask library directors or librarians to describe the library's customers, almost without exception they would note general demographic characteristics and point to those attending a program, borrowing books or DVDs, and so forth. However, the questions arise, "How closely do their perceptions actually match reality?" and "How well do the demographics match those of the community?" In the case of academic libraries, are humanities students more likely than science students to use library resources and either study or socialize in the library? Data are available to answer such questions. Librarians could examine the registered borrower file in the library's automated system. For a public library, the number of registered borrowers includes individuals from within the city or county being served as well as a number of borrowers who live outside the jurisdiction's boundaries.

There are some problems, however, with the number of total registered borrowers. For instance, most libraries purge their borrower file annually when they delete those registered borrowers who have not used the library in the last three years. Few libraries distinguish between those who live within the jurisdiction and the total number of borrowers. As a result, if a library calculates a percentage of registered borrowers in comparison to the number of individuals within the city or county, then the result looks much better than it really is. That is, the library may have 84 percent of its "official" population registered as cardholders. Yet perhaps 25 to 30 percent of the borrowers actually live outside the jurisdictional boundaries.

It seems most likely that the library would not want to equate customers with citizens or determine the number of registered borrowers who are citizens. Doing so places the library in the middle of the illegal immigration issue; alienates part of the community; and has economic, social, and legal implications.

The registered borrower file has been used to create two broad types of analysis to gain a better understanding of the library's customers. First, some libraries have used the borrower file in conjunction with a geographic information system (GIS) to discover where customers live and, by implication, to learn about their socioeconomic characteristics using the available census data or *lifestyle* demographic data from commercial firms.[3] By the way, a number of studies have shown that population characteristics such as education, family lifestyle, and physical proximity to a library have more to do with use than do age, gender, and ethnic background.[4]

A second approach is to analyze the population by *use*, which results in the often-referred-to split of users and nonusers. Using the report generation capabilities of the library's automated system, it is possible to sort the registered borrowers into three groups:

1. *Frequent customers*, who use the library on a monthly or more frequent basis. In general, 20 percent of the library's customers (the actual percentages may be slightly off in some libraries) account for 80 percent of the library's circulation.

2. *Moderate customers*, who use the library bimonthly or less frequently.

3. *Infrequent customers*, who have used the library at some time during the past year.

As libraries seek to understand better the information needs, information-seeking behavior, and service expectations of their customers, it might be fruitful to ascertain the benefits they receive from a physical or virtual visit to the library. In other words, the package of likely benefits that result from use of the library likely differs for each market segment of the population. The primary advantage of segmentation includes

- a better understanding of customers, their information needs, and their expectations; and

- a more effective targeting of resources.

Market segments are defined by the primary use of the library rather than by a reliance on demographic information. A pilot study at the Dover (Delaware) Public Library found nine identity-related reasons for a visit to the library. The nine types of users follow:

1. **Experience Seekers**, who look to the library as a venue for entertainment or as a social connection. They like being around people and may be seeking an activity to occupy their time. (Thirty-six percent of the respondents selected this reason.)

2. **Explorers**, curious individuals who love learning but do not have a specific topic or subject agenda prior to the visit. (Thirty-five percent of the respondents selected this reason.)

3. **Problem Solvers**, who have a specific question or problem they want to solve. They might be looking for health information or investment information, planning a trip, and so forth. (Twenty-three percent of the respondents selected this reason.)

4. **Facilitator**s, who support someone else in their use of the library (e.g., their children or a friend). (Sixteen percent of the respondents selected this reason.)

5. **Patrons**, individuals with a strong sense of belonging to the library. They are members of the Friends group and often volunteer to work in the library. (Sixteen percent of the respondents selected this reason.)

6. **Scholars**, who have a deep interest and a history of research work in one topic area, such as genealogy or religion. (Nine percent of the respondents selected this reason.)

7. **Spiritual Pilgrims**, who focus on the library as a place of reflection or rejuvenation. (Eight percent of the respondents selected this reason.)

8. **Hobbyists**, who pursue their interest in a particular area. (Four percent of the respondents selected this reason.)

9. **Other**, which includes those individuals who do not fit into one of the above groups; they are at the library to drop off or pick up something. In some communities, this category includes the homeless who are looking for a place to hang out and perhaps use e-mail.[5]

Other studies have come to similar conclusions, although the names given the groups differ.[6]

Another way to visualize use of the library is to conceptualize the level of customer involvement in library services, as shown in figure 7.1 (p. 114). Low-involvement services depend on the facilities available and on individuals who typically serve themselves. A customer who only uses the library's electronic resources would be another example of a low-involvement customer. Medium-involvement customers are those who use the collections intensively, but typically have little or no interaction with library staff members. High-involvement customers are those who have a high degree of interaction with librarians, collections, and the facilities.

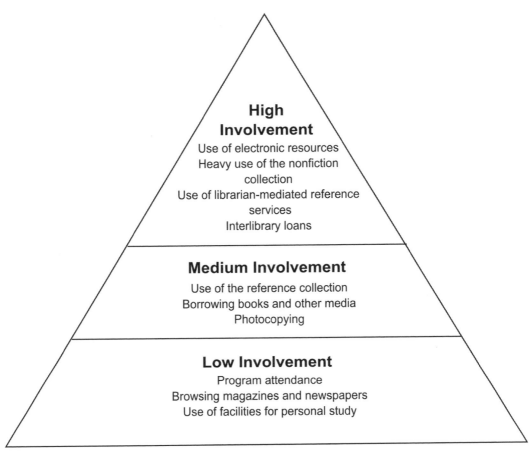

Figure 7.1. Customer Involvement with Library Services. Adapted from Pao-Long Chang and Pao-Nuan Hsieh, "Customer Involvement with Services in Public Libraries," *Asian Libraries* 9, nos. 3/4 (1997): 242–49.

A survey of 661 public library customers found that about 77 percent of the customers had low involvement, 20 percent had medium involvement, and only 3 percent had high involvement. An analysis of customer satisfaction found that high-involvement customers focused on staff empathy, medium-involvement customers were interested in the availability of materials, and low-involvement customers were interested in the amenities of the physical space.[7]

LOST CUSTOMERS

Amplifying on chapter 1, lost customers are individuals who visited the library, completed an application form, and received a library card. However, they have not used the library in the past year. Thus, though they *found* the library at one time, they are now *lost*. One of the real limitations of a library's integrated library system is that it does not help the library keep track of other uses of the library: attending programs, reading newspapers and magazines, using Wifi, and so forth. Libraries must get creative in tracking such usage in meaningful ways so they have a better understanding of all the different ways customers use the library.

Almost all organizations that spend any money on marketing know that it is easier to attract lost customers than it is to attract noncustomers—often by a factor of fifty. The costs to attract a lost customer to return to the public library are considerably less than trying to attract a nonuser who has never visited the library before. After all, the lost customer is aware of the library, knows where the library is located, and has a library card, but has not used the library for a considerable period of time.

Another Meaning of Lost Customer

Conceivably some lost customers have not obtained a library card. Perhaps they had a bad service encounter before they received the card. This particular population may be difficult, if not impossible, to determine. Any identification of this population may be time consuming and should not consume a high percentage of staff time. Still, the library should not abandon all efforts to regain them.

LIBRARY NONUSERS

Nonusers are people within a community who may or may not be aware of the location of the library and the range of services it offers. In addition to this so-called *use value*, economists recognize that individuals who do not use a public good, such as a public library, might derive satisfaction from its mere existence. The literature discussing this concept in the cultural arena has called *nonuse value* by a variety of other names (e.g., existence value, bequest value, vicarious consumption, prestige value, education value, and option value).[8]

The nonuse value of a public library can be considered as the utility that individuals obtain from libraries other than through their active use. Nonuse value or benefits can be grouped into two categories:

1. An option for an individual to use the library at some time in the future. The library is appreciated and valued as an institution that improves the quality of life in the community.

2. An option for others to use the library now and in the future. Individuals may be willing to support the library for the benefit of others.

Altruistic motivations (that is, concerns that poor people, people of color, children, and others have access to the broad range of services that the public library provides) are likely to be considered when someone is asked to reflect on the value of public libraries.

Nonuse benefits are difficult to quantify and, if they are measured, they are open to considerable debate. In addition, some individuals simply are not active readers and do not even consider use of the library. Some people, called alliterates by G. K. Beers, can read but choose not to do so.[9] The three groups of alliterates include

1. dormant readers—people who do not find the time to read but who like to read;

2. uncommitted readers—people who do not like to read but indicate they may read sometime in the future; and

3. unmotivated readers—people who do not like to read and are unlikely to change their minds.

Joan Frye Williams, a well-known library consultant, has called nonusers *civilians*.[10] Civilians can be divided into two groups: those who can be enticed to the library and those who will never, under any circumstances, use the library.

AN ACTION PLAN TO FIND LOST CUSTOMERS

Libraries should perform several activities to identify and communicate with their lost customers, including the following:

- **Identifying the lost customer.** Identifying the lost customer is a fairly straightforward activity. A report can be generated that identifies those customers who have not used the library for some period of time. The data from this report could be exported to a spreadsheet to manage and control follow-up activities. The report could be saved and run on a regularly scheduled basis.

- **Analyzing existing data about the lost customer.** Doing so provides information about the characteristics of lost customers. The library can use the lost customer data in conjunction with a geo-based information system and produce a set of maps showing the location of lost customers. Are they uniformly distributed across the jurisdictional boundaries, or can they be clumped into one or more areas? The street address can also be used to determine the census tract number in order to learn more about the socioeconomic characteristics of lost customers through the application of GIS that includes census data.

- **Learning more about the lost customer.** This is done through survey research. Library staff could distribute a brief three- to five-question survey via e-mail to a sample of lost customers. The survey would seek to determine why they have not returned to and used the library. In addition, the library could invite a few of the lost customers to visit for a free lunch and participate in focus group interviews so the library could learn more about their experiences with the library and how to better meet their information needs and expectations.

- **Communicating with the lost customer.** Given that the library has contact information for its lost customers (name, address, telephone number, and in most cases, an e-mail address), it is surprising that this information is not used to communicate on a regular basis about what is new about the library. Attractive, regular e-mail can be sent to these lost customers to encourage them to find their way back to the library. They might receive a personalized e-mail message sent through a dropbox, such as one available through a cell phone service provider (see figure 7.2). It is true that many individuals refuse to provide their e-mail addresses because of privacy concerns. The library must persuade the customer of the benefits of potential future contacts with the library and then live up to those expectations. In order to be truly customer-friendly, the library might let customers establish different levels of contact: overdue notices only, new materials alerts, forthcoming programs, and so forth.

Hi Joe,

How have you been? It's been a while since you visited your Dropbox and we don't want you to miss out on what's new.

New Downloads for iPhone, iPad, and Android

Figure 7.2. Library Dropbox

- **Attracting lost customers.** One of the results of learning more about lost customers is that the library may need to change the way in which it provides some services. Given the positive response of the community, some libraries have abandoned the use of the Dewey Decimal System and have embraced the merchandising of the collection. They are also reexamining the range of library experiences to ensure that they can better meet customer expectations. Many businesses send a discount coupon or other inducement to get lost customers to return. Other organizations send a follow-up survey to lost customers in which they ask them about their experiences. The whole idea it to better understand why they have not returned, so that the library can become more responsive to their needs. This is just another example of listening to the customer.

- **Welcoming the new (and lost) customer.** One of the ironies in any library is how little effort is made to orient new customers to the library so that they have a basic understanding of how it is organized, where they can find specific types of materials, what services are available, how they can learn about upcoming programs, and so forth. Perhaps the majority of new customers just do not *get* the library and find it overwhelming and difficult to comprehend, and thus they do not return. A library might provide a welcome package for new customers that includes a brief welcome letter from the director, a map of the physical library, information about programs, information about how to access the library's Web page, and the reasons why the library can be beneficial to them.

One study in a public library setting found that lost users and nonusers alike did not use the library due to distance, inconvenience of hours, and their preference to purchase their own materials. Further analysis revealed that adding to the collection in each location would entice lost customers to return, while building more locations and adding more hours would attract nonusers to the library.[11] However, we realize that the budget cuts that many libraries have endured since the onset of the economic recession in 2008 may make this difficult to do. Nonetheless, they should pursue other alternatives.

ADDITIONAL CUSTOMER INTERCEPTS

To increase contact with lost customers and nonusers, libraries might consider the use of community intercepts, ones that go beyond the use of exit interviews. They could contact students and other staff about friends and acquaintances who might be classified as nonusers and lost customers. To ensure the privacy of these individuals, they could ask the staff to reach out to these groups and arrange for them to attend a focus group interview, at which the managers will listen objectively to their concerns as the library starts to develop an ongoing dialogue with them. It is important that librarians pursue follow-up strategies once these group interviews have been concluded.

Other intercepts might occur in shopping malls and high traffic areas on college and university campuses. The library must carefully consider how to promote its presence and the purpose of the intercepts. Some of the strategies might also rely on social networks (as discussed in chapter 6), as these intercepts extend to the Internet. The goal is to win back lost customers, and library staff need to work with lost customers on developing effective intercepts and regaining strategies.

A REGAINING STRATEGY

Such a strategy should be part of a library's strategic plan and should recognize that the lack of customer and employee satisfaction leads to a high turnover rate of employees and of customer use. Libraries should also review what businesses are doing to regain customers lost during the economic recession. Do any of these strategies have value for libraries? Take, for instance, the academic institution that loses an important percentage of its endowment during the recession and loses additional monies to an aggressive building program that was underfinanced. The library might be forced to furlough or release staff and to make cuts in the collections budget. When the library makes staffing cuts while trying to preserve the materials budget, the result is continued employee dissatisfaction and feelings of increased stress. Library customers might accept the collection and staff cuts or might shift their loyalty to competitors. Libraries need to include regaining strategies within their strategic plans and the priorities they establish. Effective staff development should not be sacrificed during a recession and when facing decreased library budgets.

ADDING VALUE

Regardless of the market segment, the primary challenge for a library is to determine the value proposition for the customer to use the library, both physically and virtually. One helpful process is to consider Maslow's hierarchy of needs (physiological, safety, social/ belong, esteem, and self-actualization) in the context of delivering valuable services to library's customers. As shown in figure 7.3, these five needs can be collapsed when the context shifts to the delivery of library services.

At the lowest levels, customers want a clean and comfortable library as well as a well-lit parking lot and building so that their sense of safety is assured. At the next level up, successful customers find the materials they are interested in, and library staff greet them by name. And at the top, the transformational experience surprises and delights customers.

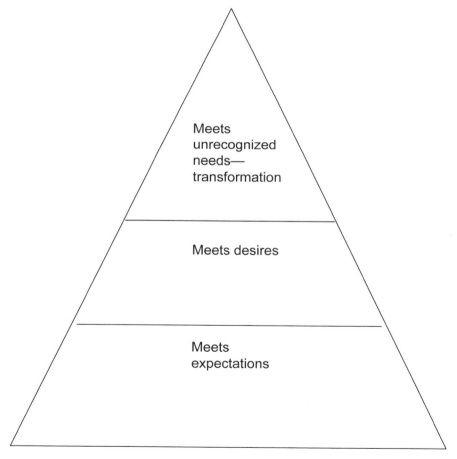

Figure 7.3. The Customer Pyramid. Adapted from Pao-Long Chang and Pao-Nuan Hsieh, "Customer Involvement with Services in Public Libraries," *Asian Libraries* 9, nos. 3/4 (1997): 242–49. See also Joseph R. Matthews, *The Customer-Focused Library: Re-Inventing the Public Library from Outside-In* (Santa Barbara, CA: Libraries Unlimited, 2009), 20.

It is vital to remember that the library must *earn* customers by somehow *improving the quality of their life*. And what improves the quality of life for any customer varies over time. Once the library has earned a customer, however, it wants that customer to keep on coming back and to recruit other customers. The goal, therefore, is to create unique and compelling value for all library customers.

CONCLUDING THOUGHTS

The quality of a library service is not what the library puts into that service, but rather what customers receive from it. Libraries need to focus on what matters, namely customers and their information needs, information-seeking behavior, and expectations. Customers and how they derive benefits should be central to every discussion about the library and its service offerings. The goal is to provide so much value that the customers are thrilled and want to share their WOW experiences with others. Accumulate enough of these delighted customers, and the library's funding decision makers will hear some consistent and very positive messages about the library.

Growing the customer base and getting existing customers to come back more frequently is the result of creating real value for them in their daily lives. Delighted customers will—on their own—recommend the library to their peers and friends. This is what a library should be focused on today and every day in the future. This is the foundation upon which every successful organization is based.

Libraries need to find their purpose and place and to focus on what truly matters—making an impact on the community served. By doing so, they will preserve a positive service reputation in the community. Furthermore, they need to tune out the distractions and noise while they focus on the delivery of customer value. To do that, librarians must listen to and value the customer.

[C]ustomers—repeat buyers one can get to know well—are becoming harder to keep every day.[12]

NOTES

1. Jill Griffin, *Taming the Search-and-Switch Customer: Earning Customer Loyalty in a Compulsion-to-Compare World* (San Francisco: Jossey-Bass, 2009), 15.

2. Joseph R. Matthews, *The Customer-Focused Library: Re-Inventing the Public Library from the Outside-In* (Westport, CT: Libraries Unlimited, 2009).

3. For an example of how this approach might work, see Marc Futterman, "Finding the Underserved," *Library Journal* 133, no. 17 (October 15, 2008): 42–45.

4. These and other related studies are discussed and summarized in chapter 7 of Joseph R. Matthews, *The Evaluation and Measurement of Library Services* (Westport, CT: Libraries Unlimited, 2007).

5. Institute for Learning Innovation, *Dover, DE Library User Identity—Motivation Pilot Study* (Dover: Delaware Division of Libraries, December 2005). The study used a convenience sample size of 113 to generate one-on-one interviews. Further, customers might belong to more than one user type.

6. Such studies have been conducted at the Carnegie Library of Pittsburgh and in Singapore. See, for instance, MAYA and their involvement with the Carnegie Library of Pittsburgh, at http://www.maya.com/portfolio/carnegie-library, accessed July 17, 2010; and Kau Ah Keng, Kwon Jung, and Jochen Wirtz, "Segmentation of Library Visitors in Singapore: Learning and Reading Related Lifestyles," *Library Management* 24, nos. 1/2 (2003): 20–33.

7. This point is referenced in Pao-Long Chang and Pao-Nuan Hsieh, "Customer Involvement with Services in Public Libraries," *Asian Libraries* 9, nos. 3/4 (1997): 242–49. The text is in Chinese.

8. Svanhild Aabo, "Valuation of Public Libraries," in *New Frontiers in Public Library Research*, ed. Carl Johannsen and Leif Kajbrg, 97–109 (Lanham, MD: Scarecrow Press, 2005).

9. G. K. Beers, "No Time, No Interest, No Way!" *School Library Journal* 42 (1996): 110–14.

10. Joan Frye Williams, as quoted in Matthews, *The Customer-Focused Library*, 14.

11. Akio Sone, "An Application of Discrete Choice Analysis to the Modeling of Public Library Use and Choice Behavior," *Library & Information Science Research* 10, no. 1 (January–March 1988): 35–55.

12. Tom Hayes and Michael S. Malone, *No Size Fits All: From Mass Marketing to Mass Handselling* (London: Penguin Group, 2009), 114.

8

Analyzing and Using the Customer's Voice to Improve Service

What does a satisfied customer look like?[1]

As previous chapters illustrate, there are numerous ways to ascertain what customers think about the library and its infrastructure (collections, staff, facilities, and technology). There are also various ways to analyze the data that the staff formally and informally gather (see figure 8.1, p. 124). In some instances, companies such as Counting Opinions provide libraries subscribing to LibSAT with statistics and their visualization in the form of graphs and charts, including, for instance, bar, pie, and quadrant charts. In other instances, libraries conduct their own studies, compile the data, and analyze patterns. As this chapter illustrates, libraries can provide detailed reports on what they discover. They can also *speak* to their stakeholders simply through the use of dashboards (gauges), which display trends, and customer rating systems. At the same time, it is important to remember that customer comments and observations are an invaluable source of insight into the reasons for customer ratings. Because these comments reflect the opinions of customers as expressed in their own words, it is important to enter them into a database and review them in batches, attempting to uncover patterns.

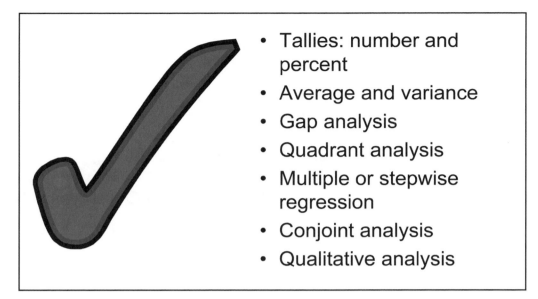

- Tallies: number and percent
- Average and variance
- Gap analysis
- Quadrant analysis
- Multiple or stepwise regression
- Conjoint analysis
- Qualitative analysis

Figure 8.1. Data Analysis Techniques Highlighted in the Chapter

STATISTICS

This chapter only highlights a few applications; readers wanting a more complete discussion of relevant analysis processes should review *Assessing Service Quality* and *Improving Your Measurement of Customer Satisfaction*.[2] For any survey it is important to determine the level of measurement (nominal, ordinal, interval, and ratio). *Nominal* refers to a scale of response options for which the attributes have an inherent order. An *ordinal* scale orders the scale or response options, but the numerical differences between adjacent attributes are not necessarily equal. In the case of an *interval* scale, there is an order, and the numerical differences between adjacent attributes are equal. Finally, in *ratio* measurement, the attributes are ordered, spaced equally, and a true zero point exists.

Tallies

Tallies, which refer to the summarization of data in the form of numbers, involve the reduction of numbers to frequency counts, percentages, and perhaps a cumulative frequency or percentage. For example, for the question, "Overall, how satisfied are you with the services of our library?" there might be a 10-point response scale (with 1 being "completely dissatisfied" and 10 being "completely satisfied"). A tally would indicate the number of respondents marking each number. If there were 400 respondents, and 50 answered with an 8, the percentage of responders selecting that number would be 12.5. Similarly, the staff might calculate the number and percentage responding in the range of 8 to 10.

Average

Instead of merely tallying the responses to the above question, management might prefer to calculate the appropriate measure of central tendency. The choices are the *mode* (the most frequently occurring number of attribute), the *median* (the midpoint of rank-ordered cases), and the *mean* (the arithmetic average). An examination of the literature of the social sciences indicates that the data for addressing the question above might be characterized in terms of the mean. The mean normally applies to interval- or ratio-level data, whereas the median applies to ordinal, interval, or ratio measurement. The mode is commonly used with nominal measurement.

Variance

Measures of central tendency define a point around which other scores tend to cluster. Measures of variability indicate how widely the scores are dispersed around the central point or average. *Variance*, which is one measure of variability, measures the amount of dispersion of a value from the mean. Another measure is the standard deviation, which is the square root of the variance. The greater the scatter of scores, the larger is the standard deviation. If all the scores in a distribution are identical, both the variance and standard deviation are zero. The standard deviation can range from zero to a small or large number.[3]

In LibSAT, for each subscribing library, Counting Opinions provides useful information about the importance of the standard deviation:

> A quality improvement process involves reducing the variability indicated by the standard deviation range where a narrower range indicates more consistency in response levels. It is especially important to focus on reducing the shaded areas below the trend line. You should use the drill-down feature to better understand the results for periods indicated by large "fangs" (produced by sudden periodic increases in variability) and address any issues cited, to help reduce the chances that these items will come back to "bite" you again.[4]

Gap Analysis

The Gaps Model of Service Quality, as discussed in chapter 3, offers a framework to identify services in the form of the gaps that exceed (or fail to meet) customer expectations. The model posits five gaps, one of which presents the discrepancy between what customers *expect* of the services and their *perception* of the service delivered. SERVQUAL, and its variation—LibQUAL+®—deal with this service gap, as does LibSAT for satisfaction. For instance, to engage in gap analysis, the staff might ask questions such as, "Overall, how important is the library to you?" and "Overall, how satisfied are you with the services the library provides?" For the first question, customers rate importance on a 10-point scale (1 being "not important" and 10 being "very important). To gauge the extent of satisfaction in the other question, they might likewise respond on a 10-point scale (1 being "not satisfied" and 10 being "very satisfied). Assuming interval measurement, the staff might compute the mean and standard deviation for both questions and compare them.

Quadrant Analysis

Quadrant analysis, a graphic correlation technique that depicts customer expectations, indicates the extent of the gap between the importance of an expectation to customers and the degree to which customers perceive a service as fulfilling that expectation (e.g., figure 8.2, p. 133).[5] Quadrant analysis shows what customers expect from a service (i.e., their ideal) and how they perceive a particular service in relation to their ideal.

A number of customer expectations can be plotted within four quadrants if the average responses on the dimensions (*ideal expectation* and *actual service*) are known. The averages (i.e., the means) for the importance of customer expectations are used to locate each expectation's position along the vertical axis. The mean of the perceived service provided is subtracted from the mean of the perceived expected measure. In other words, the gap is computed for each expectation. Using both averages as coordinates, the average location of each expectation and perception with the quadrants can be determined.

The four quadrants encompass those expectations that (1) are very important to customers, who then see the library as trying to meet those expectations; (2) are very important to customers, but the customers do not see them as being prominent features of the service; (3) are relatively unimportant to customers, and customers associate those expectations with the service; and (4) competitors are not meeting but might have some potential to cultivate. Of the expectations depicted in the visual diagram, the most important are those that are important to customers who also perceive the library as doing those things.

Conjoint Analysis

This tool, which businesses commonly use to review purchasing decisions, uses a subset of the possible combinations of product features to determine the relative importance of each feature in the purchasing decision. Because studies of service quality, including e-service quality, have identified *service* features of importance to library customers,[6] survey respondents might be asked to arrange a list of these service features in decreasing order of preference. The results complement what researchers have demonstrated when they use factor analysis to order the service features of greatest importance to library customers. It seems that the e-service features are more robust than those found in a print environment. Clearly, as conjoint analysis reminds us, it is important to look at the combination of service attributes and examine how they might be rearranged, or how additional combinations might emerge.

Reinhold Decker and Antonia Hermelbracht report on a study that applied a type of conjoint analysis:

> We systematically generated a broad range of new service ideas and developed them into concrete service concepts. Then, the service concepts, together with already existing services, were evaluated using a user survey. Knowing the individual preferences, we were able to identify the services which promise to attain a high acceptance in future. Finally, we empirically evaluated selected strategic options to support long-term service planning.[7]

They provide a detailed list and definitions of the attributes studied. They also lay out the data collection process in such a way that it can be easily replicated.

Quadrant Analysis*

A quadrant is a useful tool for its visual analysis and presentation and for its application in decision making and impact analysis. Although there are many possibilities for the vertical and horizontal axes in the quadrant chart, this discussion refers to a quadrant with a vertical axis for importance, arranged with low importance on the bottom, and high importance on the top, of the axis. Satisfaction (or performance) is located on the horizontal axis, with low satisfaction to the left and high satisfaction to the right. Therefore, looking at the quadrant clockwise from the top left sector,

- the upper left shows high importance and low satisfaction (or performance);

- the upper right shows high importance and high satisfaction (or performance);

- the lower right shows low importance and high satisfaction (or performance); and

- the lower left shows low importance and low satisfaction (or performance).

In its most basic form, the quadrant has one or more points of a combined representation of a user's perception of the importance of a service, activity, or program, and of the satisfaction or effectiveness of the performance of that service, activity, or program. A quadrant chart can therefore be used as a visual presentation of user perceptions of the importance and satisfaction of library services, programs, or other activities as framed by the question asked of users who are respondents. All of the points—categories that represent user responses—fall into one of the four sectors of the quadrant chart, and quadrant viewers can see user perceptions as measured. Viewers will see, for example, what services or programs users find important or unimportant, and with which they are satisfied (i.e., are performing well) or unsatisfied.

This snapshot of users' perceptions may also serve as a benchmark for analysis. For example, two or more quadrants created at different times can be compared days, weeks, months, or even years apart. These longitudinal, visual displays indicate shifts in user perceptions about importance and satisfaction as decision makers review the images over time.

Another gap to measure might be any differences in perceptions between library staff and users. The quadrant chart would display the importance-satisfaction points for both staff and users, and the differences in perception become visually evident for study and discussion. The perceptions of both groups should be measured as close together in time as possible and involve the same questions. Analysis of the gap between users and staff perceptions should be discussed and a rationale explaining the differences developed.

A second application of quadrant analysis focuses on decision making. By examining the visual presentation of the quadrant chart based on users' perceptions, decision makers can easily see those activities, services, and programs that fall into the lower left sector of low satisfaction and low importance. In an era of fiscal pressures and budget shortfalls, why should libraries continue to offer services or programs that have a low importance for users? Looking at the upper left sector with activities, programs, and services that have a high importance and low satisfaction to users, decision makers may want to reallocate resources from those activities, programs, or services seen as having low importance to those activities, programs, and services situated in this sector. The goal is to increase satisfaction with the activities, programs, and services that users consider important. In addition, decision makers may use the information gathered about those activities, programs, and services appearing in the upper right sector (high importance and satisfaction) to address concerns or to defend demands to cease or limit these services when internal and external stakeholders question their value or contribution to the institution or community.

A third application is the use of quadrant charts to evaluate outcomes or impacts as a result of a decision made and implemented. Library decision makers may choose to apply resources or to otherwise affect a service or program in an effort to *displace* users' perceptions from one quadrant to another. For example, user perceptions have resulted in a point landing in the upper left sector; the point therefore is important, but the satisfaction is not high. Through strategic planning, decision makers may choose to create an objective that may result in increasing satisfaction in an effort to displace the user perception of the program so that it would be relocated to the upper right sector: high importance and high satisfaction. To do so, resources are allocated to the program through the budget plan. After a predetermined period (usually stated within the objective), users are again surveyed, and, from the results presented on the quadrant chart, decision makers can see whether or not user perceptions changed and the point (importance and satisfaction) has moved to the upper right sector as targeted. This would help to demonstrate the impact of the reallocated resources, which is a measured benefit analysis. If the perception point were displaced as planned, the result would be a positive outcome. If not, the analysis can be used as an assessment from which the library can make further decisions concerning the reapplication of allocated resources intended to improve the service or program and meet its stated strategic objective. A related impact analysis would show whether the application of resources intentionally to displace a perception point resulted in another point being unintentionally displaced to a less desirable sector of the quadrant as a result of inattention to that service or program.

Decision makers may also want to ensure that a perception point remains relative within a sector over a period of time, to maintain high importance or satisfaction, or to maintain high satisfaction but low importance (e.g., the availability of programs on VHS tape). This could be referred to as *wobble*; the perception point remains within the targeted sector, moving slightly over time but not being displaced to another sector. Again, this serves as a means of measuring the impact of allocated resources.

In summary, quadrant analysis may be used to visualize current user perceptions, identify and visualize a gap between user and staff perceptions, make decisions about resource allocation, identify actionable strategic options that are framed by research results (the survey and resultant user perceptions as plotted on the quadrant), and visualize positive and negative impacts to better understand related benefits as libraries apply resources to affect outcomes in the continuous effort to improve services.

*Robert E. Dugan, Dean of Libraries, University of West Florida, Pensacola.

Qualitative Analysis

This category refers to the analysis of data collected as words and sentences. For example, in a satisfaction survey, the staff might ask:

- What do you like MOST about the library?

- What do you like LEAST about the library?

- If we could only do one thing to improve, what should it be?

Questions such as these invite respondents to share their comments. The staff then must review and characterize the responses. Most likely, they have developed predefined categories in which to place the responses.

BENCHMARK ANALYSIS

Benchmarking involves trend analysis and the comparison of customer expectations over time. Linked to strategic planning and the accomplishment of activities, benchmarking fosters and sustains organizational capacity to implement quality and process improvement initiatives successfully. Benchmarking, conducted at periodic intervals, therefore measures the progress made to improve services. These measures should be objective and reflect a performance goal against which service improvement is measured. The library self-defines and self-determines a benchmark. For example, to enable customers to use library resources without having to interact with staff, the library might create a self-paced, Web-based orientation, a tour, a guide, and a tutorial. Once they have developed each of these, they need to deploy and evaluate them; perhaps the staff might work on one activity at a time. The evaluation component is critical because it enables the staff to ensure the effectiveness of each activity and to take corrective action as necessary. They might also decide to insert widgets at various places throughout the library homepage as a means of alerting customers to their existence and to encourage their use.

An example might be useful. Adriene Lim investigated library tutorials to match the readability level of these educational tools to that of special populations that may be at risk of academic failure. She applied readability formulae to the content and shared the result with a group of experts who work with special populations. Finding a lack of well-designed, well-written, engaging library tutorials, she concludes that, "because instructions for how to use the library and how to conduct basic research are often online and predominately textbased, good readability becomes an important consideration when academic librarians design instructional content."[8] Yet libraries are producing educational tools that certain populations cannot use and that rely extensively on library jargon. The question is, "What do libraries do with this information?"

DATA DISPLAYS

Instead of merely producing and sharing tables that summarize the dataset, managers might identify key findings and portray them in the form of graphics. For example, two key satisfaction questions, willingness to recommend the services of this library to others and reuse the services of this library, might be prominently displayed on the homepage as bar or pie charts. Another option for visually displaying data is a radar chart, which graphically shows the size of the gaps among five to ten organizational performance areas. The chart shows the important categories of performance and indicates visibly concentrations of strengths and weaknesses. An additional choice is the development of digital dashboards, especially for those two key satisfaction questions. Elazar Harel and Toby Sitko ask:

> Would you drive a car without looking at the dashboard? The simple gauges on the instrument panel display what you need to know to operate the car safely and effectively: how fast you are driving, when the engine is working too hard, and how much fuel is left, for example. You cannot drive a car safely without a dashboard. The same can be said for managing a university.[9]

"Graphical dashboards," they note,

> turn voluminous business data into something easy to comprehend. A quick glance at the dashboard shows data in intuitive formats, such as charts and other gauges. Dashboards allow you to focus on business priorities by filtering out irrelevant information. Dashboards that provide drill-down capability allow tailored views of reports and data at the level of detail that an individual finds most helpful.[10]

Writing about higher education in New England, Lawrence Butler views dashboard gauges as "warning lights" and as a "quick, comprehensible overview . . . of . . . [an] institution's status . . . [,] direction . . . [,] organizational performance . . . [,] and mission effectiveness." Furthermore,

> [t]hese key performance indicators . . . are presented in consistent formats that enable institutional leaders to readily spot significant changes and trends. Like an automobile dashboard, these reports often display the equivalent of warning lights that flash on only when there is an impending problem or when certain variables stray outside of predetermined limits. In this way, the dashboard can serve as an early warning device alerting the board and senior administration when it might be important to dig deeper for greater insight.[11]

One example is the accountability dashboard developed by Minnesota State Colleges and Universities, which comprises thirty two-year colleges and seven state universities and includes indicators such as net tuition and fees as percent of median income, student persistence and completion, related employment of graduates, licensure exam pass rates, and the percent change in enrollment and condition of facilities.[12] Brent Rubin envisions dashboards for obvious metrics (e.g., graduation and retention rate); however, he implies that more attention should focus on faculty and student expectations, in particular their level of satisfaction.[13] Relevant metrics might be presented in dashboard form and placed on the opening screen of the institutional and library homepages.

Doug Lederman associates these developments with "dashboard" fever, in which higher education collects massive amounts of data. This fever links the use of dashboards to data-driven management. He even envisions faculty and others rolling out dashboards related to their productivity.[14] With all of the focus on dashboards, we ask, "What use are academic and public libraries currently making of dashboards?" An extensive search of the Internet did not reveal any dashboards that such libraries are currently using. This does not mean that they do not have them in development. Counting Opinions offers a dashboard report to its customers on the comparative questions it uses to gauge the extent of the gap between customer perceptions of importance and their expectations, and for the two questions on willingness to recommend and reuse the library. The results enable libraries to benchmark their progress (or lack thereof) over time and to make comparisons to other LibSAT subscribers.

Examples

For this section, the authors use data derived from the survey results for one library subscribing to LibSAT to illustrate different means by which to present data in a manner useful for decision makers. For that unnamed library, we viewed data for the period 2008–2010; the library started using LibSAT in 2008. LibSAT offers different ways to present the data in graphic form, namely in the form of bar and pie charts and quadrant charts. It is possible to graph data for a month or a longer time period. For illustrative purposes we chose July 2009 to July 2010, a time period for which there are more than 8,000 completed surveys.

The bar charts might compare willingness to recommend and the likelihood of reuse; for each question, there might be two bars, one for those responding during the year and the other for those answering the question overall (since the library first started using LibSAT). Similarly, there are two bars for the question about recommending the service. Among the interesting pie charts are those depicting the percentage of survey respondents who have a current library membership card, the percentage who also have a current card for another library, and how respondents rate this library in comparison to other ones they have used.

For the quadrant charts, the quadrant appearing at the bottom right reflects what is very important to customers, who then perceive the library as doing those things. This is the quadrant to which service improvement should be directed. To aid decision makers, it is possible to focus on any particular shape depicted in the quadrant and drill down to the actual comments. The smaller shapes report the overall data and the larger shapes indicate areas for improvement.

Figure 8.2, which reprints the quadrant chart for facilities, indicates the quadrant reflecting both satisfaction and importance (namely the one in the lower right). Comparing this chart with ones covering a recent period (e.g., the last month and perhaps the last three months) enables managers to monitor patterns and trends. Once they direct resources to fix a problem, it is important to know if that problem reappears—hopefully it does not.

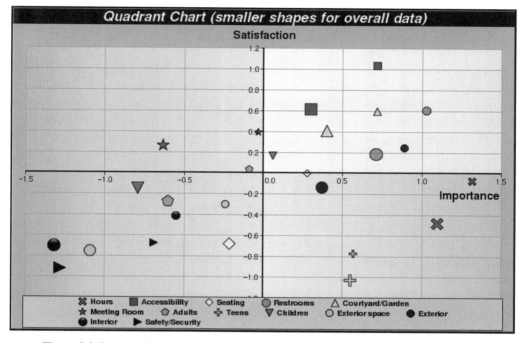

Figure 8.2. Level of Satisfaction with Library Facilities. Courtesy of Counting Opinions.

Drilling down to the actual comments, it is evident that customers are commenting on the noise level and the need for more chairs and tables. If we switch to a quadrant chart covering service, we find a number of comments about self-service checkout machines. Some customers love them, and others hate them. One of the comments offers an excellent opportunity for staff development:

> A male of European-American descent working alone . . . behind the checkout counter advised my friend, who was checking out Malcolm X books amongst other material, in this manner: "We are encouraging patrons to use the self-check machines." My friend was wondering why he was advised this, as we were the only ones in the area and nobody else was waiting to be helped with checkout materials. Was this comment made . . . because my friend was checking out Malcolm X books?

The writer of this comment suspected that the comment of the staff member reflected library policy, namely the reduction of direct interactions with customers due to budget cuts attributable to the recession and presumed compliance with the USA Patriot Act. Perhaps another reason, this person conjectured, was a political statement about having an African American president whose approval ratings were declining. The commenter concludes, "borrowers . . . should not be judged based on the books or materials they are checking out for their personal use."

ACCOUNTABILITY AND SERVICE IMPROVEMENT

As libraries cope with change and make the transition from the past to an unknown future, there is still a tendency on the part of some to view librarianship as a public good and to avoid demonstrating the impact of library services on the communities served. However, stakeholders demand accountability and, in part, expect libraries to be active partners with other parts of the institution in achieving the learning and other goals of the institution. Elizabeth J. Wood, Rush Miller, and Amy Knapp correctly label accountability as "standing up to scrutiny" and see it as "a mandate for higher education."[15]

The focus on accountability has mistakenly been called achieving a culture of assessment. In fact, assessment is a narrow but important facet of evaluation and focuses on the extent to which stakeholder expectations are met; for instance, organizations accrediting higher education programs and institutions expect student learning outcomes to be met. Still, if assessment is viewed as decision making based on evidence-based research, analysis, and other objectively gathered data, the term *culture of assessment* has broader implications. Perhaps a better label is *evidence-based planning and decision making*, with the realization that the evidence might be quantitative or qualitative.

As this book illustrates, libraries can actively collect data about what customers (e.g., current, lost, and never-gained) have to say about the library and its infrastructure. It is critical to separate what current and lost customers have to say. On the one hand, library managers should want to implement strategies aimed at regaining customers and documenting which strategies are most effective. On the other, they should also want ascertain the expectations of internal and external customers and take corrective actions as needed.

Using Information

Simply making information available does not, in and of itself, constitute a well-functioning accountability system. There are different ways to act on the data collected from listening to customers. First, the library should inject information about quality into existing processes about which management and stakeholders truly care. These processes might be reported in the context of an action plan (associated with strategic planning), with specific numerical targets for improvement and linked to budgetary priorities. When these processes provide trend data over years, they assume added importance.

CONCLUDING THOUGHTS

A logical method for reviewing customer data is to look for problem areas and the *root cause* of a problem. Once this has been accomplished, the goal is to eliminate the cause and prevent the problem from recurring. Known as *root-cause analysis*, this method has been applied to the resolution of customer complaints and returns and to the corrective action plans resulting from internal and external customer surveys. Each problem therefore is an opportunity, because it reflects why and how a problem occurred. A key tenet of root-cause analysis is to ask *why* repeatedly, until the root cause has been determined and proper corrective action taken. Clearly, the methodologies discussed in chapters 3–6 enable libraries to collect relevant data and to search for problems to which root-cause analysis can be applied.[16]

A picture is worth a thousand words—and at least ten thousand numbers.[17]

NOTES

1. Leonardo Inghilleri and Micah Solomon, *Exceptional Service, Exceptional Profit: The Secrets of Building a Five-Star Customer Service Organization* (New York: American Management Association, 2010), 7.

2. Peter Hernon and Ellen Altman, *Assessing Service Quality: Satisfying the Expectations of Library Customers*, 2nd ed. (Chicago: American Library Association, 2010); Terry G. Vavra, *Improving Your Measurement of Customer Satisfaction: A Guide to Creating, Conducting, Analyzing, and Reporting Customer Satisfaction Measurement Programs* (Milwaukee, WI: ASQ Quality Press, 1997).

3. It is advisable to produce a visualization of the data and determine whether the distribution shape conforms to a normal distribution (the familiar bell-shaped curve).

4. Counting Opinions, "What's New?" 2, accessed July 7, 2010, http://www.countingopinions.com/partners/main.php. (This is a secure customer Web site.)

5. For the framework for quadrant analysis, see Hernon and Altman, *Assessing Service Quality*, 157. The framework explains each quadrant and provides labels for interpreting each axis.

6. See Peter Hernon and Philip Calvert, "E-service Quality in Libraries: Exploring Its Features and Dimensions," *Library & Information Science Research* 27, no. 4 (2005): 377–404.

7. Reinhold Decker and Antonia Hermelbracht, "Planning and Evaluation of New Academic Library Services by Means of Web-based Conjoint Analysis," *The Journal of Academic Librarianship* 32, no. 6 (November 2006): 559.

8. Adriene Lim, "The Readability of Information Literacy Content on Academic Library Web Sites," *The Journal of Academic Librarianship* 36, no. 4 (July 2010): 302.

9. Elazar C. Harel and Toby D. Sitko, "Digital Dashboards: Driving Higher Education Decisions," *Research Bulletin* (Boulder, CO: EDUCAUSE Center for Applied Research) 19 (2003): 2, accessed July 12, 2010, http://net.educause.edu/ir/library/pdf/ERB0319.pdf.

10. Ibid.

11. Lawrence M. Butler, "Warning Lights," *The New England Journal of Higher Education* 21, no. 5 (Spring 2007): 31.

12. See Minnesota State Colleges and Universities, "Fact Sheet: System Accountability Dashboard" (St. Paul, MN: Minnesota State Colleges and Universities, 2008), accessed July 13, 2010, http://www.mnscu.edu/business/workforceeducation/accountability.html.

13. Brent D. Rubin, "Toward a Balanced Scorecard for Higher Education: Rethinking the College and University Excellence Indicators Framework," 1999, 3, accessed July 12, 2010, http://oqi.wisc.edu/resourcelibrary/uploads/resources/Balanced%20Scorecard%20in%20Higher%20Education.pdf.

14. Doug Lederman, "Dashboard Fever," *Inside Higher Ed* (October 22, 2009), accessed July 13, 2010, http://www.insidehighered.com/news/2009/10/22/cupa.

15. Elizabeth J. Wood, Rush Miller, and Amy Knapp, *Beyond Survival: Managing Academic Libraries in Transition* (Westport, CT: Libraries Unlimited, 2007), 153, 154.

16. See, for instance, Bjorn Anderson and Tom Fagerhaug, *Root Cause Analysis: Simplified Tools and Techniques* (Milwaukee, WI: ASQ Quality Press, 2006).

17. Richard M. Jaeger, *Statistics: A Spectator Sport* (Beverly Hills, CA: Sage, 1983), 23.

9

Communication

*The single biggest problem in communication is the illusion
that it has taken place.*—George Bernard Shaw[1]

Librarians have historically done little to learn about the information needs and
expectations of customers, as viewed from the customer perspective, and they have made
assumptions about the value of libraries based on being the only game in town. After all,
libraries have valuable collections of materials and have invested extensively in tools
to gain better access to those materials. Even the most passionate advocate for libraries
must acknowledge that they are complex organizations, which often appear to have an
illogical arrangement for their collections. Even if customers are confused and cannot
find what they want, they may not approach a library staff member and request assistance.
In their search for information, whether in print or digital form, they must overcome the
arrangement of various collections and jargon unfamiliar to them.

Librarians realize the complexity of the organization, for instance, when they
purchase materials available in different formats, pursue the licensing of e-materials,
preserve digital content, engage in campus-wide publishing programs, and manage
datasets for faculty who have research grants.[2] Funding bodies, students, faculty members,
administrators (e.g., in city government and higher education), or members of the general
public may perceive as high the costs of providing access to an ever-increasing body of
materials. The public and others may perceive libraries as costly and may be unwilling to
support them through increased taxation. In the case of higher education, President Barack
Obama, members of Congress, and the secretary of the U.S. Department of Education
have expressed concern about the cost or affordability of a college education. This
concern about affordability, combined with a declining graduation rate, was an impetus
for the Higher Education Opportunity Act of 2008 (P.L.110-315). Making matters worse,
many institutions of higher education, and state and local governments, have been hit hard
by the economic recession of 2008–2011 and its aftermath. The result for a number of

libraries, especially those in depressed states, has been severe budget cuts and reduction in the services offered.

Still, the amount of information available on the Internet continues to increase at an exponential rate. People find what they want by using Google or other search engines. The information they find may not be of the highest quality, but they accept it. After all, convenience is perhaps the most important criterion for many people as they seek information in a competitive environment of information provision. Given such a situation, Joe Matthews issues a reminder, namely that "the library must *earn* the customer by somehow *improving the quality of life* of that customer!" Complicating matters, libraries must do this for every customer experience, whether or not that experience involves interaction with staff. In essence, the goal is to encourage customers to return and to recruit other customers. As a result, the library needs to "create *unique* and *compelling* value" for each customer.[3]

It is time for libraries to add value to the lives of their customers as libraries compete in a shifting environment of information provision. They can do so by considering and implementing a voice-of-the-customer program. Such a program benefits the library, the customer, the staff, the library's funding bodies, and the whole community.

BENEFITS FOR THE LIBRARY

The primary benefit for the library in implementing a voice-of-the-customer program is that the staff will gain a much more detailed understanding of different customer segments. This is especially true if the library segments customers based on how they use the library rather than by using the traditional demographic approach. By listening to customers using the types of methods discussed in chapters 3 through 6, the staff can understand the information needs and expectations of the customers as they use the library, either physically or virtually. The underlying theme of this book is that librarians need to gather evidence useful to portray the library as a place to socialize, study, and learn; to review the services they currently provide; and to identify ways to improve those services or introduce new ones. Fundamental to redesigning existing services is the removal of the blinders of tradition and the need to embrace what Steven Bell calls "design thinking" or creating outstanding user experiences.[4] A wonderful customer experience occurs when one can accomplish intuitively a set of tasks without encountering one or more moments when one is unsure about how to proceed. In short, the customer experience is the sum total of all aspects of a customer's interaction with the library, its collections, staff, facilities, and services. The design of a wonderful customer experience is about anticipating what the customer needs in order to accomplish a series of tasks and making the transition from one activity to the next so fluid, logical, and automatic that the customer does not pause and ask "now what?"

The key concept of design thinking is to go beyond the bounds of the library—"go so far out of the box that you wind up in left field." It is possible to find interesting and relevant ideas from other disciplines and literatures, and then try to determine if they might work in the library setting.[5] In *Glimmer*, Warren Berger discusses the fact that designers have a different way of thinking and embrace risk and uncertainty with the objective of designing a better experience for the customer. He suggests five steps:

1. QUESTION everything, believing there is always a better way.

2. CARE about what people actually need.

3. CONNECT ideas that seem unrelated, via "smart recombinations."

4. COMMIT, or bring ideas to life through visualization and prototyping.

5. FAIL FORWARD, or try things, seek lots of feedback, and learn from one's mistakes.[6]

In addition, having a clearer understanding about the value of the library from the customer's perspective lets all library staff members, whether in public or technical service positions, have a better understanding of how their jobs and their interactions with customers add value to the life of the customers and the organization. The management literature often refers to this as "alignment." The more that library staff members know about what customers hope for and seek in terms of collections and services, the better the customer experience will be. Engaged staff members lead to engaged and delighted customers, and a library in harmony with its customers.

BENEFITS FOR THE CUSTOMER

The benefit for customers when they encounter a new and improved customer experience that "knocks their socks off" is that they become excited about the library and the value the library brings to their lives. The library, so to speak, *gets* customers, their information needs and expectations, rather than customers having to "get the library." The process of accomplishing a desired task becomes so intuitive that customers are surprised and delighted about how easy it is to use the library. Their excitement becomes contagious. They are more likely to visit the library, both in person and virtually, more frequently and for more reasons. They may become evangelists who are delighted to share their positive experiences and want others to become frequent library customers. In short, they want to share the gospel of the customer-focused library.

When library staff listen to a specific group of customers, for example in a focus group interview, they can get the participants to articulate the value that they place on the library and its services. This description of value is most likely going to be stated in qualitative terms rather than by getting the participants to assign a specific quantitative value.

BENEFITS FOR LIBRARY STAFF MEMBERS

It is important to communicate the value of a voice-of-the-customer program to all library staff members and to get them to buy into the leadership vision (see chapter 2). Staff members needs to accept the benefits of such a program to the customers, the library, and themselves. The primary benefit of a voice-of-the-customer program is that the library will gain a much better comprehension of the information needs and expectations of different customer segments. This knowledge lets the staff modify existing services and create some new ones that will be much more responsive to customers' information needs and expectations. The result is a better customer experience and the delivery of higher-quality library services. Most important, they will see how they contribute to a wonderful customer experience.

BENEFITS FOR FUNDING BODIES

Funding bodies may be direct (those associated with the institution of higher education or the local government that supplies the funding to support and maintain the library). They may also be less direct, that is, state and the federal governments, as well as private foundations and other groups. A valuable service will be used more frequently and by a large number of people and on a repeat basis. The library can communicate to funding bodies how specific customer segments receive real value when they use the library and a specific set of its services. It is important for the library to communicate a consistent message of value while at the same time receiving, processing, and acting on a rich set of data that address value for each different market segment that the library serves.

The most important part of communicating the value of the library is developing a clear understanding of what resonates with funders. For some of them, quantifying the value and impact of the library is important. As a result, a return-on-investment study might be the best approach for the library to adopt.[7] In other cases, funding bodies are more concerned about understanding how the library contributes to a better quality of life for community residents. In an academic environment, higher education administrators might be more interested in how the library helps students receive a better education and stay at the institution until they graduate (student retention rate) and helps faculty to secure grants, complete research projects, and engage in other forms of productivity.

Given the crucial role that funders and other groups play in supporting the library, library directors spend an increasing amount of time talking with those who set the budget allocation for the library, responding to how they see the library, and educating them about what the value and impact of the library are. Once the library has gathered the information showing its impact on individuals and the community, the director and other managers need to "spotlight the message," which involves communicating a consistent message by means of conventional and unusual methods. They also need to decide on the relevant set of performance metrics, be they quantitative or qualitative, and to develop compelling stories that others will find persuasive.[8]

Effectively communicating the benefits of library services may be as important as managing a well-run library. A communications strategy or plan indicates how to communicate the value of the library to a variety of stakeholders. From a stakeholder perspective, being presented with numerous facts and figures does not communicate the impact on and value that the library has for individuals and the community itself. As a result, it is important to determine what information will be persuasive and in what form: graphics, quadrant charts, bar charts, dashboards, or some other way. Amos Lakos issues an important reminder: "A profession that sees itself as 'doing good' is less concerned with assessing its outcomes and impacts since it sees its own activities as inherently positive."[9] Yet various stakeholders (e.g., the federal and state governments and program and institutional accreditation organizations) expect accountability, and increasingly they want accountability to be explained in terms of impact and effectiveness. They do not want anecdotal evidence and mere claims of success. Instead, they want evidence that can withstand objective scrutiny.

A COMMUNICATIONS STRATEGY

In putting together a communications strategy, it is important to understand the audience the library wants to reach, the context in which the evidence is presented, the positive perceptions that resonate with those providing the funding, the need for credibility of both the message and messenger, how effectively that message is conveyed, and when to release information. Furthermore, it is important to ask a variety of stakeholders to review and critique the library's communication strategy and the particular presentation skills of any presenter. After all, different groups vary in the ways in which they prefer to receive and absorb information; the choices might be visual, through a conversation, listening to a formal presentation, reading a brief synopsis, and so forth. A critical question therefore is, "How effective are directors and members of the senior management team in getting people to listen to what they say and to engage in an actual conversation?" Naturally, this question assumes these people are leaders and not merely administrators and micromanagers.

Understand Your Audience

One of the primary reasons information about the value of the library is not well received or understood is that the information being presented does not satisfactorily address the audience's perspective. For instance, the funding body for the local public library, be it a city manager, the mayor, city council members, members of the board of supervisors, a library board, or other key individuals, is the principal audience for the message concerning the value of the public library. The funding body wants to know that the library uses its financial resources in a responsible and cost-efficient manner and that the community values and appreciates the services available at the local library.

A national survey of library directors and public officials demonstrates a wide gap in perception when comparing the value of the public library to other community services (police, fire, streets, and parks and recreation). While three-fourths of the library directors believe that they initiated positive interactions with local public officials, slightly more than one-half of the local officials agree. There is, however, general agreement about the extent to which library directors and public officials agree on the goals, importance, and quality of the public library.[10]

The director of any type of library needs to develop a good working relationship with those making funding decisions and to understand what information they prefer to receive and how they prefer to receive it. Some decision makers are auditory learners, some are visual (graphic) learners, and others prefer to read textual material. Consequently, it is important to visit with them outside the library and learn about their current problems and priorities in order to determine if the library can provide information or services that will be of value.

The choice of metrics, be they output (the extent of activity) or outcome (the impact of library services) metrics, must show how library services benefit the larger organization/institution or community served. Those metrics must go beyond input (resource allocation) metrics that portray the library on its own terms and address what is relevant to institutional planning and decision making. Whatever the library communicates to others must avoid the use of library jargon and acronyms. For example, most stakeholders will not appreciate the value of "circulation per capita." However, mentioning "the number of items borrowed per capita" or "the number of items checked out per capita" will have more meaning to the funding decision makers if a context is provided by comparing the library's numbers to those of other similarly sized libraries.[11]

Provide Context

Providing raw statistical data has little meaning to those to whom the library is trying to demonstrate its accountability or is trying to impress. There is a need for context or comparisons about what a particular statistic means. For instance, mentioning that "circulation per capita" is among the highest 10 percent in the state for comparable libraries has greater meaning than the raw number itself. Comparing the weekly or monthly attendance at the public library to attendance at sporting events or the local movie theater may provide a more meaningful impression about how frequently the library is used. It is beneficial to develop one-liners such as "public library services for 'x' cents per day per citizen" or "we provide library services for 'y' cents per use," or "the entire population of 'your city' visits the library every 'z' days!" In the case of academic libraries, showing that the total value that students receive for their tuition dollars from their use of library services for the academic year is at least $449.64 resonates with higher education administrators, students, and their parents, and for that matter, with anyone concerned about the affordability of higher education.[12]

In some cases, especially for larger public libraries, providing the statistical information on a map has real appeal, since this is something that local stakeholders see on a fairly frequent basis. It is relatively easy to import data into a geographical information system (GIS) and then produce some fairly striking maps revealing library use across the jurisdiction.

Perceptions That Resonate Positively

Statements that describe public libraries and their services resonate well with the general public, according to a 2002 survey conducted on behalf of the American Library Association. The statements in support of libraries that were either "very convincing" or "somewhat convincing" include the following:

- Libraries are changing and dynamic places (91 percent).

- Libraries are places of opportunity (90 percent).

- Libraries are unique (88 percent).

- Libraries are a place of lifelong learning (88 percent).

- Libraries are your neighborhood's "how to" resource (88 percent).

- Librarians are information navigators (86 percent).

- Libraries bring you the world (85 percent).

- Librarians are the ultimate search engine (84 percent).

- Free people need free libraries (83 percent).

- Librarians are techno-savvy (81 percent).[13]

For academic libraries, the focus tends to be on the convergence and collaboration of campus information services. As Peter Hernon and Ronald R. Powell explain:

> Convergence ... involves, but is not limited to, the integration of information, communications, and comparing resources and services that seamlessly traverse multiple infrastructures and deliver content to multiple platforms or appliances. This integration, which supports learning and meets the information needs of the constituencies served, includes collaboration that is effective and mutually advantageous to the parties involved.
>
> Specific examples of convergence include centers for teaching excellence and writing centers, information arcades, facilities for multimedia production and delivery, information and learning commons, cafés, photocopying centers, centers for distance education, participation in the use of course management software . . . to make library resources available to classes digitally and to make students more information literate, publishing . . . , counseling and career centers, and services for students for whom English is a secondary language (mostly in community colleges).[14]

Be Credible

Expertise and trustworthiness influence the credibility of an organization and its leadership. One of the key qualities for leaders, especially during difficult economic times, is retention of the trust that followers place in them and their ability to carry through on their promises. As well, leaders build trust within the community served, with those to whom they report, and with stakeholders. Library directors need to develop and maintain trust with institutional leaders and stakeholders. Effective presentations are a form of dialogue and trust building. When presenting information about the library and its value, the director might advance metrics, either quantitative or qualitative, that are of interest to the particular audience. Furthermore, it is important to

- ensure that survey findings are accurate and that the survey does not contain methodology problems (e.g., concerns about sampling error);

- document the process of how the data were collected;

- compare the findings with those reported by comparable libraries in the state, geographical region, or nation; and

- contrast the findings with those reported in similar studies noted in the literature.

For whatever metrics the library chooses to gather, it is important to display trends over time just as corporations do in their annual reports. Coverage of the past five years will typically provide enough time and data to demonstrate trends.

Improve Presentation Skills

Effective communication, which occurs when the message is received and accepted, requires an appropriate choice of the communication medium for the size and sophistication of the group the library is trying to reach (see figure 9.1). For any presentation, it is important to have a clear goal of the message(s) conveyed. Presenting information in graphic form is an effective way to communicate the library's message. However, care must be exercised in the use of graphics, as the availability of such programs as PowerPoint has made graphical presentations too routine and humdrum. Suggestions for improving the use of graphical presentations include

- making the number of graphics small;

- making sure the graphic can stand on its own and minimize text;

- selecting a simple and memorable graphic over a complex one; and

- testing each graphic, making certain it communicates the intended message.[15]

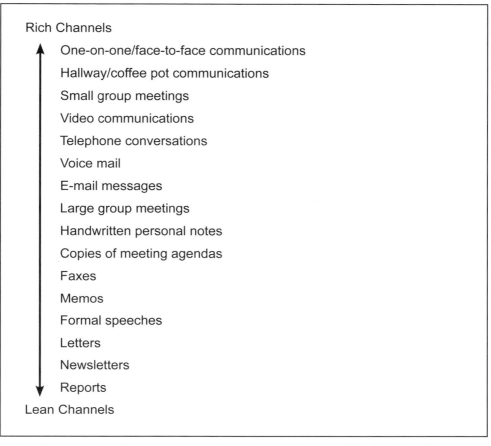

Rich Channels

- One-on-one/face-to-face communications
- Hallway/coffee pot communications
- Small group meetings
- Video communications
- Telephone conversations
- Voice mail
- E-mail messages
- Large group meetings
- Handwritten personal notes
- Copies of meeting agendas
- Faxes
- Memos
- Formal speeches
- Letters
- Newsletters
- Reports

Lean Channels

Figure 9.1. Communication Continuum. Reprinted from Joseph M. Miniace and Elizabeth Falter, "Communication: A Key Factor in Strategy Implementation," *Planning Review* 24, no. 1 (January–February 1996): 29.

Stage the Release of Information

The process of communicating the value of the library should occur throughout the year and consist of more than the release of a library's written annual report. A combination of written and oral messages should be conveyed by means of press releases and formal and informal presentations before local organizations, interested groups and stakeholders, and those making funding decisions. Managerial leaders can prepare formal presentations (using a few carefully selected PowerPoint slides and handouts) and be prepared to give informal, brief talks to small-group meetings. The hallmark of good salespeople is the ability to deliver a succinct "elevator speech" that conveys the library's mission and perhaps vision and addresses the value of the library. When appropriate, that speech should encourage customers to provide input into planning new services and improving existing ones. The library director and members of the senior management team should be comfortable delivering such speeches. They should expect any member of the staff to deliver an elevator speech to anyone on campus or in the community that addresses the library's mission statement and shows what the library is all about. For example, the mission of the Purdue University Libraries "is to foster a dynamic information environment that advances learning, discovery, and engagement." The statement goes on to clarify the meaning of the following terms:

- **Learning.** "The Libraries' faculty and staff apply sound pedagogical approaches to create innovative and effective learning experiences which foster the core competencies of critical thinking, communication skills, information literacy, information technology, and methods of inquiry. These competencies are integrated into disciplinary learning through collaborative efforts with colleagues engaged in teaching."

- **Discovery.** "The Libraries' faculty and staff are grounded in the principles and practices of library and information science, and of specialized information-related disciplines. They bring their library science expertise to collaborative initiatives with colleagues in other fields to more effectively undertake interdisciplinary research which expands the realm of knowledge."

- **Engagement.** "Contributions to the engagement mission of the University arise from the Libraries' strength in support of learning and discovery, and a commitment to help meet the information needs of the residents of Indiana."[16]

The staff may have to practice their delivery of very short speeches that cover the critical parts of the mission statement. It is important for them to receive critical feedback on their performance; however, this must be done in a way that is neither offensive nor alienating.

The library can produce a range of written materials to communicate effectively any messages that relate the value of the library to the community, stakeholders, and those making funding decisions. Some of the activities that the library might consider are

- human interest stories that appeal to the press and bloggers, print, digital, television, and radio;

- an executive summary of the library's annual report (no more than two pages) that is well designed and has visual appeal (consider using colorful graphics, charts, and so forth);

- the library's monthly newsletter, with its coverage of how the library meets its goals and the extent of customer satisfaction with the library and its services;

- bookmarks that convey a message; and

- an article appearing in one of the professional library journals documenting staff experiences and study findings.

Storytelling puts the information contained in human interest stories and the library's newsletter in context and makes facts and figures come alive. Stories have a human voice, help people to communicate in a way that listeners can remember the message better, and are a way for people to make sense of things. The staff should collect "war stories" and use selective ones to convey the message about the value of the library and its information services. Even when the director and senior managers deliver a presentation, they might begin by saying, "Let me tell you a story . . . ."

The Customer Experience: Jacksonville Public Library Learns to Listen*

Listening to the library user is a basic tenet of providing quality library services. Simple, right? Not so. Listening requires a mechanism to hear and a methodology to respond to what is said. The Jacksonville Public Library (JPL) has been on a multiyear journey of learning to listen to its customers. Milestones along the way include a community-based strategic plan, an online customer comment management system and satisfaction survey, development of a balanced scorecard, and a capacity planning process.

That journey of learning to listen was begun under the leadership of Library Director Barbara A.B. Gubbin with the development of a community-based strategic plan. The library sought to determine the future direction of the JPL after completion of a building program that had added six new branches and a new main library by the end of 2005. The heart of the strategic planning process, listening to the community, was accomplished by engaging the community in a dialogue about the future of the public library. Input was solicited from users and nonusers alike using various methods, including a community summit, surveys, interviews, and focus group interviews.

The community summit was a one-day event that featured a panel of national library leaders who facilitated an exploration of public library services with participants through presentations, panel discussions, and participant breakout sessions to discuss library services. Topics presented included trends in urban public libraries, the library as a place of discovery, electronic resources, community partnerships, and technology. More than 200 people attended the summit and offered opinions about the programs and services that were most important to them for the future.

Additional planning elements used to solicit input from the community during the strategic planning process included surveys, interviews, and focus groups. Customer ideas, priorities, and recommendations were compiled and presented to a committee of community leaders, board members, and senior library staff who incorporated those ideas into the strategic plan. One of the most difficult tasks that the committee faced was adopting a new mission statement that would incorporate the priorities of the community: *To connect people with ideas that enlighten, encourage, inspire, enrich, and delight.* Although the mission statement broadly represents community direction, the major goals adopted by the committee more specifically addressed the priorities that were identified: *As the Library fulfills its mission, the community will recognize it as a springboard for educational and occupational success, a partner in creating learning experiences, the center of community life, and an outstanding public investment.*

The strategic plan has provided a multiyear, customer-based framework for decision making and organizational direction that is used by the board, the library administration, and library staff. The four areas of focus adopted for the plan (customers, organizational effectiveness, human resources, and funding) have formed the basis for JPL's service plans, strategies, and metrics each year since the plan was adopted in fiscal year (FY) 2007 and most recently have formed the basis for the library's balanced scorecard adopted for FY 2011. The board of trustees formally adopted a service philosophy in 2009 that refers to the strategic plan as the basis for service decisions. The community input gathered four years ago for the strategic plan continues to inform service decisions and directions.

For current input, the library hears from individual customers via an online customer satisfaction survey and comment management system. This system was implemented three years ago to replace an unwieldy manual system of paper comment cards. Due to the volume and diversity of the written comments, complaints, and suggestions received, the library was, in effect, listening and responding to one customer at a time. There was no mechanism to identify trends or track input on specific subjects. The library administration recognized that we were missing an opportunity to mine a rich source of data that speaks directly to customer satisfaction with the library experience.

The system purchased by JPL is LibSAT, a Web-based product that allows management of customer comments, provides continuous customer feedback from an online satisfaction survey, allows peer comparisons, and provides the ability to write reports. JPL's marketing of the survey and online comment system has been successful with customers; annual comments have increased 56 percent over three years, to 6,500, and survey responses have increased 67 percent, to 5,510.

However, there have been two challenges in using this tool effectively: staff resistance to the validity of the satisfaction survey data and staff reluctance to embrace customer comments as a tool for improvement. Though there are many reasons for staff resistance to customer satisfaction surveys, in the final analysis, as Joseph R. Matthews suggests, "When it comes to customer satisfaction, the perception of the customer—right or wrong, informed or uniformed—is the only 'reality' that counts."[1]

Although survey responses have increased significantly, the results for overall satisfaction have remained constant or have improved slightly (FY10/FY08):

Satisfaction with services	(8.7/8.7)
Quality of services	(8.7/8.6)
How like to reuse services	(9.2/9.2)
Importance of library	(9.3/9.3)
Recommend the library	(9/8.9)
Services compare to expectations	(8.5/8.4)

To overcome resistance from staff and incorporate the wealth of customer perception data into the organizational culture, the administration pushed the data down to the library managers, up to the board of library trustees, and out to the city departments responsible for information technology and facilities.

To push ownership of the satisfaction survey down, library managers are given annual satisfaction survey targets to manage. They have also been given increasing responsibility each year for managing and responding to customer comments. Managers are expected to include customer satisfaction trends on their regular meeting agendas for discussion and report on all service improvements made in response to customer comments.

The first year, managers were only responsible for categorizing their comments, reviewing survey scores, and reporting their metrics for customer satisfaction performance targets. After more than three years of working with the system, managers are now responsible for answering all comments. The expectation is that they will take the time to meet personally with customers to listen, resolve difficulties, or accept suggestions instead of having staff refer customers to a comment form. Since implementing this change, the number of customers requesting a written response has declined, as have the number of paper comment cards received.

Information from the customer satisfaction survey is also reported up, to the board of library trustees. They value these data and have formally adopted monitoring and review of the survey and comment data as a board committee responsibility. The board receives reports on survey-based performance metrics, significant changes in customer satisfaction YTD (year-to-date) reports provided to other city agencies, and other pertinent data. A recent board decision to disallow any fees, fines, or overdue materials if customer accounts were to be "in good standing" led to unexpected consequences in the form of difficulties for online users who could not pay accounts online after library hours. Customer comments about the negative impact of the new board policy on their library experience were heard and acted on by the board in the form of a grace period for online customers.

Satisfaction and comment reports are provided monthly to both the city information technology and facilities departments. Providing topic-specific reports to outside city agencies helps the library communicate the opinions of our customers and the value of library services to the community. These reports also support our position when requesting funding and resources. Both departments are provided with YTD satisfaction metrics, monthly metrics, and monthly comments.

Although the mission, goals, and objectives as set forth in the strategic plan were customer based, the administrative team struggled each year to develop relevant metrics to support a customer focus. Service plans, strategies, and objectives were routinely supported by performance metrics that were based on inputs, process, and outputs. These were easy to select and to measure and were focused internally on the organization. Instead of inspiring the staff to focus on the library mission, these metrics tended to focus staff on meeting the numeric targets for a successful performance evaluation.

The JPL strategic plan was based on a balanced scorecard. In order to help shift the library's focus toward achieving our customer-based mission and strategic plan, the library engaged a consultant to provide training to managers and administrative staff in the development of a balanced scorecard.[2] A year's work resulted in a balanced scorecard that expands the four focus areas originally identified in the strategic plan to five perspectives (customers, information resources, internal processes, organizational readiness, and financial). The theme of the library's balanced scorecard is "the customer experience," as reflected in the scorecard's customer-centered strategic aims. JPL defines *customer experience* for the scorecard as "providing personalized services, treating customers well, and facilitating successful library visits."

Listening to the customer is built into the balanced scorecard strategies and performance targets. By keeping the scorecard on the agenda for discussion at staff meetings, town hall meetings, and leadership meetings, the library is beginning to shift the conversation from what the organization does, to what the customer experiences. And, in order to understand what the customer experiences, we have to listen. For the first time, we have successfully incorporated a multiple-year outcome-based strategy into the mix. JPL will track library cards issued to children at targeted outreach events over three years to determine if the cards remain active during this time.[3] We want to hear what the outcome is for the children who receive library cards at these events.

Finally, Jacksonville Public Library has embarked on a capacity planning project to determine the capacity of the library to provide services in a rapidly changing information environment, given reduced and uncertain funding, and to obtain direction from the community about which service priorities are the most important for the future. The board recognizes that the library cannot continue to operate on a *business as usual* basis when funding is reduced each year. In addition to evaluations of all library facilities, including information technology, a review of statistical data, and market segmentation analysis, a key component of the planning process will be the communications plan.

The communications plan encompasses four public meetings to gather input from customers at the beginning of the process, and additional public meetings to roll out the plan and get reactions from the community at the end of the process. The response to the capacity plan public meetings has been both passionate, fueled by reactions to a reduction in hours at several libraries, and encouraging. Hundreds of community residents provided input about their priorities for service and ideas for cost savings at the public meetings and by an online comment solicitation. JPL expects similar input in response to the capacity plan recommendations as they are developed. All of this input will be incorporated into the final plan.

The capacity plan process will bring JPL full circle by asking the community to tell us their priorities in the face of new economic realities. We will listen. The priorities will be incorporated into our goals and strategies for providing services and creating customer experiences that fulfill our mission to "connect people with ideas that enlighten, encourage, inspire, enrich, and delight."

Notes

1. Joseph R. Matthews, *The Evaluation and Measurement of Library Services* (Westport, CT: Libraries Unlimited, 2007), 249.

2. Joseph R. Matthews, *Scorecard for Results: A Guide for Developing a Library Balanced Scorecard* (Westport, CT: Libraries Unlimited, 2008).

3. Cards that are not used for one year are identified as "inactive."

*Melonee Lotterhos Slocum, Manager for Strategic Initiatives, Jacksonville Public Library, Jacksonville, FL.

CONCLUDING THOUGHTS

Central to the communications' process is the message that the library conveys about the customer experience. That message might address the emotional, physical, and analytical needs of customers. Emotional needs connect people through a sense of satisfaction, appreciation with the service received, or spiritual reverence. Physical needs refer the perception of customers about a welcoming, caring, inviting, and comfortable environment, and analytical needs focus on the fulfillment of information needs. It is critical to communicate that the library is more than a warehouse or provider of books. As shown in figure 9.2, librarians might communicate various facets of program awareness, interaction with a caring and knowledgeable staff, the ability to be self-sufficient, getting to the library, navigating the building, and similar topics. Collectively, these topics concentrate on the library's infrastructure (collections, staff, technology, and facilities).

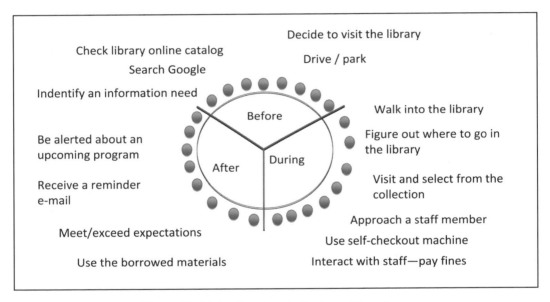

Figure 9.2. Understanding the Customer Experience

As the library director and members of the management team communicate with stakeholders, staff members, and customers, they should

- understand that the organizational culture and what resonates with key decision makers is as important as measuring library outcomes;

- cultivate the library's stakeholders, even when they do not need anything;

- overdeliver, not oversell, library services,[17] and look for ways to personalize the services that customers experience, in person or online;[18]

- convey the message about the value of the library vividly but succinctly, and convert the library's annual budget to a cost per day per capita and identity the number of days it takes for the entire population of the community to visit the library (total population divided by daily gate count times "x" number of days);

- talk to library stakeholders one-on-one whenever possible;

- put information into a context; that is rather than using dry statistics, provide some context that will be understandable in the environment within which the library operates (e.g., convert annual number of people visiting the library (in person and online) to the number of times a nearby auditorium would be filled; and

- present information in terms the audience understands. Translate numbers, be they dollars or statistics, into terms that have a real associative meaning, so that the bottom-line message of the library is heard, understood, and remembered.

In essence, the library director and members of the management team communicate the value of the library; this should be "Job no. 1" for the library director. They need to devote the time and energy to the delivery of the library's message and practice doing so without any props, including notes.

The very word "communicate" means "share," and inasmuch as you and I are communicating at this moment, we are one. Not so much a union as a unity.[19]

NOTES

1. ThinkExist.com, Quotations, "George Bernard Shaw," accessed August 13, 2010, http://thinkexist.com/quotation/the_single_biggest_problem_in_communication_is/155222.html.

2. See Association of Research Libraries, "Press Releases & Announcements: E-Science and Data Support Services" (Washington, DC: Association of Research Libraries, 2010), accessed August 12, 2010, http://www.arl.org/news/pr/escience-12august10.shtml; Association of Research Libraries, *E-Science and Data Support Services*, prepared by Catherine Soehner, Catherine Steeves, and Jennifer Ward (Washington, DC: Association of Research Libraries, 2010), accessed August 12, 2010, http://www.arl.org/bm~doc/escience_report2010.pdf.

3. Joseph R. Matthews, *The Customer-Focused Library: Re-Inventing the Public Library from the Outside-In* (Santa Barbara, CA: Libraries Unlimited, 2009), 19.

4. Steven Bell, "'Design Thinking' and Higher Education," *Inside Higher Ed* (March 2, 2010), accessed August 13, 2010, http://www.insidehighered.com/views/2010/03/02/bell; StevenBell.Info, Steven Bell's Resource Center, "Design Thinking & User Experience," 2007, accessed August 13, 2010, http://stevenbell.info/design.htm.

5. See, for instance, Paco Underhill, *Why People Buy: The Science of Shopping* (New York: Simon & Schuster, 2000).

6. Warren Berger, *Glimmer: How Design Can Transform Your Life and Maybe Even the World* (New York: Penguin Press, 2009).

7. See Robert E. Dugan, Peter Hernon, and Danuta A. Nitecki, *Viewing Library Metrics from Different Perspectives* (Santa Barbara, CA: Libraries Unlimited, 2009), 142–44.

8. See ibid.

9. Amos Lakos, "The Missing Ingredient—Culture of Assessment in Libraries," *Performance Measurement and Metrics* (sample issue) (August 1999): 3–7.

10. The Library Research Center, "A Survey of Public Libraries and Local Government," *Illinois State Library Special Report Series* 4, no. 1 (1997): 1–62.

11. See also Dugan, Hernon, and Nitecki, *Viewing Library Metrics from Different Perspectives*, 283–94.

12. Ibid., 125.

13. KRC Research & Consulting, "@Your Library: Attitudes toward Public Libraries Survey," June 2002, accessed August 13, 2010, http://www.ala.org/pio/presskits/nlw2002kit/krc_data.pdf.

14. Peter Hernon and Ronald R. Powell, eds., *Convergence and Collaboration of Campus Information Services* (Westport, CT: Libraries Unlimited, 2008), 1–2.

15. Richard S. Wurman, *Information Anxiety 2* (Indianapolis, IN: Que, 2001).

16. Purdue University Libraries, "Strategic Plan. 2006–2011" (West Lafayette, IN: Purdue University, 2006), accessed August 12, 2010, http://www.lib.purdue.edu/admin/stratplans/plan2011.html.

17. Tom Peters, *Thriving on Chaos* (New York: Pan Books, 1989).

18. Kevin Davis, "The Changing Role of the Business Librarian," *Knowledge Management* (December 1998), accessed August 13, 2010, http://enterprise.supersites.net/knmagn2/km199812/fc1.htm.

19. Colin Cherry, *On Human Communications: A Survey and a Criticism*, rev. ed. (Cambridge, MA: MIT Press, 1980), 84.

10

Valuing Library Customers

A majority of Americans report that quality customer service is more important to them in today's economic environment.[1]

Academic and public libraries are not inexpensive organizations for institutions, municipalities, and other sources of funding to support. The salary and benefits of staff, for instance, are a recurring expense. During the economic recession of 2008–2010 and its aftermath, a large number of libraries have combated budget cuts, in part, by furloughing staff members, terminating the employment of some (most often part-time staff), redesigning positions, and increasing the workload of professional and nonprofessional staff. Libraries may also have reduced the number of hours open to the public and eliminated some branch libraries. Such actions have a negative impact on both the managerial and nonmanagerial staff. Everyone feels greater workplace stress and expresses concern about his or her future. With the stock market and global financial system in a volatile state, a number of these individuals may have concerns about their personal finances. The challenge for a library's managerial leadership is to maintain employee motivation, morale, engagement, and commitment, without letting customer service and the mission of the organization be adversely affected.

Customer service refers to both the *process* and *outcome* of any service transaction.[2] The process, which is the way the service provider treats the customer, includes factors such as courtesy, clear communication, and attention to the customer's request. Process might also address self-sufficiency, as not all customers interact directly with library staff. What customers think about both the process and the outcome of that transaction are important issues for them. Customer service focuses on the ability of an organization, such as a library, constantly and consistently to meet or exceed the expectations of those individuals visiting the library either physically or virtually. In essence, every part of the organization should have an impact on customer service, not just those parts that involve face-to-face customer contact.

INFORMATION NEEDS AND CUSTOMER EXPECTATIONS DIFFER

People find themselves in situations where they need information to make a decision, answer a question, locate a fact, solve a problem, or understand something. An *information need* refers to the gap between the individual's knowledge about the problem or topic and what the person needs to know to make a decision, and so forth. That information need cannot be separated from the situation that created the need and the individual who perceives the need. The person's *information-seeking behavior* refers to the process that person goes through to locate the information needed to make that decision, and so forth.

As they seek information and interact with information providers, people form expectations or impressions of those providers and their experience with them. Service quality, which is an antecedent of customer satisfaction, is not the same thing as satisfaction. *Satisfaction* is a sense of contentment that results from an actual experience in relation to an expected experience. *Service quality* is a global judgment relating to the superiority of a service as viewed in the context of specific statements that the library is willing to act on if customers find them of great value. "The inference is that the satisfaction levels from a number of transactions or encounters that an individual experiences with a particular organization fuse to form an impression of service quality for that person. The collective experiences of many persons create an organization's reputation for service quality."[3] Because both service quality and satisfaction involve listening to customers and gathering meaningful feedback from them, the key question is, "How does the library use the evidence gathered to improve service and delight customers?"

CUSTOMER SERVICE PLEDGES

During the administration of President William J. Clinton, the federal government was actively engaged in improving the quality of services that government employees provide the public and in creating a customer service climate for the services that government departments and agencies provide to the public. As government departments and agencies developed service pledges, some libraries followed suit. A weakness of pledges such as the partial, hypothetical one in figure 10.1 is that they may contain general statements—platitudes—that cannot be measured. For example, "We will take time to listen to you." What does this statement mean? Furthermore, statements such as "we will empower our customers as they engage in lifelong learning" are important to librarians, but how important are they to customers? Missing from the hypothetical pledge is coverage of digital services and the library's homepage. After all, the provision of customer service is not limited to those physically visiting staff and asking questions. Expanding the collection of e-books and e-audiobooks, for instance, calls for modification of statements such as "we will make new books available within three weeks of receipt and provide priority delivery when necessary," "we will process current serials within twenty-four hours of receipt," and "we will reshelve library materials within twenty-four hours of use and regularly maintain shelving order." Prompt reshelving of materials is a key expectation documented in service quality research.

The library is firmly committed to providing excellent customer service. We will continually evaluate and update this commitment, and we value your opinion throughout that process.

Commitment to Excellence

- We will display a welcoming, courteous, respectful, helpful, and professional attitude to all customers.
- We will carefully listen to what you say as we strive to meet your needs and expectations.
- We will provide prompt and reliable service.
- We will maintain a clean and safe environment for our customers.

General Services

- We will acknowledge you immediately at the service desk, respond to your needs, and call for additional staff if we are unable to serve you promptly.
- We will answer the phone within five rings and, if we are unable to deal with the question at that time, we will offer to call back at an agreed time.
- We will identify ourselves and the section of the library when answering the phone.

Specific Services

- We will place and acknowledge faculty acquisition orders within ten working days and provide priority delivery when necessary.
- We will make new books available within four weeks of receipt and provide priority delivery when necessary.
- We will check customer e-mails at least once a day and answer all inquiries within two business days.
- We will process current serials within twenty-four hours of receipt, new books for circulation within three business days, and the newest media within five business days.
- We will reshelve library materials within twenty-four hours of use and regularly maintain shelving order.
- We will report equipment failures immediately and advise customers appropriately.
- We will respond to your signed suggestions within three working days.

Figure 10.1. Customer Service Commitment. For actual examples, see the Hong Kong Polytechnic University, Pao Yue-kong Library, "Library Performance Pledges 2010/2011," 2010, accessed September 8, 2010, http://www.lib.polyu.edu.hk/about_library/performance_pledges; Renfrewshire Community Website, "Libraries," 2010, accessed September 8, 2010, http://www.renfrewshire.gov.uk/ilwwcm/publishing.nsf/Content/els-pl-renfrewshire-libraries-customer-pledges; Falmouth Public Library, "Customer Service Policy" (Falmouth, MA: Falmouth Public Library, 2010), accessed September 8, 2010. http://www.falmouthpubliclibrary.org/?/services/policies/customer-service-policy/; Fayetteville Public Library, "Customer Service Standards" (Fayetteville, AR: Fayetteville Public Library, 2007), accessed September 8, 2010, http://www.faylib.org/information/pdf/customerservicestandards.pdf; Cleveland Heights-University Heights Public Library, "Pledge to Our Customers" (Cleveland Heights, OH: Cleveland Heights-University Heights Public Library, 2010), accessed September 8, 2010, http://www.heightslibrary.org/page/customer_pledge.

Examples of pledges appeared in the first edition of *Assessing Service Quality*.[4] Since then, similar pledges tend to lessen the accountability aspect and merely inform customers about the services provided. Most likely, libraries do not have pledges such as that in figure 10.1. Furthermore, with 10 to 13 percent of college students having a disability, does the pledge cover them, or must customers find a special Web page devoted to disability?

The absence of customer service pledges does not mean the absence of customer service; rather, a pledge is an opportunity for staff across all library departments to meet and discuss customer service and what they are willing to do collectively. The discussion becomes a tool for the staff, perhaps together with input from some customers, to identify areas where they might exceed customer expectations. As part of that review, those participating in staff development programs might share comments that customers made through formal surveys and social networks. The contents of any pledge, even if it is not publicly shared, should look at service from the customer's, not the organizational, perspective. The key is to include what really matters to customers and will help the library to attract new ones.

MYTHS

There are a number of myths in librarianship about the information-seeking behavior of different customer segments. For example, one myth is that college and university students change their behavior once they interact with librarians and use self-help guides. In fact, students tend not to use library services that require direct interaction with librarians; they prefer to use online library and other resources and to rely on Google and *Wikipedia* for information on assorted topics. Course readings are their first choice for information seeking, and they turn to their instructors for the identification of additional sources.[5]

Another myth, applicable to university libraries whose institutions have membership in the Association of Research Libraries (ARL), is that the number of reference questions posed in person at a reference desk remains stable or is increasing. In fact, these libraries report an 80 percent decrease in the number of questions asked. Some of the library deans even question the role and value of offering general reference desk service. To an extent, in these libraries there is a shift from in person to various forms of digital reference service. Further, as the scenario for academic libraries in chapter 1 shows, a university library might embed librarians in research teams and in program instruction, leaving clerical and paraprofessional staff to handle general reference questions.

A third myth is that college and university students rely on the library's online public access catalog (OPAC) for its coverage of monographs and other resources. In fact, the students do consult the library homepage, but for access to the databases available there. They skip use of the OPAC, a resource whose development libraries have made a huge investment in. To correct this situation and make it easier for students and others to obtain information from the homepage, a number of libraries have invested in Aquabrowser or an equivalent as the interface to library collections. Although Aquabrowser has its critics, it is a search tool intended to let customers have access to a wider array of resources than they would find from a general search of the OPAC. Without such an interface, use of the OPAC would remain far behind use of databases.

A related aspect of this myth is that lack of reliance on library resources and the OPAC is presumed to be a problem for academic, but not for public, libraries. In 2003, the Council on Library and Information Resources issued a report that provides an overview of more than 200 recent research studies (conducted between 1995 and 2003) concerning use and users of electronic library resources. Conclusions from this report, such as that college and high school students use the Internet more than the library for conducting research, underscore the movement toward reliance on digital information.[6] Moreover, as Joe Matthews discusses in *The Customer-Focused Library*, "only a small proportion of library customers use the library's online catalog, and because the catalog does not return 'Google-like results,' people are often confused."[7] The social OPAC, he points out, is a method to rectify the situation. Customers can rate, comment, and tag items in the library catalog. "The whole idea of a social OPAC is to unleash the power of the 'we' through the active participation of those who use the catalog."[8]

Another myth is that library use is decreasing. Numerous reports and stories about public library use during the economic recession portray the opposite picture; people may be turning to the library, for instance, for free use of computers and for programming (e.g., workshops on job seeking and resumé preparation). For academic libraries, especially those with information and learning commons, the library is part of a student social network and a place to engage in group work. The evidence suggests there is a shift in academic libraries from studying and working alone to participating in groups.

A number of librarians assume that customer service does not apply to libraries. They mistakenly argue that customers do not pay a real cost for use and are not making a purchase decision. Contrary to this myth, purchase decisions correspond to their willingness to visit the library and use collections and facilities. It is hoped that customers become avid library supporters. Customer service might mistakenly be associated with the concept that the customer is always right. The fundamental principle of service quality is to concentrate resources on meeting high customer expectations, not fulfilling *all* customer expectations. Another misperception is the association of customer service with disgruntled or problem customers.

The final myth to highlight here is that circulation counts adequately convey the amount of use the public makes of the library. Increasingly, library use as a concept involves in-house use (occupancy rate, material use, and equipment use), Web site/database/OPAC hits and sessions (frequency and downloads), and the other components included in figure 9.2 in *Assessing Service Quality*.[9]

Given the existence of such myths, the question is, "How does knowledge of them result in the provision of better customer service?" This is a question that library staff should ponder and address as they review and discuss the customer service pledges. Any pledge item, such as "we will empower our customers in their search for lifelong learning," merits ample discussion as the staff decide whether or not it is a platitude or is actually achievable. Complicating an affirmative answer is the fact that the United States now ranks twelfth among thirty-six developed nations "in the number of 25- to 34-year-olds with college degrees."[10] Other problems include the low high school graduation rate, especially among people of color; comparison ratings showing how U.S. students compare internationally in areas such as science and mathematics; poor student understanding of

U.S. and world history; and questioning by society, government, and educators about the poor quality of education that students receive in primary and secondary schools.

THE MANAGEMENT CONTEXT

The balanced scorecard is a strategic planning and management system that aligns business activities with the vision and strategy of an organization, improves internal and external communications, and monitors organizational performance in relationship to strategic goals. The framework provides managers with a balanced view of organizational performance. Matthews points out that the scorecard helps the library demonstrate accountability by measuring its true performance beyond the simple counts of the number of activities performed.

At the bottom of the scorecard for him is the financial perspective, which identifies the financial and other resources provided to the library as well as to the infrastructure. Upward is the organizational readiness perspective, which refers to staff. At the third level, there are two, side-by-side perspectives: the information resources perspective and the internal process perspective. The information resources perspective includes print and electronic collections, selected quality Web links, interlibrary loan, and document delivery. The goal of the internal process perspective is to understand the process and activities critical to enabling the library to satisfy customer needs and expectations and to add value that the customers actually see. The combination of organizational readiness, information resources, and the efficient internal processes delivers a mix of products and services upward to the top of the scorecard, which is the customer perspective.[11]

The customer side of the balanced scorecard might draw, in part, on mystery shopping and the observations of trained shoppers (see chapter 3). Mystery shopping is not intended to replace the use of other market research techniques; rather, the goal is to add a new dimension to customer service evaluation.

An example of a mature process for using the balanced scorecard is found at the University of Virginia Library (http://www2.lib.virginia.edu/bsc/index.html), where the scorecard has been in use since 2001. Its scorecard uses perspectives different from those advocated by Matthews. To address the user perspective, the library relies on customer ratings as derived from periodic surveys, data about materials use, and turnaround time for patron requests.[12] On its surveys, the library "asks respondents to rate three aspects of customer service: speed, courtesy, competence." The scores are "combined into one composite number" and compared to two targets:

1. At least 4.25 out of 5.0 from each of the user groups: undergraduate students, graduate students, humanities faculty, social science faculty, and science faculty.

2. A score of at least 4.00 from each of the major user groups.[13]

In contrast, the Orange County Library System has five perspectives for its balanced scorecard, one of which is labeled "customer satisfaction," and it addresses

How well are library customers served according to the Library Mission? What does this mean to you? We want to be sure that we are meeting your needs. We have set some standards to measure customer satisfaction. These include the following:

Availability: days & hours the Library is open and the Website is available.

Customer feedback: We look at customer surveys and have a secret shopper program to find out your opinions on how we are doing.

Usage: We measure how many people have library cards and how many people are visiting the library.

Programs and services. We count how many people attend library events.[14]

As these examples illustrate, libraries can decide what methods of data collection they will include for the customer perspective. Ideally, as the scorecard for the Orange County Library System indicates, more than one methodology should be included. Methods such as surveys and mystery shopping complement each other and provide a fuller view of customer expectations. Other methodologies presented in chapters 3 through 6 might be added.

KEY METRICS

Bill Price and David Jaffe claim that "most of the metrics that the customer service industry has captured and tracked over the past twenty years are rubbish." They believe that the metrics have too often focused on speed (of the answer or the service encounter), do not factor "in differences among customers, issues, and agent skills," or "are simply incomplete or hard to calculate and therefore easy to 'fix' or game."[15]

In *Viewing Library Metrics from Different Perspectives*, Robert Dugan, Peter Hernon, and Danuta Nitecki, in effect, respond to Price and Jaffe's criticism. They identify various output metrics that libraries can use to demonstrate accountability and improve service delivery.[16] Additional metrics, some of which Price and Jaffe discuss, emerge, including the following:

- **Resolution rate** (for the comments made, the percentage of problems solved). This metric might be subdivided by survey comments, e-mail comments, comments posted in suggestion boxes, and so forth.

- **Return rate** (from survey responses, the percentage expressing a willingness to return or responding with a 9 or 10 on a 10-point scale).

- **Recommend rate** (from survey responses), the percentage indicating they have recommended the library or a particular service to others. They might respond with either a yes or no. As an alternative, respondents might be asked, "Would you recommend the services of this library to others?," with a 9- or 10-point scale. The results then might be reported as the net promoter score (see chapter 3).

- **Delight rate** (from survey responses, the percentage of respondents choosing 9 or 10 on a 10-point scale to the question, "Overall, how important is this library to you?" and/or "Overall, how satisfied are you with the services of this library?").

Such metrics might be displayed in dashboard form on the library homepage and included in annual and other reports as well as in any community forum. They might also be shared with the press as the library demonstrates how it uses the metrics for accountability and service improvement.

Libraries might also engage in behavior monitoring and use different metrics to characterize how they treat customers. It is possible to create different categories for positive and negative treatment and to subdivide responses based on survey responses and comments made via e-mail, in person, and so forth. Most likely, such metrics would not appear in the form of dashboards. Instead, they become internal metrics that library managers revisit on a regular basis.

Price and Jaffe caution against the adoption of metrics that staff members can manipulate or that are designed solely to create a favorable image of the organization. For instance, they mention branch queue time as reported through queue tickets and dockets: During quiet times, branch staff go up to some self-service machine and create fake responses that reflect positively on the organization.[17]

Finally, as libraries invest in developing and using metrics that reflect outputs, the amount of service provided and how well customer expectations are met, they should not forget the importance of outcomes that reflect the impact of library services on the public. Although some stakeholders do not recognize any connection between satisfaction and service impacts, there is undoubtedly a correlation, even if it is a weak one. It seems logical to assume that individuals who are satisfied or delighted will be more likely to use and value library services. They have a positive attitude that undoubtedly contributes, in some way, to making them receptive to the library's impact on their lives. Further, it might be worthwhile to examine those unemployed workers who attended library programs on résumé writing and job seeking and believe that these programs contributed to them getting employed. Have they become delighted customers who are willing to let the library develop stories about the success of its community role?

Some Examples*

Examples of key metrics include the various reports available using LibSAT and LibPAS from Counting Opinions. Libraries can quickly assess some of their major opportunities for improvement using metrics such as the Net Promoter Score (NPS; see chapter 3) and the Opportunity Index (OI). Determining the NPS for various customer profiles can lead to some valuable insights. Consider the differences in NPS for customers who have or have not had contact initiated by staff in the past year. The differences are startling. Despite the fact that these same customers (>40 percent) prefer to locate information at the library on their own, the effort made by the library to initiate contact with customers is a valuable way to influence their affinity and satisfaction.

In response to the question, "Did library staff meet, greet, or initiate contact with you at any time in the past year?," the following represent the NPS scores for a typical library customer. Note that the "Peers" column indicates the outcomes for all libraries using LibSAT, whereas the "Total" column represents all results for this library. The values shaded in black are indicative of above the overall average for all respondents, while the values in the NO chart (see Total and Peers) indicate below average results.

YES						NO				
	Month	Quarter	Total	Peers			Month	Quarter	Total	Peers
Promoters	82.5	83.44	83.8	78.55		Promoters	43.75	43.75	57.01	53
Passives	12.5	6.75	11.2	14.35		Passives	18.75	20.31	21.18	21.27
Detractors	5	9.82	5	7.1		Detractors	37.5	35.94	21.81	25.74
NPS	77.5%	73.62%	78.8%	71.44%		NPS	6.25%	7.81%	35.2%	27.26%

The analysis provides an opportunity to drill down from the underlined values (see above) to the specific comments from those respondents, enabling the library to monitor progress over time and provide some constructive context for potential improvements in service levels. The Opportunity Index (OI) provides additional insight into which aspects of service represent a priority for improving customer satisfaction. The following figure, which represents the results from LibSAT for all customer responses from public library subscribers, represents a macro view of some of the challenges confronting public libraries in terms of satisfying their customers.

Opportunity Index

Type: | Public ▼ | -- All Libraries -- ▼

Context: | -- All Contexts -- ▼ | -- All Options -- ▼

Service	Opportunity Index
Books and other materials available to borrow/reference	11.85
Comprehensive list of items in the collection	11
This library's web site	10.9
Hours of access and operation	10.64
Borrowing items (books and/or other materials)	10.32
Holds/Renewals	9.97
Lending policies	9.96
Accessing library services from a location other than the library (online or over-the-phone)	9.89
Personal safety and security	9.81
CheckIn/CheckOut	9.8
Overall Importance and Satisfaction	9.77

The results depict aspects of service with a higher OI than represented by responses to questions about the overall importance of and satisfaction with the library. Each library can view its own results, which can be filtered by various customer segments. Notice in the following figure how the range and ranking of high-priority opportunities for public library customers who are best described as "in the workforce" differ from the overall results.

Opportunity Index

Type: | Public ▼ | -- All Libraries -- ▼

Context: | Status ▼ | in the workforce ▼
You are ... (select the best fit)

Service	Opportunity Index
Books and other materials available to borrow/reference	11.1
Hours of access and operation	10.67
Borrowing items (books and/or other materials)	10.4
Comprehensive list of items in the collection	10.33
This library's web site	10.24
Accessing library services from a location other than the library (online or over-the-phone)	10
Holds/Renewals	9.93
Lending policies	9.9
Overall Importance and Satisfaction	9.86

Using key metrics can provide valuable insight. The challenge for most libraries is sustaining the effort required to take the measurements and analyze (over time) the impact on customer satisfaction of various investments the library makes to improve service levels. The key metrics are ideally available on a steady, ongoing basis (i.e., continuous customer satisfaction feedback); otherwise it is too difficult to measure the impact and outcomes of specific changes in service levels. In the following example (representing an actual LibSAT subscriber), the library is provided with a dashboard interface that enables it to monitor key metrics against set targets for improvement. The library can drill-down to service location rankings (not shown) and trends for all or selected locations (shown). From here it can also drill down to associated open-ended feedback for any time period by selecting the associated point on the chart. Using set targets, monitoring trend lines/variances and accessing constructive and relevant feedback can simplify the process of monitoring of key metrics with a focus on continuous improvement. Often this type of ongoing focus on key metrics is simply not available using traditional approaches.

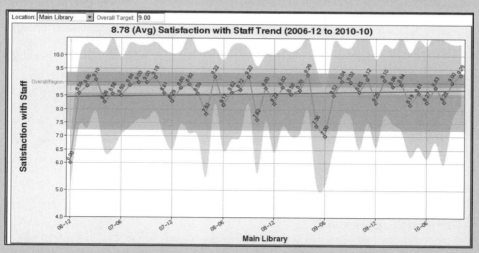

It also merits mention that Counting Opinions, in cooperation with the Association of Research Libraries (ACRL), makes available Academic Library Survey data that the U.S. Census Bureau (http://www.census.gov/econ/overview/go1700.html) collects for the National Center for Education Statistics (NCES). The dataset in this fee-based service dates from 2000, and it enables libraries to produce trend data (see http://www.acrlmetrics.com).

*Carl Thompson, President, Counting Opinions, Toronto, Canada.

RETURNING TO THE LIBRARY OF THE FUTURE

Chapter 1 presents two possible scenarios for the future, one for an academic and the other for a public library. Such scenarios contain elements or threads that libraries can use as they piece together a story relevant to local circumstances, linked to strategic planning and change management. The goal is to produce a story that the organization can use to examine surprises and discontinuities in the planning process and to obtain staff buy-in to the vision that the senior management team projects to the staff and the community. One such surprise might be that, during the aftermath of the economic recession, the local board of supervisors, such as the one in San Joaquin County, California, might consider privatization of the management and services of the public library.[18] Any private company would likely seek profits and curtail the number of services provided, the number in the workforce, and the commitment to the provision of outstanding customer service, preferring "good-enough" service.

In order to survive and thrive in the future, libraries must be able to adapt to and evolve with their customers' changing expectations. This means that for any future scenario that a library explores, there must be consideration of customer expectations and how to best meet them. In other words, any viable scenario must cover services that will meet changing customer expectations and information-seeking behavior. Those services need to build on the existing strengths of libraries, namely their emphasis on

- "Access: virtual and physical access to services, wherever the customer may be";

- "Support: the information and support customers need to achieve their objectives";

- "People-focus: working out with customers what they need and then providing it";

- "Personalized service: the services they require, whatever their needs";

- "Responsive service: always listening to the users"; and

- "Dynamic service: flexible, adaptable."[19]

The focus of each bulleted item could easily be expanded and connected to service quality and customer satisfaction.

An Alternative Approach

Since 2000, city funding for the Milwaukee Public Library, "adjusted for inflation, has fallen more than 20%. During this time, fuel and energy costs and health care costs have increased, and demand for computers and electronic resources has increased." In addition, "the City has seen a substantial decrease in state shared revenue." To address these gaps, the library has

- improved efficiencies,

- reduced energy consumption,

- reduced the materials budget,

- reduced service hours, and

- reduced staff through layoff and attrition.

Seeking a remedy to these problems, the management of the library is taking a different approach. Instead of envisioning a future scenario, the managers have taken a more limited, immediate approach. They are involving the community in a discussion of the future of the library and "different ways to provide the best library service and products to the residents of Milwaukee, while identifying efficiencies of service." In a series set of Web pages, the staff lay out how the library has changed since it first opened in the nineteenth century. They identify the current services as

- reference services offered (in-house, by phone, via e-mail, and 24/7 live chat);

- Books2Go outreach to childcare providers/Ready to Read pre-reading skills;

- computer training classes;

- job/résumé help; and

- automated checkout/self-checkout.

Noting that the library must make choices, such as "maintaining the current system of Central and neighborhood libraries will require a reduction in services and hours," the page announces that the "administration and the Library Board of Trustees have explored new long-term options that are affordable and sustainable" and offers four options that are "less expensive" but still enable the library to provide "excellent library service." These options, for which they list the savings, will "transform the neighborhood library system into one the taxpayers can afford." Furthermore, "all of these options assume the continued operation of the Central Library as well as the Center Street Library, which is currently funded by Community Development Block Grants," and, for each option, there is a comparison to the present situation. Table 10.1 (p. 168) reprints one of the options, and table 10.2 (p. 169) projects the cost savings for all the options.

The final Web page invites the community to revisit the set of Web pages for any updates, to send e-mail comments, and to attend a community forum where these options will be presented. The conclusion is a quote from Winston Churchill: "There is nothing wrong with change, if it is in the right direction."[20]

Table 10.1. Option One (Milwaukee Public Library)*

Estimated Annual Savings of $600,000

4 Neighborhood Libraries

7 Mixed Use/Co-location Libraries

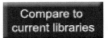

Neighborhood Library	Mixed Use Villard Avenue example

Square Footage:
   12,000–20,000 sq. ft.
	Square Footage:
	   8,000–12,000 sq. ft.

Collection:
   60,000–80,000 items
	Collection:
	   40,000–50,000 items

Computers:
   20–40
	Computers:
	   20–25

Features:
   Open 45–54 hours/week
   Comfortable reading/seating areas
   Community Room
   Child & Teen areas
   Reference staff
   Self-service Checkout
	Features:
	   Open 45 hours/week
	   Comfortable reading/seating area
	   Community & Study Rooms
	   Child & Teen areas
	   Reference staff
	   Self-service Checkout

Benefits:
   Remains similar to current model.
	Benefits:
	   Access to technology, popular collections, reduced operating costs.

Drawback:
   Neighborhood libraries that are removed from service will need to be repurposed.
	Drawback:
	   Smaller locations will have fewer services and smaller collections

*Source: Milwaukee Public Library, "Rethinking Libraries in the 21st Century," n.d., accessed July 25, 2010, http://www.mpl.org/file/community_p6.htm.

Table 10.2. Long-Term Savings for the Four Options (Milwaukee Public Library)*

	5 Years 2015	**20 Years 2030**	**30 Years 2040**	**36 Years 2046**
Option 1	$2,260,199	$10,866,866	$18,176,741	$22,677,331
Option 2	$667,672	$1,653,879	$8,214,953	$12,380,926
Option 3	$2,686,602	$11,917,178	$24,429,193	$32,165,732
Option 4	$643,210	$1,423,045	$4,124,801	$5,860,520

(Estimated Savings over Current System, by Option**)

* Source: Milwaukee Public Library, "Rethinking Libraries in the 21st Century," n.d., accessed July 25, 2010, http://www.mpl.org/file/community_p8.htm.

**Includes operating expenses and capital debt service.

THE WORKFORCE OF THE FUTURE

Any vision of the future requires a consideration of the staffing necessary to make that scenario into a reality. Succession planning, which is more than replacement planning, ensures the identification, development, and long-term retention of talented individuals at the upper level of management. It also looks at all professional positions in the organization and the type of talent and expertise that will be needed. Those engaged in succession planning analyze the job market and their competitors, try to anticipate possible retirements within the library for the next five years, examine long-term organizational needs, and set budget priorities. Positions vacated by retirement or departures might be restructured to reflect better the current and future needs of the organization.

A number of libraries whose institutions have ARL membership need a wider level of knowledge, abilities, and skills than graduates of programs of library and information science (LIS) possess. They want a workforce with better knowledge, for instance, of information technologies, marketing, teaching and learning pedagogy, development, and entrepreneurship. As other types of libraries seek different knowledge and abilities, they will also move away from a workforce comprised solely of individuals from master's programs in LIS. Projected over time, that master's degree may well become even less important. In fact, both of the authors of this book envision a time when a workforce with other degrees and knowledge may dominate.

The workforce must understand and be skilled with evaluation and assessment research (problem solving) and critical thinking; have good communication skills and good people skills; show a willingness to work within the larger institutional environment; make a commitment to high-quality customer service; and be flexible, able to be partners with faculty and the community in meeting the library's mission, and able to embrace change. The workforce should also contain managers and leaders able to manage institutional knowledge and datasets and to carry through on the organizational vision.

CONCLUDING THOUGHTS

As Matthews writes:

> Service is a key part of the customer experience. The service experienced by a customer is not a one-time event, but rather a journey that consists of numerous touchpoints between the customer and the organization. These touchpoints must be carefully designed and managed; each touchpoint has a potential for innovation. . . . A great library experience must incorporate the totality of the organization. Do everything right but get one touchpoint wrong, and you've eliminated the possibility for delivering a great experience.[21]

Although design is most frequently associated with a business and its product, it can also refer to understanding how customers interact with the library's infrastructure (staff, facilities, collections, and technology) and using the insights gained to improve the customer experience. The Hillman Library, University of Pittsburgh, was innovative in its infrastructure design. Rather than relying on signage that often explained locations using library jargon, the dean of libraries hired a consulting company to interact with library customers and recommend a means of visual communication about floor layout and services offered. As a result, the walls were colorfully painted and huge letterforms were added throughout the building. In addition, user-friendly floor maps and directories convey location.[22]

Customer-driven (or customer-focused) organizations focus on customers and their information needs, information-seeking behavior, and expectations. Historically, it has been common for libraries to adapt a library-centric perspective and fail sufficiently to consider the customer as the heart of the service organization, and thus for problems to arise when the staff do not recognize and act on customer needs and expectations. This book offers strategies for recognizing customer expectations and using the data generated to improve the delivery of services. The goal is to retain delighted customers, while reaching out to new customers and regaining lost ones. To do so, library staff need to understand the level of customer service they are delivering and to ascertain if their own standards for good customer service are considerably lower than what their customers expect.

A wonderful definition of a library catalog is a place where bibliographic records get lost alphabetically. A parallel definition for a library's physical collection is a place where items get lost on the shelves in call number order. The challenge for a library is to listen to its customers, especially at those points where the customer gets lost, and then to experiment to find ways to make the customer's experience truly wonderful. It is important to utilize a great many methods to gather voice-of-the-customer conversations so that the library receives and understands the message. One of the challenges to overcome, as noted by Andrew Booth, is that by participating in a focus group interview, making a complaint, or engaging in some other type of interaction, the customer ceases to be a *typical anonymous user*. As such, it is incumbent on the library to receive a broad cross-section of comments in order to prevent potential biases from impacting future decisions.[23]

Keeping the Antennae Up:
How Listening Improves Service*

Much of my undergraduate studies is long forgotten. Fortunately, what I do recall tends to be among the most valuable content to which I was exposed. One of those bits of memorable wisdom was learned in an unlikely course, an introduction to poetry. Though I lacked genuine talent for poetry writing, the value of the course was that it taught the importance of drilling down beyond the surface of the words. One cannot overestimate the importance of learning to read in a way to understand the author's message. My instructor said something that I still remember: "The poet is the antennae of society." He actually told us to visualize the poet with stalks protruding from that person's head, capturing all manner of information from the world around. Then the poet would write in a way that inspires others to explore life through poetry. Poets needed to be astute observers of the world around them.

Librarians must not underestimate the power of listening. To excel at it, they must always have their antennae up, picking up the signals user community members emit all around us. Doing so allows them to gain sensitivity to user needs and expectations. Simply put, listening leads to a better library experience. Although the act of listening sounds simple, doing it effectively in a way that leads to positive change is anything but. The major challenge is that in day-to-day work we become so involved in our routines that we become oblivious to much of the nonroutine activity happening all around us. Those things that are problematic to library users and that prevent them from having the best possible library experience are what library workers are likely to miss. In order to become good listeners, library staff must make a conscious effort to become more attuned to the sounds and sights around them. When the antennae are up, it can make all the difference.

Two Old Standbys

Librarians tend to fall into ruts when it comes to finding out what user community members think about library services. Two of our favorite old standbys are user surveys and focus group interviews. The former is an indirect form of listening, while the latter is all about listening. At Temple University we use both techniques and view them as connected. Academic librarians are accustomed to conducting all types of surveys, from quick-and-dirty Web site polls to ones that are more elaborate. All of these efforts provide good insights and generate questions such as these:

- Why did they say the Web site confuses them?

- How come so few respondents know we already are open past midnight?

- Does what we hear tell us there is a communication gap?

To enhance our ability to conduct surveys, both simple and complex, we recently became a subscriber to Counting Opinion's LibSAT software. One of the challenges of satisfaction surveys is developing the questionnaire and collecting the data. LibSAT reduces the amount of time required to create a survey and provides more options for inviting community members to participate. It will also enable a new type of survey, the post-service survey. Think about a recent hotel stay or a retail purchase. A few days later a request to complete a survey arrives in your inbox. This type of survey, sent to a targeted user right after a reference or an interlibrary loan transaction, provides direct feedback about an actual service interaction. In conjunction with annual "how are we doing" satisfaction surveys, this will amplify our ability to listen to what community members want to tell us about our services and resources. Surveys are good starting points. They help us refine our interests so that instead of trying to listen to all the buzz and noise, which ultimately overwhelms us, we can point ourselves in the proper direction.

Equipped with this sense of where we need to direct our energy, it is a logical step to learn more through focus group interviews. In the past, like many libraries, we used focus group interviews to understand better the less than satisfactory ratings showing up on satisfaction surveys. More recently, we enlisted a team from our institution's Leadership Academy, an internal professional development institute, to conduct focus group interviews with students and faculty, both library users and nonusers, to provide insights for the early stages of a building planning process. Though we want to listen to users, in this instance we opted to designate the actual listening to a nonlibrary focus group team. Concerned that having librarians present in the focus group might bias responses, we thought it best to do the listening secondhand. With tapes, transcripts, and reports, it is almost the same as being there. Focus group interviews are not without their problems. As Gerry McGovern, Web usability expert, stated in a column about focus groups, "The biggest problem: what users say in a focus group interview rarely matches what they do in a real-life setting. Users' opinions about a site or product are rarely consistent with how they behave when they actually interact with it" (see http://www.gerrymcgovern.com/nt/2010/nt-2010-11-01-Focus-groups.htm). Although listening is important, what is said in focus group interviews should be viewed with a touch of skepticism.

That is one reason for the growing popularity of anthropological techniques. Well known as an instrument used by corporations to understand better how consumers use their products, field studies add observation to listening. Consider the following example from the corporate world. A company that made body wash products asked its customers what they like and dislike about the product. No men ever mentioned in the focus group interviews what was learned by observing them as they used the products. Many men shampooed their hair with the body wash, a good example of consumers using a product in ways it was never intended. The result was all-in-one body wash/shampoo products targeted to men, which are quite successful. Had the company stopped with focus group interviews, they might have lost out on a great opportunity. That is an important lesson for librarians. We need to pay attention to what we hear, but also to what we see.

Take the focus group report mentioned above. Many participants indicated they wanted the library to be open 24/7. If librarians listened only to focus group participants, perhaps every library would be open 24/7, but, from actual observation, we know that as it nears the midnight hour the library grows deserted. This is a classic example of people asking for things in focus group interviews that they would rarely, if ever, truly use. That is why more limited, self-access 24/7 spaces have grown in popularity in academic libraries. It is a cost-effective, lower-risk solution to the challenge of listening to the few whose needs hardly represent the average college student. If Temple were to build a new library facility, members of the library would listen carefully to the community members, but chances are we would base some decisions on observations of user behavior.

Other Formal Listening Devices

In addition to the survey and focus group interviews, librarians can organize more formalized sounding boards in the effort to seek out advice, ideas, and feedback related to decisions and planning. The most common approach is to organize committees that allow for representation from community members. At Temple we have several different types of advisory groups. In addition to those groups organized at the administrative level, many subject specialists tap into their own networks in their assigned disciplines so that they too serve as remote listening outposts. Our two primary advisory groups are the Faculty Senate Library Committee and the Student Library Advisory Board. Each group meets two or three times per semester. The meetings are mostly for bidirectional information sharing, but also to create positive connections between the library and its constituents. Although there are some common topics at each meeting, such as a report on the library facility, the two groups focus on the issues of concern to the groups they represent.

The faculty are most concerned about collections and services that support teaching and research. The students want to know what we are doing to make the library better for their fellow students. For both groups we offer a glimpse at pieces of the budget; they all want to know if the administration is treating us decently. The danger of these groups is that the tendency exists for them to become more about us and less about them. Rather than tell them what we are doing, we need to know how they use what we have and what they would like to see. That means getting them to do the talking while we listen, and we are usually able to come up with good questions to get them going. As much as the groups are a sounding board for our ideas, we need to learn from them. They are the voice of the community. They allow us to extend our antennae into that community.

Informal Techniques

With the formal methods described above, there are limitations on the effectiveness of listening. Today, technology allows us to extend our ability to listen into cyberspace. To listen to our community members in that space, librarians leverage technology to establish new outposts for tapping the virtual conversation. Take a simple example, the library Web site. Libraries always offered suggestion boxes conveniently located by the entrance or circulation desk. Some still do, but many more now have a virtual equivalent, the suggestions blog, on their Web sites. We call ours "What's Your Suggestion," and it allows any community member to let us know what is on his or her mind, be it a complaint or an idea for improvement. Either way, we take it seriously and pay attention to what we are hearing through the messages received. Sometimes we can take action with a positive response, such as when we were asked to provide more single student study carrels in quiet zones. At other times we cannot, such as when we are asked to provide more electrical outlets, but even then we are able to post an explanation of why we may not be able to satisfy the request. The suggestion blog then becomes an ongoing record of all the requests and explanations, along with comments from students. Above all, it shows the community that we are listening.

Social media (e.g., Facebook and Twitter) also offer ways to communicate with community members. Though they provide a good channel for announcing updates and events, they are perhaps even better as listening posts. By monitoring the tweets and status updates, the library staff and administration can stay alert to any complaints, problems, or other issues of which they might not otherwise hear. We have all heard stories about corporations using social media to monitor consumer reactions to their products and services—and responding quickly when problems arise. We can do the same thing. It is fairly easy to set up alerts on search engines and with other Web tools that allow the social media to be monitored 24/7. In 2008, we introduced some new furniture. When we had it available on display for review and community comment, there was none, so we went ahead and bought some of it. To our surprise, a student made a video complaining about the new furniture and then posted it on YouTube. Rather than get upset, we took it as an opportunity to make some minor corrections that would improve the furniture and respond to the complaints. Now everyone likes the furniture.

That is why listening to the community is so important. We are professional librarians. We are experts at acquiring, storing, organizing, and retrieving information. We are not experts on design, customer relations management, or many of the other elements that add up to a great library experience for the community member. It is often the case that they know what is best. If we fail to listen and pick up these signals, we also fail at delivering the great library experience that builds loyal community members, keeps them coming back, and, most important of all, encourages them to tell their friends to use the library. Following social media to detect what is being said about the library is proving to be a powerful way to listen and quickly respond to demonstrate that the library does care.

Carpet Time

New technology tools and social media can improve the ability of librarians to listen, but there is still much to be said for good old fashioned low-tech listening. Good listening approaches that involve no technology could fit into the category that Nicholas Webb, author of *The Innovation Playbook*, refers to as "carpet time." It is a simple concept that emphasizes the importance of spending quality time with the people who use your services and products. Webb says that to "understand what customers really care about—or what could be going wrong in the course of delivering meaningful value—you have to spend carpet time . . . to see them, feel them and experience them." If you are a library administrator, you cannot experience members of the community from your corner office; you need to walk the floor or get out for face time with your constituents. Here is an example.

In our LibQUAL+® surveys we consistently get low ratings from faculty on information content. To learn more, I started visiting department chairs, along with the subject specialist for that discipline. We are occasionally joined by the departmental liaison to the library and possibly a graduate student. When I engage them in conversation about our collection, I rarely hear anything but praise for the quality of the collection in that discipline. If anything, I might hear some requests for specific journals or electronic resources. It may be that when being surveyed anonymously, faculty are much more critical, or it may be that when we take the time to ask questions and listen we get a completely different perspective. I am not sure what accounts for this inconsistency, but in the end, regardless of the strength of the collection in a discipline, by demonstrating our willingness to engage in dialogue and listen we are improving our ability to serve our faculty. It is much better to hear about problems directly from the faculty than to be surprised when the LibQual+® report turns up. (I will be interested to see if our carpet time has an impact on faculty responses when we do our next LibQUAL+® survey in 2012.)

Carpet time works just as well in the library as it does beyond the walls of the building. We were thinking about creating some flexible study spaces using freestanding wall dividers. Our building has too few formal study rooms. I had one space in mind in our computer commons where there were no electrical outlets, which usually ended up as the place where students lounged and ate meals. This was sometimes a problem as there was more noise and mess than we would like. I thought we could turn it into more productive space. There was, however, some concern that students would prefer the space as is. So what did I do? Conduct a survey? Run focus group interviews? Neither. I simply spent some time on the carpet, literally, talking to students and asking them what they thought of the idea. I also observed the extent to which students were already forming study groups in the computer commons. I asked those groups what they thought of the flexible study space idea. Nearly every student I spoke with thought having a flexible space was the best of both worlds, study space when needed and lounge space when it was not. That encouraged my administration to make a modest investment in adding electrical outlets, a wall-mounted flat-panel monitor, and two collapsible wall dividers. Now the space can easily and quickly become an enclosed, private study area when needed that has all the features of traditional study rooms. Surveys and focus group interviews may have worked equally well, but carpet time was faster, simpler, and more direct. By listening and observing, we were able to make a good decision that will improve the library experience for students.

Keep the Antennae Up

The best thing about listening to the user community is that it is something any library worker can do. No special training is needed. There are no listening workshops. The more staff members we can enlist to think of themselves as individual listening posts, the better positioned the library is to both discover what is broken and quickly fix it and detect ideas for new services. When an undergraduate walks up to the reference desk and asks the librarian on duty why it is not possible to send a text message from the library catalog, the antennae should start buzzing and the ideas should start flowing. If we do a good job of picking up the signals, there is no end to the ways in which we can enhance the library experience for our community members. What we need to do, as staff, is engage in a conversation about the importance of listening and observing what happens all around us every day, rather than just going through the motions and being oblivious to the experiences that community members are having as they work, study, relax, socialize, game, or whatever it is that motivated them to come to the library. It all starts with getting those antennae up.

* Steven J. Bell, Associate University Librarian, Temple University Libraries.

In summary, we propose that libraries consider the following actions as a voice-of-the-customer checklist:

- The director and top management of the library provide enthusiastic support and make an ongoing commitment to listening to customers and acting on what they learn.

- The library is obsessive about really listening to all its customers and learning more about their information needs and expectations.

- The library builds a definite profile of each customer segment.

- The library uses that profile to design customer-focused services.

- The library gathers all of its voice-of-the-customer data into a single repository.

- A staff member is responsible for ongoing analysis and presentation of the voice-of- the-customer data.

- The library only hires staff who are *people persons* and take delight in serving customers.

- The library provides staff with training to improve their customer-listening skills.

- The library is committed to being the most customer-focused library possible.

> *Most companies tell their customers they come first[,] but in reality their policies put the company first.*[24]

NOTES

1. "American Express Rolls out Customer Service Barometer," *The Washington Post,* July 13, 2010, n.p. Available from *General BusinessFile ASAP.*

2. Mary M. LoSardo and Norma M. Rossi, *At the Service Quality Frontier* (Milwaukee, WI: ASQ Quality Press, 1993).

3. Peter Hernon and Ellen Altman, *Assessing Service Quality: Satisfying the Expectations of Library Customers*, 2nd ed. (Chicago: American Library Association, 2010), 5.

4. Peter Hernon and Ellen Altman, *Assessing Service Quality: Satisfying the Expectations of Library Customers* (Chicago: American Library Association, 1998), 39–42. See also Peter Hernon and Ellen Altman, *Service Quality in Academic Libraries* (Norwood, NJ: Ablex, 1996), 59–60; Peter Hernon and John R. Whitman, *Delivering Satisfaction and Service Quality: A Customer-Based Approach for Libraries* (Chicago: American Library Association, 2001), 72–73.

5. Alison J. Head and Michael B. Eisenberg, *Lessons Learned: How College Students Seek Information in the Digital Age* (Seattle: University of Washington, The Information School, 2009), accessed July 23, 2010, http://projectinfolit.org/pdfs/PIL_Fall2009_Year1Report_12_2009.pdf.

6. Carol Tenopir, *Use and Users of Electronic Library Resources: An Overview and Analysis of Recent Research Studies* (Washington, DC: Council of Library and Information Resources, 2003), accessed July 24, 2010, http://www.clir.org/pubs/reports/pub120/contents.html.

7. Joseph R. Matthews, *The Customer-Focused Library: Re-Inventing the Public Library from the Outside-In* (Santa Barbara, CA: Libraries Unlimited, 2009), 55.

8. Ibid., 56.

9. Hernon and Altman, *Assessing Service Quality*, 2nd ed., 125.

10. Tamar Lewin, "Once in First Place, Americans Now Lag in Attaining College Degrees," *The New York Times,* July 23, 2010, A10.

11. Joseph R. Matthews, *Scorecard for Results: A Guide for Developing a Library Balanced Scorecard* (Westport, CT: Libraries Unlimited, 2008).

12. University of Virginia Library, "Overview about the Balanced Scorecard" (Charlottesville, VA: University of Virginia Library, n.d.), accessed July 25, 2010, http://www2.lib.virginia.edu/bsc/overview.html.

13. University of Virginia Library, "Balanced Scorecard 2007–09: Balanced Scorecard Metrics" (Charlottesville, VA: University of Virginia Library, n.d.), accessed July 25, 2010, http://www2.lib.virginia.edu/bsc/metrics/all0708.html#user.

14. Orange County Library System, "Performance Scorecard for Annual 2008/2009" (Orlando, FL: Orange County Library System, n.d.), accessed July 25, 2010, http://www.ocls.org/about/balancedscorecard/default.asp.

15. Bill Price and David Jaffe, *The Best Service Is No Service: How to Liberate Your Customers from Customer Service, Keep Them Happy, and Control Costs* (San Francisco: Jossey-Bass, 2008), 253–54.

16. Robert E. Dugan, Peter Hernon, and Danuta A. Nitecki, *Viewing Library Metrics from Different Perspectives* (Santa Barbara, CA: Libraries Unlimited, 2009), 99–116, 279–82.

17. Price and Jaffe, *The Best Service Is No Service*, 257.

18. Beverly Goldberg, "California Groups Oppose Library Privatization Talks," *American Libraries* (July 14, 2010), accessed July 25, 2010, http://www.americanlibrariesmagazine.org/news/07142010/california-groups-oppose-library-privatization-talks.

19. Laser Foundation, "Libraries: A Vision (The Public Library Service in 2015)," n.d., 5, accessed July 25, 2010, http://www.ohionet.org/pdf/vision2015.pdf.

20. Milwaukee Public Library, "Rethinking Libraries in the 21st Century," n.d., accessed July 25, 2010, http://www.mpl.org/file/community_index.htm; http://www.mpl.org/file/community_p9.htm.

21. Matthews, *Customer-Focused Library*, 83.

22. See University of Pittsburgh, University Library System, "Wayfinding at a Glimpse," n.d., accessed July 25, 2010, http://www.landesbergdesign.com/work/signage/hillman/hillman.shtml.

23. Andrew Booth, "In Search of the Mythical 'Typical Library User'," *Health Information and Libraries Journal* 25, no. 3 (September 2008): 233–36.

24. Ian Brooks, "Who Do Your Policies Serve? Are Your Customer Service Policies Putting the Company's Needs Ahead of the Customer's? Dr. Ian Brooks Explains How That Costs You Dearly in Lost Business," *NZ Business* 24, no. 5 (June 2010): 56. Available from *General BusinessFile ASAP*.

Bibliography

ARTICLES

Beers, G. K. "No Time, No Interest, No Way!" *School Library Journal* 42 (1996): 110–14.

Booth, Andrew. "In Search of the Mythical 'Typical Library User'." *Health Information and Libraries Journal* 25, no. 3 (September 2008): 233–36.

Blowers, Helene. "Public Library of Charlotte & Mecklenburg County." *LibraryJournal.com* (March 15, 2007). Accessed August 13, 2010. http://www.libraryjournal.com/article/CA6423431.html.

Butler, Lawrence M. "Warning Lights." *The New England Journal of Higher Education* 21, no. 5 (Spring 2007): 31–33.

Chang, Pao-Long, and Pao-Nuan Hsieh. "Customer Involvement with Services in Public Libraries." *Asian Libraries* 9, nos. 3/4 (1997): 242–49.

Czopek, Vanessa. "Using Mystery Shoppers to Evaluate Customer Service in the Public Library." *Public Libraries* 37, no. 6 (November/December 1998): 370–71.

Decker, Reinhold, and Antonia Hermelbracht. "Planning and Evaluation of New Academic Library Services by Means of Web-based Conjoint Analysis." *The Journal of Academic Librarianship* 32, no. 6 (November 2006): 558–72.

DiNucci, Darcy. "Fragmented Future." *Print* 53, no. 4 (1999): 32.

Dixon, Matthew, Karen Freeman, and Nicholas Toman. "Stop Trying to Delight Your Customers." *Harvard Business Review* 78, nos. 7/8 (July-August 2010): 116–22.

Futterman, Marc. "Finding the Underserved." *Library Journal* 133, no. 17 (October 15, 2008): 42–45.

Gabridge, Tracy, Millicent Gaskell, and Amy Stout. "Information Seeking through Students' Eyes: The MIT Photo Diary Study." *College & Research Libraries* 69, no. 5 (November 2008): 510–23.

Garibay, Cecilia, Humberto Gutiérrez, and Artuor Figueroa. "Evaluation of a Digital Library by Means of Quality Function Deployment (QFD) and the Kano Model." *The Journal of Academic Librarianship* 36, no. 2 (March 2010): 125–32.

Given, Lisa M., and Gloria J. Leckie. "'Sweeping' the Library: Mapping the Social Activity Space of the Public Library." *Library & Information Science Research* 25, no. 4 (2003): 365–85.

Hernon, Peter, and Philip Calvert. "E-service Quality in Libraries: Exploring Its Features and Dimensions." *Library & Information Science Research* 27, no. 4 (2005): 377–404.

Horan, Mark. "What Students See: Sketch Maps as Tools for Assessing Knowledge of Libraries." *The Journal of Academic Librarianship* 25, no. 3 (May 1999): 187–201.

Keng, Kau Ah, Kwon Jung, and Jochen Wirtz. "Segmentation of Library Visitors in Singapore: Learning and Reading Related Lifestyles." *Library Management* 24, nos. 1/2 (2003): 20–33.

Knorr, Eric. "Fast Forward 2010–The Fate of It." *CIO* (May 15, 2004): 14–19.

Lakos, Amos. "The Missing Ingredient—Culture of Assessment in Libraries." *Performance Measurement and Metrics* (August 1999): 3–7.

Leckie, Gloria J. "Three Perspectives on the Library as Public Space." *Feliciter* (In special issue devoted to "Library Space, Planning, and Architecture") 50, no. 6 (2004): 233–36.

Leckie, Gloria J., and Jeffrey Hopkins. "The Public Place of Central Libraries: Findings from Toronto and Vancouver." *Library Quarterly* 72, no. 3 (July 2002): 326–72.

Lewin, Tamar. "Once in First Place, Americans Now Lag in Attaining College Degrees." *The New York Times* (July 23, 2010): A10, A12.

Lim, Adriene. "The Readability of Information Literacy Content on Academic Library Web Sites." *The Journal of Academic Librarianship* 36, no. 4 (July 2010): 296–303.

Lubans, John, Jr. "Where Are the Snows of Yesteryear? Reflections on a Suggestion 'Box' That Worked." *Library Administration & Management* 15, no. 4 (Fall 2001): 240–45.

Matthews, Joseph R. "Customer Satisfaction: A New Perspective." *Public Libraries* 47, no. 6 (November/December 2006): 52–55.

Miniace, Joseph N., and Elizabeth Falter. "Communication: A Key Factor in Strategy Implementation." *Planning Review* 24, no. 1 (1993): 26–30.

Neal, James G. "Raised By Wolves: The New Generation of Feral Professionals in the Academic Library." *Library Journal* 131, no. 3 (February 15, 2006): 42–44.

Parasuraman, A., Valarie A. Zeithmal, and Leonard L. Berry. "A Conceptual Model of Service Quality and Its Implications for Future Research." *Journal of Marketing* 49, no. 4 (Fall 1985): 41–50.

Sines, Robert G., and Eric A. Duckworth. "Customer Service in Higher Education." *Journal of Marketing for Higher Education* 5, no. 2 (1994): 1–16.

Smyth, Jolene D., Don A. Dillman, Leah Melani Christian, and Michael J. Stern. "Comparing Check-All and Forced-Choice Question Formats in Web Surveys." *Public Opinion Quarterly* 70, no. 1 (2006): 66–77.

Snyder, Steven J. "The Customer-Service Express Lane." *Time* 176, no. 4 (July 26, 2010): 56.

Sone, Akio. "An Application of Discrete Choice Analysis to the Modeling of Public Library Use and Choice Behavior." *Library & Information Science Research* 10, no. 1 (January–March 1988): 35–55.

Von Hippel, Eric. "Lead Users: A Source of Novel Product Concepts." *Management Science* 32, no. 7 (1986): 791–805.

BOOKS

Anderson, Bjorn, and Tom Fagerhaug. *Root Cause Analysis: Simplified Tools and Techniques*. Milwaukee, WI: ASQ Quality Press, 2006.

Anton, Jon, and Debra Perkins. *Listening to the Voice of the Customer*. New York: Alexander Communications Group, 1997.

Barlow, Janelle, and Claus Møller. *A Complaint Is a Gift: Recovering Customer Loyalty When Things Go Wrong*. San Francisco: Berett-Koehler Publishers, 2008.

Bennis, Warren, and Patricia W. Biederman. *Still Surprised: A Memoir of a Life in Leadership*. San Francisco: Jossey-Bass, 2010.

Berger, Warren. *Glimmer: How Design Can Transform Your Life and Maybe Even the World*. New York: Penguin Press, 2009.

Blackshaw, Pete. *Satisfied Customers Tell Three Friends, Angry Customers Tell 3,000*. New York: Doubleday, 2008.

Butler, Pierce. *An Introduction to Library Science*. Chicago: University of Chicago Press, 1933.

Carlzon, Jan. *The Moments of Truth*. New York: Harper, 1989.

Cherry, Colin. *On Human Communications: A Survey and a Criticism.* Rev. ed. Cambridge, MA: MIT Press, 1980.

Christensen, Clayton M. *The Innovator's Dilemma: When New Technologies Cause Great Firms to Fail.* Cambridge, MA: Harvard Business School Press, 1997.

Dugan, Robert E., Peter Hernon, and Danuta A. Nitecki. *Viewing Library Metrics from Different Perspectives.* Santa Barbara, CA: Libraries Unlimited, 2009.

Foster, Nancy F., and Susan Gibbons. *Studying Students: The Undergraduate Research Project at the University of Rochester.* Chicago: American Library Association, 2007.

Griffin, Jill. *Taming the Search-and-Switch Customer: Earning Customer Loyalty in a Compulsion-to-Compare World.* San Francisco: Jossey-Bass, 2009.

Grönfeldt, Svafa, and Judith Strother. *Service Leadership: The Quest for Competitive Advantage.* Thousand Oaks, CA: Sage, 2006.

Hackman, J. Richard. *Leading Teams: Setting the Stage for Great Performances.* Boston: Harvard Business School Press, 2002.

Hayes, Tom, and Michael S. Malone. *No Size Fits All: From Mass Marketing to Mass Handselling.* London: Penguin Group, 2009.

Hernon, Peter, ed. *Shaping the Future: Advancing the Understanding of Leadership.* Santa Barbara, CA: Libraries Unlimited, 2010.

Hernon, Peter, and Ellen Altman. *Assessing Service Quality: Satisfying the Expectations of Library Customers.* Chicago: American Library Association, 1998.

Hernon, Peter, and Ellen Altman. *Assessing Service Quality: Satisfying the Expectations of Library Customers.* 2nd ed. Chicago: American Library Association, 2010.

Hernon, Peter, and Ellen Altman. *Service Quality in Academic Libraries.* Norwood, NJ: Ablex, 1996.

Hernon, Peter, Joan Giesecke, and Camila A. Alire. *Academic Librarians as Emotionally Intelligent Leaders.* Westport, CT: Libraries Unlimited, 2007.

Hernon, Peter, and John R. Whitman. *Delivering Satisfaction and Service Quality: A Customer-Based Approach for Libraries.* Chicago: American Library Association, 2001.

Hernon, Peter, and Ronald R. Powell, eds. *Convergence and Collaboration of Campus Information Services.* Westport, CT: Libraries Unlimited, 2008.

Hernon, Peter, Robert E. Dugan, and Danuta A. Nitecki. *Engaging in Evaluation and Assessment Research.* Santa Barbara, CA: Libraries Unlimited, 2011.

Inghilleri, Leonardo, and Micah Solomon. *Exceptional Service, Exceptional Profit: The Secrets of Building a Five-Star Customer Service Organization.* New York: American Management Association, 2010.

Jaeger, Richard M. *Statistics: A Spectator Sport*. Beverly Hills, CA: Sage, 1983.

LoSardo, Mary M., and Norma M. Rossi. *At the Service Quality Frontier*. Milwaukee, WI: ASQ Quality Press, 1993.

Matthews, Joseph R. *The Customer-Focused Library: Re-inventing the Public Library from the Outside-In*. Santa Barbara, CA: Libraries Unlimited, 2009.

Matthews, Joseph R. *The Evaluation and Measurement of Library Services*. Westport, CT: Libraries Unlimited, 2007.

Matthews, Joseph R. *Scorecard for Results: A Guide for Developing a Library Balanced Scorecard*. Westport, CT: Libraries Unlimited, 2008.

Matthews, Joseph R. *Strategic Planning and Management for Library Managers*. Westport, CT: Libraries Unlimited, 2005.

Miller, Delbert C. *Handbook of Research Design and Social Measurement*. Newbury Park, CA: Sage, 1991.

Northouse, Peter G. *Leadership: Theory and Practice*. 5th ed. Thousand Oaks, CA: Sage, 2009.

Peters, Tom. *Thriving on Chaos*. New York: Pan Books, 1989.

Price, Bill, and David Jaffe. *The Best Service Is No Service: How to Liberate Your Customers from Customer Service, Keep Them Happy, and Control Costs*. San Francisco: Jossey-Bass, 2008.

Quenqua, Douglas. *Starbucks' Own Good Idea*. Chicago: American Marketing Association, 2009.

Underhill, Paco. *Why People Buy: The Science of Shopping*. New York: Simon & Schuster, 2000.

Vavra, Terry G. *Improving Your Measurement of Customer Satisfaction: A Guide to Creating, Conducting, Analyzing, and Reporting Customer Satisfaction Measurement Programs*. Milwaukee, WI: ASQ Quality Press, 1997.

Wood, Elizabeth J., Rush Miller, and Amy Knapp. *Beyond Survival: Managing Academic Libraries in Transition*. Westport, CT: Libraries Unlimited, 2007.

Wurman, Richard S. *Information Anxiety 2*. Indianapolis, IN: Que, 2001.

BOOK CHAPTERS

Aabo, Svanhild. "Valuation of Public Libraries." In *New Frontiers in Public Library Research*, edited by Carl Johannsen and Leif Kajbrg. Lanham, MD: Scarecrow Press, 2005.

Martin, Elaine. "Team Effectiveness and Members as Leaders." In *Making a Difference: Leadership and Academic Libraries*, edited by Peter Hernon and Nancy Rossiter. Westport, CT: Libraries Unlimited, 2007.

Mayer, John D., and Peter Salovey. "What Is Emotional Intelligence." In *Emotional Development and Emotional Intelligence: Educational Implications*, edited by Peter Salovey and David J. Sluyter. New York: Basic Books, 1997.

DISSERTATIONS

Cook, C. Colleen. "A Mixed Methods Approach to the Identification and Measurement of Academic Library Service Quality Constructs: LibQUAL+™." PhD diss., Texas A&M University, 2001.

Kyrillidou, Martha. "Item Sampling in Service Quality Assessment in Service Quality Assessment Surveys to Improver Response Rates and Reduce Respondent Burden: The LibQUAL+® Lite Randomized Control Trial." PhD diss., University of Illinois at Urbana-Champaign, 2009. Accessed September 2, 2010. http://libqual.org/documents/LibQual/publications/lq_gr_2.pdf.

GOVERNMENT PUBLICATIONS

Kutz, Gregory D. *For-Profit Colleges: Underscore Testing Finds Colleges Encouraged Fraud and Engaged in Deceptive and Questionable Marketing Practices*, GAO-10-948T. Washington, DC: Government Accountability Office, 2010. Accessed August 8, 2010. http://www.gao.gov/products/GAO-10-948T.

REPORTS

Institute for Learning Innovation. *Dover, DE Library User Identity—Motivation Pilot Study* Dover: Delaware Division of Libraries, December 2005.

The Library Research Center. "A Survey of Public Libraries and Local Government." *Illinois State Library Special Report Series* 4, no. 1 (1997): 1–62.

WEB RESOURCES

AllBusiness.com. "Customer Service Experience: Employee Empowerment Contributes to the Customer Service Experience." Accessed August 12, 2010. http://www.allbusiness.com/sales/customer-service/3876268-1.html.

"American Express Rolls out Customer Service Barometer." *The Washington Post,* July 13, 2010. Available from *General BusinessFile ASAP.*

Association of College and Research Libraries. *Environmental Scan 2007.* Chicago: Association of College and Research Libraries, 2008. Accessed July 1, 2010. http://www.ala.org/ala/mgrps/divs/acrl/publications/whitepapers/Environmental_Scan_2007%20FINAL.pdf.

Association of Research Libraries. *E-Science and Data Support Services.* Prepared by Catherine Soehner, Catherine Steeves, and Jennifer Ward. Washington, DC: Association of Research Libraries, 2010. Accessed August 12, 2010. http://www.arl.org/bm~doc/escience_report2010.pdf.

Association of Research Libraries. "LibQUAL+®: Publications." Washington, DC: Association of Research Libraries, 2010. Accessed September 2, 2010. http://www.libqual.org/publications.aspx.

Association of Research Libraries. "Press Releases & Announcements: E-Science and Data Support Services." Washington, DC: Association of Research Libraries, 2010. Accessed August 12, 2010. http://www.arl.org/news/pr/escience-12august10.shtml.

Bell, Steven. "'Design Thinking' and Higher Education." *Inside Higher Ed* (March 2, 2010). Accessed August 13, 2010. http://www.insidehighered.com/views/2010/03/02/bell.

Boston College University Libraries. "Message from the University Librarian: Welcome to the Boston College Libraries." 2009. Accessed September 22, 2010. http://www.bc.edu/libraries/about/universitylibrarian.html.

Brooks, Ian. "Who Do Your Policies Serve? Are Your Customer Service Policies Putting the Company's Needs Ahead of the Customer's: Dr. Ian Brooks Explains How That Costs You Dearly in Lost Business." *NZ Business* 24, no. 5 (June 2010): 56. Available from *General BusinessFile ASAP.*

Carnegie Library of Pittsburgh. "MAYA Design." Accessed July 17, 2010. http://www.maya.com/portfolio/carnegie-library.

Cleveland Heights-University Heights Public Library. "Pledge to Our Customers." Cleveland Heights, OH: Cleveland Heights-University Heights Public Library, 2010. Accessed September 8, 2010. http://www.heightslibrary.org/page/customer_pledge.

Colorado State University Libraries. "Comments and Suggestions." 2009. Accessed July 3, 2010. http://lib.colostate.edu/help/comments.html.

Counting Opinions. "What's New?" (secure Web site). Accessed July 7, 2010. http://www.countingopinions.com/partners/main.php.

Davis, Kevin. "The Changing Role of the Business Librarian." *Knowledge Management* (December 1998). Accessed August 13, 2010. http://enterprise. supersites.net/knmagn2/km199812/fc1.htm.

De Rosa, Cathy, Joanne Cantrell, Diane Cellentani, Janet Hawk, Lillie Jenkins, and Alane Wilson. *Perceptions of Libraries and Information Resources*. Dublin, OH: OCLC, 2005. Accessed July 26, 2010. http://www.oclc.org/reports/pdfs/ Percept_all.pdf.

Epstein, Jennifer. "Congress's 'Secret Shopper'." *Inside Higher Ed* (August 3, 2010). Accessed August 8, 2010. http://www.insidehighered.com/ news/2010/08/03/gao.

Falmouth Public Library. "Customer Service Policy." Falmouth, MA: Falmouth Public Library, 2010. Accessed September 8, 2010. http://www. falmouthpubliclibrary.org/?/services/policies/customer-service-policy/.

Fayetteville Public Library. "Customer Service Standards." Fayetteville, AR: Fayetteville Public Library, 2007. Accessed September 8, 2010. http://www. faylib.org/information/pdf/customerservicestandards.pdf.

Gilmore, Susan. "Survey Shows: At 7.3 Million Visits a Year, Seattle Loves Its Public Libraries." *The Seattle Times* (July 30, 2010). Accessed August 8, 2010. http://www.resourceshelf.com/2010/07/31/public-libraries-community-survey-results-released-seattle-wants-more-from-its-libraries/.

Goldberg, Beverly. "California Groups Oppose Library Privatization Talks." *American Libraries* (July 14, 2010). Accessed July 15, 2010. http://www. americanlibrariesmagazine.org/news/07142010/california-groups-oppose-library-privatization-talks.

Harel, Elazar C., and Toby D. Sitko. "Digital Dashboards: Driving Higher Education Decisions." *Research Bulletin* [Boulder, CO: EDUCAUSE Center for Applied Research] 19 (2003). Accessed July 12, 2010. http://net.educause. edu/ir/library/pdf/ERB0319.pdf.

Head, Alison J., and Michael B. Eisenberg. *Lessons Learned: How College Students Seek Information in the Digital Age*. Seattle: University of Washington, The Information School, 2009. Accessed July 23, 2010. http://projectinfolit.org/ pdfs/PIL_Fall2009_Year1Report_12_2009.pdf.

Heathfield, Susan M. "Perform Exit Interviews: Exit Interview Questions." *About. com: Human Resources*. 2010. Accessed June 9, 2010. http://humanresources. about.com/od/whenemploymentends/a/exit_interview_2.htm.

Hong Kong Polytechnic University, Pao Yue-kong Library. "Library Performance Pledges 2010/2011." 2010. Accessed September 8, 2010. http://www.lib.polyu. edu.hk/about_library/performance_pledges.

How Sociable? Brand Visibility Metrics (WorldPress.com). "How Visibility Score." 2008. Accessed August 20, 2010. http://howsociable.wordpress.com/.

Kagan, Marta. "What Is Social Media Now?" Accessed August 9, 2010. http:// www.slideshare.net/mzkagan/what-is-social-media-now-4747765.

King, David Lee. "The Social Web and Libraries: Twitter Alerts" 2008. Accessed July 10, 2010. http://www.davidleeking.com/2008/08/09/the-social-web-and-libraries-twitter-alerts/.

Klein, Karen E. "Building Customer Relations by Listening." *Bloomberg Businessweek* (June 1, 2007). Accessed August 2, 2010. http://www. businessweek.com/smallbiz/content/jun2007/sb20070601_858776.htm.

KRC Research & Consulting. "@Your Library: Attitudes toward Public Libraries Survey." June 2002. Accessed August 13, 2010. http://www.ala.org/pio/ presskits/nlw2002kit/krc_data.pdf.

Laser Foundation. "Libraries: A Vision (The Public Library Service in 2015)." n.d. Accessed July 25, 2010. http://www.ohionet.org/pdf/vision2015.pdf.

Lederman, Doug. "Dashboard Fever." *Inside Higher Ed* (October 22, 2009). Accessed July 13, 2010. http://www.insidehighered.com/news/2009/10/22/ cupa.

"Lesson #1: Be a Good Leader." Accessed August 10, 2010. http://www. evancarmichael.com/Famous-Entrepreneurs/592/Lesson-1-Be-A-Good-Leader.html.

Milwaukee Public Library. "Rethinking Libraries in the 21st Century." n.d. Accessed July 25, 2010. http://www.mpl.org/file/community_index.htm; http://www. mpl.org/file/community_p6.htm; http://www.mpl.org/file/community_p8.htm; http://www.mpl.org/file/community_p9.htm.

Minnesota State Colleges and Universities. "Fact Sheet: System Accountability Dashboard." St. Paul: Minnesota State Colleges and Universities, 2008. Accessed July 13, 2010. http://www.mnscu.edu/business/workforceeducation/ accountability.html.

Namjoshi, Jyoti, and Archana Gupte. "Service-Oriented Architecture for Cloud-Based Travel Reservation Software as a Service." IEEE International Conference on Cloud Computing, 2009. Accessed June 19, 2010. http://www. patni.com/media/345097/SOA_for_Cloud_based_Travel_Reservation_SaaS. pdf.

OCLC. *From Awareness to Funding: A Study of Library Support in America.* Dublin, OH: OCLC, 2008. Accessed October 3, 2010. http://www.oclc.org/reports/funding/.

Oder, Norman. "Survey in Seattle Shows Satisfaction, Generational Change, Huge A/V Circ." *LibraryJournal.com* (August 3, 2010). Accessed August 8, 2010. http://www.libraryjournal.com/lj/home/886208-264/survey_in_seattle_shows_satisfaction.html.csp.

Orange County Library System. "Performance Scorecard for Annual 2008/2009." Orlando, FL: Orange County Library System, n.d. Accessed July 25, 2010. http://www.ocls.org/about/balancedscorecard/default.asp.

Planetfeedback. "Complimenting the Staff." 2001. Accessed July 2, 2010. http://www.planetfeedback.com/mcdonalds/employees/complimenting+the+staff/20861.

Purdue University Libraries. "Strategic Plan. 2006-2011." West Lafayette, IN: Purdue University, 2006. Accessed August 12, 2010. http://www.lib.purdue.edu/admin/stratplans/plan2011.html.

"Quality Function Deployment: Overview." Accessed July 31, 2010. http://thequalityportal.com/q_know01.htm.

Quintessential Marketing Consulting Pty Ltd ®. "Customer Feedback: The Customer Complaint Iceberg." 2006. Accessed May 17, 2010. http://www.quinntessential.com.au/customer-feedback.htm.

The Quotations Page. "Mark Twain." Accessed August 10, 2010. http://www.quotationspage.com/quote/30207.html.

Reh, F. Jon. "Customer Satisfaction Survey." About.com: Management, n.d. Accessed July 8, 2010. http://management.about.com/od/competitiveinfo/a/CustomerSatSurv.htm.

Renfrewshire Community Website. "Libraries." 2010. Accessed September 8, 2010. http://www.renfrewshire.gov.uk/ilwwcm/publishing.nsf/Content/els-pl-renfrewshire-libraries-customer-pledges.

Rogers, Curtis R. "Social Media, Libraries, and Web 2.0: How American Libraries are Using New Tools for Public Relations and to Attract New Users." In *German Library Association Annual Conference in Frankfurt, June 2nd to 5th, 2009.* Accessed August 9, 2010. http://www.slideshare.net/crr29061/social-media-libraries-and-web-20-how-american-libraries-are-using-new-tools-for-public-relations-and-to-attract-new-users-second-survey-november-2009.

Rubin, Brent D. "Toward a Balanced Scorecard for Higher Education: Rethinking the College and University Excellence Indicators Framework." 1999. Accessed July 12, 2010. http://oqi.wisc.edu/resourcelibrary/uploads/resources/Balanced%20Scorecard%20in%20Higher%20Education.pdf.

Rutledge, Merryn "The Listening Organization." *Revisions: Ideas for Leaders* 6, no. 1 (Winter 2003). Accessed August 12, 2010. http://www.revisions.org/newsletters/ReVisionsIdeas_v06n01.pdf.

San Diego Reader Website. Accessed July 1, 2010. http://www.sandiegoreader.com/news/2008/jun/18/cover/.

Search Engine Journal (blog). Accessed July 1, 2010. http://www.searchenginejournal.com/blogging-in-2010-what-you-need-to-know/18886/.

The Seattle Public Library. "About the Library: Mission Statement." Seattle, WA: Seattle Public Library, 2010. Accessed May 22, 2010. http://www.spl.org/default.asp?pageID=about_mission.

The Seattle Public Library. *Community Survey Summary.* Seattle, WA: Seattle Public Library, July 28, 2010. Accessed August 8, 2010. http://www.spl.org/pdfs/about/community_survey_summary.pdf.

Staley, David J., and Karen J. Malenfant. *Futures Thinking for Academic Librarians: Higher Education in 2025.* Chicago: Association of College and Research Libraries, 2010. Accessed July 1, 2010. http://www.ala.org/ala/mgrps/divs/acrl/issues/value/futures2025.pdf.

StevenBell.Info, Steven Bell's Resource Center. "Design Thinking & User Experience." 2007. Accessed August 13, 2010. http://stevenbell.info/design.htm.

Tennant, Roy. "An Industry in Search of Failure." *Digital Libraries* (blog). July 13, 2010. Accessed September 19, 2010. http://blog.libraryjournal.com/tennantdigitallibraries/2010/07/13/an-industry-in-search-of-failure/.

Tenopir, Carol. *Use and Users of Electronic Library Resources: An Overview and Analysis of Recent Research Studies.* Washington, DC: Council of Library and Information Resources, 2003. Accessed July 24, 2010. http://www.clir.org/pubs/reports/pub120/contents.html.

Thinkexist.com, Quotations. "George Bernard Shaw." Accessed August 13, 2010. http://thinkexist.com/quotation/the_single_biggest_problem_in_communication_is/155222.html.

Thinkexist.com, Quotations. "Will Durant, American Writer and Historian." Accessed July 2, 2010. http://thinkexist.com/quotation/inquiry_is_fatal_to/157487.html.

Thinkexist.com, Quotations. "Zora Neale Hurston, American Folklorist and Author." Accessed July 2, 2010. http://thinkexist.com/quotes/zora_neale_hurston/.

University of New Hampshire Library. "Comments." Accessed July 3, 2010. http://www.library.unh.edu/comments/viewcomments.php.

University of Pittsburgh, University Library System. "About Us: The University Library System (ULS) Mission." Pittsburgh, PA: University of Pittsburgh, 2007. Accessed May 22, 2010. http://www.library.pitt.edu/uls/mission.html.

University of Pittsburgh, University Library System. "Wayfinding at a Glimpse." n.d. Accessed July 25, 2010. http://www.landesbergdesign.com/work/signage/hillman/hillman.shtml.

University of Texas at Austin, Library. *LibQUAL+® 2008 Survey*. Washington, DC: Association of Research Libraries, 2008. Accessed July 3, 2010. http://www.lib.utexas.edu/sites/default/files/vprovost/2008_LibQUAL_Institution-Results.pdf.

University of Virginia Library. "Balanced Scorecard 2007–09: Balanced Scorecard Metrics." Charlottesville: University of Virginia Library, n.d. Accessed July 25, 2010. http://www2.lib.virginia.edu/bsc/metrics/all0708.html#user.

University of Virginia Library. "Overview about the Balanced Scorecard." Charlottesville: University of Virginia Library, n.d. Accessed July 25, 2010. http://www2.lib.virginia.edu/bsc/overview.html.

Webjunction. Survey Results. Accessed August 9, 2010. http://blog.webjunctionworks.org/index.php/2010/07/06/library-staff-report-their-use-of-online-tools/?utm_source=WhatCountsEmail&utm_medium=Crossroads&utm_campaign=2010-07+Crossroads.

UNPUBLISHED MATERIAL

Hernon, Peter, and Joseph R. Matthews. "Public Libraries in the Year 2025." Unpublished manuscript, 2011.

Moss, Debbie. "And the Survey Says . . . Strengthening Services through Surveying." Presentation at the American Library Association Annual Meeting, Washington, D.C., June 28, 2010.

Index

About the Authors

Peter Hernon is a professor at Simmons College (Graduate School of Library and Information Science, Boston, Massachusetts), where he teaches courses on government information policy and the evaluation of library services. He is the principal faculty member for the doctoral program, Managerial Leadership in the Information Professions, where he teaches and guides student research. He received his PhD from Indiana University and has taught at Simmons College, the University of Arizona, and Victoria University of Wellington (New Zealand).

Hernon is the coeditor of *Library & Information Science Research* and the author of more than 300 publications, 50 of which are books. *Viewing Library Metrics from Different Perspectives* (Libraries Unlimited, 2009) received the 2010 Greenwood Press award for outstanding contribution to the literature of library and information science. His coauthored work (with Ellen Altman) *Assessing Service Quality* was the recipient of the 1999 Highsmith award. He is the 2008 recipient of the Association of College and Research Libraries' (ACRL) award for Academic/Research Librarian of the Year.

Joseph R. Matthews is a consultant specializing in strategic planning, assessment, the evaluation of library services, customer service, the use of performance measures, and the Library Balanced Scorecard. He was an instructor at the San Jose State University School of Library and Information Science and lives in Carlsbad, California.

In addition to numerous articles, Joe is the author of *Library Assessment in Higher Education*, *The Customer-Focused Library*, *The Evaluation and Measurement of Library Services*, *Scorecards for Results*, *Strategic Planning and Management for Library Managers*, and *Measuring for Results*, among other books.